Renewing the Sunday School
and the CCD

Renewing the Sunday School and the CCD

Edited by
D. CAMPBELL WYCKOFF

Religious Education Press
Birmingham, Alabama

Library of Congress Cataloging-in-Publication Data
Main entry under title:

Renewing the sunday school and the CCD.

   Includes bibliographies and index.
   1. Sunday-schools—Addresses, essays, lectures.
2. Confraternity of Christian Doctrine—Addresses, essays,
lectures.   I. Wyckoff, D. Campbell.
BV1521.R46   1985   268′.0973   85-19419
ISBN 0-89135-053-5

Religious Education Press, Inc.
1531 Wellington Road
Birmingham, Alabama 35209
10 9 8 7 6 5 4 3 2

Religious Education Press publishes books exclusively in religious
education and in areas closely related to religious education. It is
committed to enhancing and professionalizing religious education
through the publication of serious, significant, and scholarly works.

PUBLISHER TO THE PROFESSION

Contents

Introduction

Renewing the Sunday School and the CCD is a major rethinking of these two enterprises, intended to spark reform in them. As a renewal and reform book, it examines them without compromise and without apology, carefully assesses their accomplishments and weaknesses, and makes concrete suggestions for improvement.

In order to provide a responsible and thorough treatment, there are four major sections. The histories of the Sunday school and the CCD are traced by Jack L. Seymour (Chapter 1) and Mary Charles Bryce (Chapter 2). Warren J. Hartman and Andrew D. Thompson provide hard empirical data on their status and effectiveness in Chapters 3 and 4. Participant leaders speak informatively and critically on the basis of their experience: Locke E. Bowman, Jr., on the general Protestant Sunday school (Chapter 5), Robert J. Dean on the evangelical Sunday school (Chapter 6), Nathan W. Jones on the CCD (Chapter 7), Mary A. Love on the black Sunday school (Chapter 8), and Alfred W. Hanner, Jr., on the Sunday school and the CCD in the Armed Forces (Chapter 9). On the basis of these data, James Michael Lee (Chapter 11) and I (Chapter 10) assess the overall situation and explore the possibilities for genuine and effective renewal. The authors have maintained a sharp focus, giving the work a unity not always characteristic of a symposium.

In the normal course of events, a study like this is called for periodically. But the state of the Sunday school and the CCD today cannot be described as normal. They have been weakened by severe criticism and by structural changes, creating a situation of urgency. Yet they serve millions of children, youth, and adults,

1

with a potential for even greater service if realistically assessed and redirected. This book is intended to contribute to that assessment and redirection.

D. CAMPBELL WYCKOFF

Chapter 1

A Reforming Movement: The Story of Protestant Sunday School

JACK L. SEYMOUR

Throughout its two-hundred-year existence, the Sunday school has meant many things to many people. For some it is the evangelistic arm of the church, for others it is the context for serious study and instruction, and for still others it is an intimate, caring fellowship. Its life has engendered deep feelings of pride and caustic criticisms. Assessments of its work have always been varied. For every positive statement made about the Sunday school, there seems to be comparable criticism.

The Sunday school has motivated literally hundreds of thousands of volunteers to share the faith with others, yet it was called in the 1950s in a *Life* magazine article "the most wasted hour" in the United States.[1] It has introduced methods of biblical study and provided an occasion for faith sharing among millions of people, yet its results have disparagingly been called "Sunday school faith." The Sunday school has been a significant agency for evangelism in the church, yet too often it is segmented from the total life of the church and inadequately supported.

The Sunday school has inspired extremes of feeling—sarcastic criticism and inordinate praise. The tone of the criticism is reflected in the riddle of one church educator, who ridiculed the Sunday school by asking: How is the Sunday school like a mule? and then answering, because it has no pride in its ancestry and no hope for posterity. The praise has been equally exaggerated. Charles G. Trumbull, a delegate to the 1905 International Sunday School Convention, concluded in a speech about the future of the Sunday school:

1. Wesley Shrader, "Our Troubled Sunday Schools," *Life* 42 (February 11, 1957), p. 110.

3

The magnitude and glory of [its] cause . . . [is today], under God, enlarged and exalted. . . . The simple, God-ordained ideal of the Sunday school, Bible study for character building, is unchanged. The organizing machinery of the great, world-encircling movement is improved and extended. The methods of work within the school are not essentially new; and they are not likely to grow more complex, but rather simpler, as the years go on. The goal will remain the same until the Kingdom shall have come: to bring every unsaved soul to Christ and to train every saved soul in Christ through his word.[2]

Of course, both of these comments seem undeserved and simplistic in this day. The Sunday school is neither a "mule," nor an "ideal." Yet, both reflect the context of diverse and deeply held opinions about the Sunday school. Any book or effort seeking to reform this institution must recognize this context. Too many past efforts at reform in church education have either participated in the rhetoric of criticism or have ignored the deeply held convictions people have about their Sunday schools.

In addition, both of these quotations reflect the fundamental commitment to reform which has permeated the history of the Sunday school. Its leaders have understood themselves as reformers in church and society. Their passion has been grounded in the convictions of the necessity of the Sunday school for church and society, and in their desire to make it equal to its task.

In its initiation the Sunday school was understood as an effort to reform society through the education of working-class children. As it became an agency of the church, leaders saw it as a way of reforming society by gathering persons into the church, and as a way of reforming the church by increasing the quality and knowledge of church members. The comments of one pastor, F. D. Huntington, to a state convention of Sunday school teachers in 1860 illustrates this dynamic of reform.

The Sunday school appears to take on the character of an endless experiment. By the grandeur of its objective, by the inexhaustible interest it touches, by the immortality of the souls it

2. Charles G. Trumbull, "The Nineteenth Century Sunday School," in International Sunday School Association, *The Development of the Sunday School, 1780-1905: The Official Report of the Eleventh International Sunday-School Convention* (Boston: International Sunday School Association, 1905), pp. 17-18.

nourishes, as well as by the variety of conditions by which it exists.[3]

Even though Huntington's comments seem quaint today, it is true that each generation of Christian educators has seemed to criticize the weaknesses of the previous generation in order to "fill out" the "unfinished experiment" in its own ways. In fact, the literature of the Sunday School in Protestant America seems preoccupied with what future can be created for education. Each generation has been concerned to create a *new* future for the Sunday school. Yet, in so doing, its designs have often ignored the actual dynamics and contributions of the Sunday school in the past and in their present, and moreover have offered "novel" directions which in actuality were repetitions of efforts of previous generations.[4] Many of the efforts at reform or innovation have been frustrated because of a lack of understanding of the historic dynamics of the Sunday school itself.

This essay is an attempt to survey the spirit of reform which has motivated the Sunday school in the United States. By such an emphasis, it may be possible to ground a new effort at renewal, of which this very book is one evidence, in both the possibilities and limitations which have manifested themselves in the life of the Sunday school. The thesis of this essay is that conversation about the character and structure of the Sunday school, since it became an agency of the church in the middle of the nineteenth century, has continually been fueled by the motive of reform. Usually, the concern for reform has been rooted in a sense of inadequacy, a feeling that the Sunday school could not fulfill its expectations. The result has been a tendency to berate the Sunday school, rather than realistically assess what it can contribute. Moreover, the spirit of reform has tended to blind many educators to basic, continuing issues which must be addressed for reform to take root. The task for the present is to assess the continuities that have maintained the vitality of this institution for the last 150 years and to clarify the continuing issues that have had to be

3. F. D. Huntington, *The Relation of the Sunday School to the Church* (Boston: Henry Hoyt, 1860), pp. 3-4.
4. For a description of the tendency to ignore continuity in Christian education, see my monograph *From Sunday School to Church School: Continuities in Protestant Church Education in the United States, 1860-1929* (Washington, D.C.: University Press of America, 1982).

addressed over this time. It is important for church educators to clarify the relationship of their rhetoric about the Sunday school with its contributions. In such a manner, a place for it within the program of education may be clarified and its relationship with other agencies of Christian religious education may be assessed.

No matter what else is said of the Sunday school, all must admit that it is one of the major structural innovations in Protestant church education in the United States. The Sunday school has won a place for itself in most Protestant denominations. From an agency external to the daily life of the church two hundred years ago, it has become an accepted part of church life in the United States. It has not only changed the way Christian education is conducted, but it has changed the shape of the church.

As a relatively new innovation, adopted by the church only in the middle of the nineteenth century, the Sunday school has profoundly affected church architecture, lay leadership, and the concern for knowledge. Above all else, the Sunday school is an attempt at popular education with all of the strengths and weaknesses of such education. The Sunday school does have a future and can be renewed, but an effort at renewal must be rooted in its history and aware of its dynamics.

Becoming the Church's School

The major structural change in the history of the Sunday school occurred in the middle of the nineteenth century when it was adopted by the church as the church's own agency for education. This major change is illustrated by formal action at the meeting of the Third National Sunday School Convention in 1859. For the first time, a major interdenominational gathering claimed the Sunday school as the church's school. The resolution of the convention was not unanimous, but its effect is significant. The resolution read: "Resolved, that we regard the Sunday-school, *in connection with* the teachings of the Family and the Pulpit, reliable as an agency for bringing the *entire youth* of our country under the saving influence of the Gospel."[5] Before twenty more years had elapsed the major United States denominations had

5. Henry Clay Trumbull, "Historical Introduction," in *The Fifth National Sunday School Convention* (New York: Aug. O Van Lennep, 1872), p. 16. The emphasis is mine.

accepted the directions of this resolution in practice, and by the latter part of the century the Sunday school had become an intrinsic part of Protestantism in the United States.

Note the three themes which are emphasized in this resolution, for they reflect the structure embedded in the Sunday school which had endured in practice. First, the Sunday school was not conceived as an institution to stand on its own separated from other forms of influence and education. The Sunday school was thought to be effective only when related to a context of Christian formation represented in family influence, church life, and worship and preaching. Second, a grandiosity of aim has always tended to plague the Sunday school with hope that it would be able to affect the entire population of the church and country. The rhetoric has tended to the extreme and has made church leaders feel inadequate to the task. Third, the task of the Sunday school has been defined as significantly relating gospel and life. Despite varying interpretations of the gospel as solution, religious formation, or biblical instruction, the struggle has been to create an institution whose focus is religious and whose effect is linking faith and life.

The Sunday school began in England during the last twenty years of the eighteenth century. Despite the fact that Sunday instruction had been attempted in several places, tradition has it that Robert Raikes "invented" the institution. His work is paradigmatic of those early efforts. A philanthropist particularly involved in prison reform, Raikes saw the Sunday school as a means to provide education for poor and factory-working children. He hoped by such education to provide a vehicle by which crime could be reduced.

The Sunday school was initiated as an agency of social betterment that would reform society. It was with the same vision that the Sunday school spread to the new nation of the United States. Sunday schools began in several of the cities as vehicles for education particularly in reading and writing to provide better life chances for the poor. When church leaders and members raised concerns about Sunday instruction, which seemed to violate their conviction that Sunday was only a day of religion to worship God, Sunday school leaders were uniform in their defense that the purpose of this Sunday education was to form "useful" citizens, without which "the peace of society" would be threatened. The teaching of reading using the Bible as text was for them a means

of influencing and "moralizing" the character of the poor, and
thereby "improving the social fabric."[6]

When the new organization, the American Sunday-School
Union, an organization to stimulate Sunday school work in the
United States, initiated the "Mississippi Valley Enterprise" in
1830, the Sunday school was extended into the frontier of the
new nation as a means of social and moral reform. The task was
to "endeavor to plant a Sunday school wherever there is a population," to find the illiterate, and to evangelize them with the influence of the Gospel.[7] Biblical formation was seen as the unique
means of humanizing and moralizing the frontier, thereby pro-
tecting and extending the values of democracy to all the citizens.
These initial efforts on the frontier were even extended to native
Americans and blacks making their most profound impact in
what was to become the Mid-West.

The influence of the Sunday school was effective enough that
by the late 1820s and in the 1830s it began to be incorporated into
some churches. Church leaders began to worry that the benefits
of its education had not been extended to the relatively affluent
and to church members. The leadership of the American Sunday-
School Union was to conclude that it is an erroneous assumption
that

> they are intended only for the poor. . . . These schools are
> intended as much for the affluent as the indigent. The great
> object is religious instruction; it is, indeed, given without mon-
> ey and without price—is it, therefore, of no value to those who

6. These quotations are from early minutes of Sunday school organizations and are quoted in Anne Mary Boylan, "The Nursery of the Church:
Evangelical Protestant Sunday Schools, 1820-1880" (Ph.D. dissertation,
University of Wisconsin, 1973), pp. 8, 14-15. Boylan gives an excellent
overview of these developments in Chapter 1, "Sunday Schools as Missionary Institutions," pp. 5-54.

7. Edwin Wilbur Rice, *The Sunday-School Movement 1780-1917 and
the American Sunday-School Union 1817-1917* (Philadelphia: American
Sunday-School Union, 1917), p. 79. Although an older volume, Rice's
work is the only comprehensive chronology of the effort of the American
Sunday-School Union. For a more contemporary and popular treatment
of its effort, see Robert W. Lynn and Elliott Wright, *The Big Little School,
The Two Hundred Years of the Sunday School*, 2nd ed. rev. (Birmingham
and Nashville: Religious Education Press and Abingdon Press, 1980), pp.
40-67.

have the means and who, if it were vendible, would secure it by purchase.[8]

These sentiments increasingly were spoken by church and denominational leaders and Sunday schools were opened to church members. By 1827, a Sunday-School Union had been established for the Methodist Episcopal Church. Although no other denomination would officially organize a Sunday school effort until later in the century, several local churches began to experiment with the Sunday school.

From the 1820s through the 1860s, the Sunday school began to exist in a dual form as both *mission schools* for poor and frontier children and *church schools* for the children of church members. In much of the literature from the 1840s, these two emphases became so intertwined that it is almost impossible to tell to which a writer is referring.[9] With the gradual increase of public efforts at education and the success of extra-congregational Sunday schools that served the affluent as well as Sunday schools supported by churches, the focus and structure of the Sunday school as we know it—as the church's means of education—was born and solidified.

Changes in the focus of the American Sunday-School Union clearly illustrate this shift. By the 1840s the task of the Sunday school was clearly to be religious. Everything of a secular nature was dismissed to the point that the Annual Report of the Union in 1842 read: "If we find a child who does not know how to read, we ascertain what means of instruction are within his reach, and endeavor to persuade him or his parents to avail themselves of such means."[10] The Sunday school was becoming a church institution to instill religious knowledge and character into the children of the church.

Several church leaders worried about the shift which replaced mission to the poor with evangelization of church members. Henry Ward Beecher, pastor of Plymouth Congregational Church in Brooklyn and a child of the socially and theologically influential

8. Rice, *Sunday School Movement*, p. 68.
9. For a discussion, see my *From Sunday School to Church School*, pp. 29-34.
10. From the *Eighteenth Annual Report* of the American Sunday-School Union, quoted in Boylan, "Nursery of the Church," p. 54.

Beecher clan, challenged his contemporaries not to forget the outreach character of the Sunday school. To him the Sunday school was a powerful means by which the work of the church "as reservoirs of moral influence" was carried "into neighborhoods, and into streets, and into households."[11] Yet in spite of his and others' pleas, mission schools almost disappeared by the 1870s, and the Sunday school became the church's school, "the nursery of the church."[12] In this form, the Sunday school grew into the place it occupies today.

The Spirit of Reform

Even in this new form, the grandiose agenda and spirit of reform were maintained and extended. Significant efforts in three periods, the Sunday school of the late 1800s, the progressive church school in the early twentieth century, and the "theological" church school of the middle twentieth century maintained the early passion for the Sunday school's agenda as reforming church and society, and therefore struggled to be faithful to it.

The Sunday School of the Late 1800s

The meeting of the Fifth National Sunday School Convention in Indianapolis in 1872 was a watershed in the history of the Sunday school. It was here that the church's Sunday school formally received its national (one could even say international) goal and solidified its form. B. F. Jacobs, a Baptist layperson from Chicago, provided the convention with a grand vision for Sunday school work. Jacobs was convinced that the Sunday school was the church's agency for biblical formation; therefore, he attempted to overcome its inadequacies and, in a military metaphor, provided it with its marching orders. The rallying cry was unity and uniformity which was in turn embodied in Jacobs' strategy, the Uniform Lesson system.

11. Henry Ward Beecher, "The Mission Work of the Sunday-School," in *Third National Sunday-School Convention of the United States, 1869* (Philadelphia: J. C. Garrigues and Co., 1969), p. 69. (This convention was erroneously called the third convention; it was later renumbered in 1872 as the fourth).

12. For a fuller description of the meaning of this phrase, see Boylan, "Nursery of the Church," pp. 76-77. See also E. Morris Fergusson, *Historic Chapters in Christian Education in America* (New York: Fleming H. Revell Co., 1935), p. 128.

Jacobs' vision was to provide an orderly system of biblical passages, published in quarterlies, that could be taught at the same time across all the ages in a congregation, across all the churches in the United States, and eventually across all the churches in the world. The system was so designed that every person in every place, no matter how "destitute," could study the same biblical passage at the same time. Jacobs provided the convention with the dream, "For the Sunday-schools of the country not only; but, blessed be God! we hope, For the World!"[13]

What Jacobs actually provided was a structure by which the church could claim the Sunday school as an agency of biblical instruction and evangelism to the whole world. His vision coincided well with the conviction that the Sunday school complemented the emerging United States system of public education with a moral and religious focus. It was to become a means to extend and protect the values of American democracy which many felt were embedded in evangelical Protestant Christianity.

The grand aim often led to nativist outbursts such as Jacobs' comments at the Seventh International Sunday School Convention that "the ballot, the school, the Sabbath, the church and the Bible are assailed" in the United States by the threat of immigration.[14] To him, the Sunday school and the Bible were the two great arms of the church to protect *Protestant* civilization and democracy. While such a Protestant imperialism must be rejected, the vision did give Sunday school leaders a way of broadening the role of the Sunday school in the church, and developing a national and even international convention system to support Sunday school work.[15] In fact, within a few years of the 1872 convention other denominations like Congregationalists, Baptists, and Presbyterians were formally to found Sunday school denominational structures. Most other Protestant denominations joined them by the end of the nineteenth century. This new strategy gave church educators a means to respond to the inadequacies that they saw

13. Simeon Gilbert, *The Lesson System* (New York: Phillips and Hunt, 1879), p. 37. See also Jacobs' presentation in "The Uniform Lesson Question," in *Fifth National Sunday-School Convention*, pp. 84-88.

14. B. F. Jacobs, "Report of the Executive Committee," in *Seventh International and World's Second Sunday School Conventions* (Chicago: Executive Committee, 1893), p. 136.

15. For a discussion and chronology of the international Sunday school effort, see Gerald E. Knoff, *The World Sunday School Movement: The Story of a Broadening Mission* (New York: Seabury Press, 1979).

in the previous period which they called the "Babel period" because of its many forms of Sunday school, many differing curricula, and multiple expectations. At the same time, however, it enabled them to claim the Sunday school for the church and still feel they were being faithful to the mission agenda rooted in its past.

This late nineteenth century was a period of great enthusiasm and passion as the Sunday school grew geometrically and its influence expanded. For example, Henry Clay Trumbull declared in 1888 in his lectures at Yale University, "the Sunday-school has become the prime church agency for pioneer evangelizing, for Bible teaching, and for the religious instruction and care of the children in every denomination of Protestant Christians in America."[16] The social effect of its effort was applauded by many secular as well as religious leaders. In 1910, President William Howard Taft even called it "one of the two or three great instrumentalities for making the world better, for making it more moral, and for making it more religious."[17]

Uniformity provided the vision, the convention system provided the means, and Sunday school leaders worked to improve the methods the local church was to use in carrying out its task. One Methodist Episcopal leader was to prod his own denomination in a manner that is illustrative of many Sunday school leaders. He called for the perfecting of the educational quality and structure of the Sunday school.

> There is a general consciousness that we need a higher grade of teaching than we have had in the past. Common school facilities are constantly increasing, and care must be taken that there be not too marked a contrast between the style of teaching our children receive during the week, and that which they get on the Sabbath.

To respond to his own concern and to allay the fears of Sunday school workers, he continued with an answer.

16. Henry Clay Trumbull, *The Sunday-School: Its Origin, Mission, Methods, and Auxiliaries* (Philadelphia: John D. Wattles, 1888), p. 131.

17. William Howard Taft, "The President's Estimate of the Sunday-School," in World-Wide Sunday-School Association, *World-Wide Sunday-School Work: The Official Report of the World's Sixth Sunday-School Convention,* ed. William N. Hartshorne (Chicago: Executive Committee of the World's Sunday-School Association, 1910), p. 125.

> This reflection ought not to bring discouragement to any right-minded person who desires to do good in the Sunday-school, for the facilities for self-improvement now offered to Sunday-school teachers are such that pious persons of ordinary good sense, though having but little culture, can by determined perseverance become qualified for the duties to be performed.[18]

What was referred to here was improvement in denominational and interdenominational curricula, and the birth of national and regional training centers to "perfect" Sunday school leaders in pedagogical practice. Sunday school leaders were elated that the new Sunday school was finding a place for itself in the church and that it had outgrown its primitive mission beginnings in the country.

Consistently, Sunday school leaders called for improvement in structure. J. M. Gregory in an essay on the future of the Sunday school listed the four structural issues which needed addressing: (1) providing comfortable classrooms, (2) developing a better system of classifying pupils, (3) securing higher quality teachers, and (4) preparing more adequate methods of instruction.[19] With the creation of a Sunday school building and a style of church architecture (the Akron plan), with the creation of the Uniform Lessons, and with the establishment of teacher training patterns, leaders sought to respond to these needs.

The Progressive Church School of the Early Twentieth Century

In fact, by the beginning of the twentieth century many leaders were confident that their work was succeeding and the appropriate machinery was in place. It was their confidence that caused Charles Trumbull to call the Sunday school "the God-ordained ideal."[20] However, others were less confident and they initiated a new movement of reform. They insisted that passion and commitment were not sufficient for Sunday school work and new efforts at reform were needed. For example, one leader characterized the Sunday school as an "old-time collection of indifferent children and ignorant teachers meeting in the church auditorium or base-

18. J. M. Freeman, "Growth of the Sunday-School Idea in the Methodist Episcopal Church," *Methodist Quarterly Review* 52 (July, 1871), p. 412.

19. J. M. Gregory, "The Future of the Sunday School," *The Sunday School Teacher* 2 (June, 1867), p. 173.

20. See again note number 2.

ment."[21] Another mused, "The great wonder is that our Sunday schools continue to exist in many instances."[22]

Both were referring to the fact that the Sunday school seemed not to continue to reflect a "modern" image. Several leaders were disgruntled with its quality of education and its effect. The Sunday school seemed out of step with modern psychology, modern public school practices, and modern methods of organization.

These new reformers were also dissatisfied with the speed by which older members of the International Sunday School Convention responded to these modern developments. Because of what they saw as the recalcitrance and backwardness of these leaders, they formed a competing organization in 1903, the Religious Education Association. Its purpose was to make work in religious education modern—

to inspire the educational forces of our country with the religious ideal: inspire the religious forces of our country with the educational ideal: and to keep before the public mind the ideal of Religious Education and the sense of its need and value.[23]

Further splintering of Sunday school effort was to continue in that first decade of the twentieth century as individual denominations covenanted together to support each other, but in ways that preserved denominational freedom and integrity. They formed the Sunday School Council of Evangelical Denominations in 1910 to represent a higher standard for Sunday school education.[24]

Armed with liberal Protestant theology, the new breed of reformers sought to listen to research in psychology and pedagogy and to shape the Sunday school in relation to modern public school practices. The new spirit of reform seemed well on its way by 1911 when Northern Baptists changed the name of the institu-

21. Henry F. Cope, *The Modern Sunday School in Its Present Day Task* (New York: Fleming H. Revell Co., 1901), pp. 190-191.

22. J. D. Springston, "The Application of Modern Educational Theory to the Sunday School," *Religious Education* 3 (August, 1908), p. 90.

23. "The Purpose of the Association," *Religious Education* 1 (April 1906): 2. For a significant assessment of the work of the REA see Stephen A. Schmidt, *A History of the Religious Education Association* (Birmingham, Ala.: Religious Education Press, 1983).

24. "Constitution: The Sunday School Council of Evangelical Denominations," in Sunday School Council of Evangelical Denominations, *Minutes, Third Annual Meeting* (New York: Office of the Secretary, 1913), pp. 70-73.

tion from Sunday school to "School of the Church."[25] The church school was thus born as a modern pedagogical vehicle to build curriculum in relationship to research on human development; to organize itself on the model of the public school with local church superintendents called Directors of Religious Education and local church boards of education; to improve the quality of instruction by rigorous teacher-training procedures and standards of excellence; and to coordinate all local modes of education such as Sunday sessions of church school, youth and children's work, and women's and men's work into a unified program of education.[26] When in 1922 the competing Sunday School Council of Evangelical Denominations and the International Sunday School Association settled their differences and united their efforts in the International Sunday School Council of Religious Education, many leaders optimistically concluded that the church school would achieve what the Sunday school had merely hinted at—an effective educational agency to extend Christian faith into all education and thereby to protect American democracy.[27]

In the exuberance of this period, Eugene Exman was to describe the changes as significant and positive. He was inspired by the programs at Hyde Park Baptist Church in Chicago, Riverside Church in New York, and Madison Avenue Presbyterian Church in New York. He seemed particularly "taken" by the three-hour school program at Riverside with its seventeen-story building and elevators. He wrote that these church schools

> represent a new attitude on the part of church leaders, substituting trained teachers and attractive courses for rally days and class pins. In objective they have much in common with the old-time Sunday school. Their aim is to put religion to work, to make it contribute to day by day living. It is in method they differ using project as well as precept and weaving religion into the fabric of common experience.[28]

25. Henry Frederick Cope, "Ten Years Progress in Religious Education," *Religious Education* 8 (June 1913), p. 126.

26. For a fuller description of the style and innovations of this period see *From Sunday School to Church School*, pp. 101-153.

27. *Report of Committee on Education of the International Sunday School Council of Religious Education*, by Walter S. Athearn, Chairman (Kansas City: International Sunday School Council of Religious Education, 1922).

28. Eugene Exman, "Sunday Schools Have Changed Too," *School and Society* 47 (June 11, 1938), pp. 765-766.

The church school was to be the new reform, a new incarnation of an old ideal, but a more accurate methodological expression of that ideal.

Only one hint of anxiety remained on the horizon for these educators. Their tendency to begin the study of religion with the religious needs of children, and consequently to appear to give the Bible a secondary place was resisted by many evangelical denominations. For example, the influence of David C. Cook, Jr., an independent publisher, spread in the 1920s to represent the evangelical view that Christian educators must insist that the Bible be in the primary focus of all educational efforts. Evangelicals responded to the concern for method of the church school reformers, but maintained the Bible as the primary text for instruction.[29] The fundamentalist-modernist controversy thus divided the education work of denominations in two directions along theological lines. For the evangelical denominations, the Sunday school had to preserve its focus on conversion, for the Sunday school was the primary entry point into the church. Modern methods were to be used, as liberals had emphasized, but these were not to block efforts at evangelism through the Sunday school which were rooted in the study of the truths written in the Word of God, the Bible.

The "Theological" Church School of the Middle-Twentieth Century

The great Depression with the resulting curtailment of local church expansion in education and the termination of many directors of religious education; the diminishing of Sunday school enrollments in several of the denominations most supportive of liberal religious education reform such as the Methodist Episcopal Church, Disciples of Christ, Presbyterians, U.S.A.; and the ascendency of neo-orthodox theology in Protestantism—all these factors initiated a third period of reform in Sunday school education in the 1930s and 1940s.[30] The expressed optimism of liberal reli-

29. For an example of how the concern for method was maintained by these evangelicals along with their concern for scripture and conversion see David C. Cook, Jr., *How to Write the Child Life Story* (Elgin: David C. Cook Publishing Co., 1922). The extensive use of Dewey, Hall, and Coe contrasts with many contemporary misconceptions of Cook's work.

30. For a brief description see Lynn and Wright, *The Big Little School*, pp. 133-136.

gious educators seemed unequal to the task presented by the Depression and the Second World War.

H. Shelton Smith was only one voice among many who argued that "the theological roots of Liberal Protestant nurture must also be examined and reconstructed."[31] Neo-orthodox educators sought to reform the religious education of the previous decades and remake religious education into a Christian theological education. They thought it was imperative to make the church's school into a real school where members acquired a comprehensive and accurate foundation in the knowledge and beliefs of Christian faith. The liberal concern for nurture had led many, they believed, to miss the rigor and thoroughness needed to learn the history of the church, methods of biblical exegesis, and the doctrines of Christian theology.

Again the call for reform was stated in an extreme fashion and newer reformers sought to distinguish themselves from the past—both the past of the simplistic pedagogy of the Sunday school period, and the optimistic nurture of the church school period. James Smart, a biblical scholar and the director of the new Presbyterian effort at neo-orthodox education, is illustrative of the feelings of these newer reforms.

In many of our churches our education of the younger generation in the Christian faith is so grossly inadequate and ineffective that to continue on the present level is to invite disaster. . . . The Church must, in the fullest sense of the word, become a teaching church.[32]

The action of the Presbyterian Church, U.S.A., is most representative of this shift. In 1941 it withdrew from the Graded Lesson Outline Committee of the International Council of Religious Education in an effort to become a teaching church. By 1948 the Presbyterian Church offered its new Christian Faith and Life Curriculum as a comprehensive effort at theological education for

31. H. Shelton Smith, *Faith and Nurture* (New York: Charles Scribner's Sons, 1941), p. 32.

32. James Smart, "The Why? What? When? of the New Curriculum entitled Christian Faith and Life, A Program for Church and Home," quoted in William B. Kennedy, "The Genesis and Development of the Christian Faith and Life Series" (Ph.D. dissertation Yale University, 1957), p. 446.

the whole of the church.[33] Its success was so significant that many other denominations embarked on equally expansive efforts to unite psychology, biblical scholarship, theology, and education.

Throughout the 1950s Sunday church schools saw almost phenomenal growth. There was again great optimism about what this theological approach to church education could achieve. The vision was of a teaching church where theology was to become the task of church laity and the benefits of seminary theological education were to be extended throughout the church. However, this vision was not realized. Declining memberships and Sunday church school enrollments in the late 1960s and the reduction of denominational staff in Christian education caused educators to search again for what they must be doing wrong.

The story of both the feelings of positive regard for the Sunday school and of criticisms of "Sunday school faith" could be continued throughout the 1960s and 1970s. The search for adequate understandings and new models proliferated with conferences on the Sunday school and celebrations of its 200-year existence.[34] The spirit of reform which birthed the Sunday school continued to give it life through 200 years, and we seem again at a place where the reforming spirit is pervasive. We need to assess this "endless experiment" and ground it in its past.

Assessing the Spirit of Reform

In all of the above periods of Sunday school reform are reflected enduring issues and characteristics that define the identity and shape of the church's Sunday school for Protestantism. However, the spirit of reform itself has tended to blind many Christian educators to these characteristics and continuities.

Most social institutions move into the future with an accumulated tradition and wisdom from the past. While many leaders of social institutions must fight to free themselves from a restrictive bondage to the past, they also realize there are opportunities in that past. In contrast, Sunday school leaders have seemed not to

33. The story of this curriculum is told in Kennedy "Genesis and Development of the Christian Faith and Life Series."

34. See for example the report and papers of a conference "Confrontation: Sunday School" in *The Duke Divinity School Review* 40 (Fall, 1975); and "The Sunday School Revisited" issue of *Religious Education* 75 (January-February, 1980).

recognize a positive relationship to the past. Throughout the history of the Sunday school, leaders have so separated themselves from the past that many have missed the opportunities provided for them in that very past.

What has resulted is a separation of the visions of Sunday school leaders from the accumulated past that actually maintains the Sunday school in the local church. Local church workers are often confused by the criticisms leveled and the expansive visions provided by Christian educators. To the local church people who experience the Sunday school, it can neither be as bad as they hear nor as grand as it is envisioned. Therefore, to understand the impact and power of this institution, it is necessary to explore three enduring continuities rooted in its past. These were identified earlier in this chapter as a grandiosity of aim for the Sunday school, a concern to link gospel and life, and the relationship of the Sunday school to the total context of Christian formation.

Grandiosity of Aim

Comments such as "the only hope for American democracy," "the moral complement of the system of American education," "the salvation of the 'Entire youth of our country,'" and "the theological seminary for the laity" seem exaggerated and out of touch with the experience of laity in the Sunday school. While it may have been necessary to paint such grand visions in order to have the idea of the Sunday school accepted by the church and culture in the nineteenth and early twentieth centuries, today the visions function more to confuse than to clarify.

Of course there is a kernel of truth in each of these visions and it is important for the Sunday school to be as thorough and competent as possible, but the tendency to separate rhetoric and practice has been and continues to be problematic. In fact, it has tended to place Christian education leadership over against the very institutions they have sought to serve. One example is illustrative of this tendency. In 1933 Hugh Hartsborne and Earle Ehrhardt at the Institute of Social and Religious Research of Yale University published a major analysis of the educational programs of ten outstanding churches. Their desire was to discover how effective the enthusiasm of progressive religious education had been in changing local church educational practices. The findings of the study were disheartening to them and other progressives. They wrote:

The process of accretion whereby the traditional school has
been broadened and enlarged its work *seems to have effected
little change in the underlying historic assumptions;* in fact,
the acceptance of innovation has depended largely upon their
probable worth as agencies for strengthening and perpetuating
the accepted stereotypes.[35]

While their findings are probably accurate, their words were
heard as a defeat of efforts at renewal, rather than a clarification
of new directions needed to take the reality of the Sunday school
seriously and develop a program in light of it. Rather than being
defeated by "underlying historic assumptions," they could have
used them to clarify directions for renewal.

What is needed is a realistic assessment of goals for the Sunday
school. In a captivating phrase, D. Campbell Wyckoff has called
the Sunday school "as American as crabgrass."[36] What Wyckoff
reminds us is that while the Sunday school may not be "pretty" in
achieving all of the goals developed for it, the Sunday school has
been enduring and has been a vital institution for many people.
Above all else the Sunday school is a movment of popular education in the United States—spreading knowledge widely throughout the public. To understand it as such provides a picture of both
its strength and weaknesses.

Linking Gospel and Life—A Movement for Popular Education

During the Third National Sunday-School Convention in 1869 in
Newark, New Jersey, the keynote speaker, Theodore Runyon, noted with pride how the Sunday school was spreading the knowledge of Christian faith throughout the United States. Central to
his argument was the conviction that it had become a substantial
"means of popular education" influencing all classes of society. To
him it was the "leaven of society."[37]

Runyon was convinced that the Sunday school was a movement
with a social impact and a strategy for popular education. The

35. Hugh Hartshorne and Earle V. Ehrhardt, *Church Schools of Today*
(New Haven: Yale University Press, 1933), p. 218.

36. D. Campbell Wyckoff, "As American as Crab Grass: The Protestant
Sunday School," *Religious Education* 75 (January-February, 1980),
pp. 27-35.

37. Theodore Runyon, "The Address of Welcome," in *Third National
Sunday-School Convention*, p. 7.

import of Runyon's analysis is that the Sunday school had a clear social goal—to spread and increase public knowledge about Christian faith. It is this movement characteristic which gave the Sunday school much support and focus. The conviction was that the Sunday school was responsible for spreading knowledge and perspectives about Christian faith widely throughout society. Faith knowledge and experience were not therefore to be restricted to those who had the leisure and education for sophisticated theological study but in contrast were to be made broadly available. One leader, Warren Randolph, the chair of the International Lesson Committee, directly expressed the popular character of Sunday school education in his report in 1890. Randolph argued that the Sunday school could not be expected to parallel a theological curriculum. Rather "a wide general range" of knowledge "with direct personal application" was what was to be expected from the Sunday school.[38]

Any strategy for popular education has the advantage of giving people a sense of an understanding and a broad acquaintance with a field of study. It also has the disadvantages of not dealing with the subtleties and depth of that field of study and with being inefficient. Both the advantage and disadvantages are true for the Sunday school. In fact, they are what makes it "as American as crabgrass." The Sunday school made available knowledge and experience about the Christian faith for people who had not previously explored the faith's content, but it was also usually unable to do that with depth. To expect the Sunday school to do more is probably to expect too much of the Sunday school. Only in conjunction with other agencies of education is the total goal possible.

To acquire a sense of the power of popular education today, it is only necessary to see, for example, how knowledge about psychology and human development have been extended. Books, newspaper and magazine articles, self-help courses, church studies, and adult continuing education in parenting and human growth have given people a broad acquaintance with research and perspectives in psychology. It is not at all strange to hear conversations filled with psychological references. Sophisticated concepts have

38. Warren Randolph, "Report of the Lesson Committee for 1890," in *Sixth International Sunday School Convention of the United States and British North American Provinces* (Chicago: Executive Committee, 1890), p. 101.

been popularized in this manner and are used regularly to help persons understand their lives and experiences. A similar case could probably be made for the ways innovations in public health, medicine, child-rearing, and even organizational management as well as concerns for human rights and equal access are made available to people through popular education. For example, the present concern for a nuclear freeze has been stimulated by means of popular education including the leadership of church and public organizations.

In a similar way, the Sunday school has given a great many people concepts to understand their lives and experiences in terms of the faith. These understandings are often not as sophisticated or as complex as many educators would desire, but they are at least made available to many people in ways that they can use.

A task for Christian educators stimulated by the history of the Sunday school is to study in more depth the power and effect of strategies of popularization. It is not useful to criticize the weaknesses of the Sunday school without recognizing its character as a movement for popular education.

In a recent study of adult Sunday schools, Dick Murray has been helpful in dispelling many of the myths about the Sunday school. Murray's argument is that the Sunday school is best in giving people an experience which helps them know *of* the faith. While it may be weak in giving a comprehensive knowledge *about* the faith, it does give them a focus and place to start in experiencing the faith and its meaning. Murray concludes:

> The Sunday school is a unique school—a school in which we tell stories, share life, seek answers to the deepest questions, and laugh at one another's joy and cry at one another's pain— not a "real" school—but possibly the most *real-real* school there can be.[39]

In these comments, Murray describes the power of popularization and community experience in Sunday school.

What must be remembered is that the Sunday school was never called to do the whole task of Christian religious education. It should be accepted for what it can do, and a program of education built within that can play a unique and appropriate role.

39. Dick Murray, *Strengthening the Adult Sunday School Class* (Nashville: Abingdon, 1981), p. 26.

The Sunday School in a Program of Education

A key to understanding the effectiveness and focus of the Sunday school in the nineteenth century is the realization that the Sunday school was one institution in a broader system of Christian religious education. It was never intended by its early leaders to carry the total task of Christian education. Within the church itself the work of the Sunday school was to be complemented by worship, preaching, church fellowship, and Bible classes.

One of the early leaders and the editor of the Methodist Episcopal Church's Sunday school resources, John Vincent, argued persuasively that it was a "defect" in thinking to turn over the total "responsibility of Biblical and religious training" to the Sunday school alone.[40] With other contemporaries Vincent argued that Sunday school, family, and pulpit worked together to provide a program of education. He even went further to describe how the Sunday school was effective because it fit within the framework of other cultural institutions such as the press, school, library, clubs, and philanthropic agencies to provide a comprehensive context for Christian education.

What Vincent was advocating has been described by the contemporary Sunday school historian, Robert Lynn, as an ecology of education where revival, church press, public school, Sunday school, and church worked together to provide a comprehensive program of education.[41] The relation of these institutions made its education effective. The Sunday school was never to stand alone in the nineteenth century.

Early twentieth century Christian educators were even clearer in how the Sunday school was to be one aspect of a broader church education program coordinating local church efforts at education (represented in Sunday school, preaching, junior and youth societies, and women's and men's organizations) with other public agencies dealing with religious education. Several designs for programs coordinating all church and cultural modes of education were advanced.[42] While the designs seem too bureaucratic and expansive for our day, within them was the recognition that the Sunday school played only one part in a total program of education.

40. John H. Vincent, *The Modern Sunday School*, rev. ed. (New York: Eaton and Mains, 1900), p. 254.//
41. Lynn and Wright, *The Big Little School*, pp. 146-168.//
42. See for example Walter Athearn, *Religious Education and American Democracy* (Boston: Pilgrim Press, 1917), pp. 2-21.

It is to this conviction that educators must return today. Too much is expected of the Sunday school when it is seen to carry the total burden of religious instruction and faith formation. The contribution of the Sunday school as a nurturing agency and a means of popular education can be celebrated when it is recognized that other agencies carry other aspects of religious formation.

The challenge for Christian educators is to look comprehensively at the various agencies that carry Christian religious education and to evaluate and relate their individual contributions to a total program.[43] For example, the whole life of a parish works together to communicate what it means to be a Christian person in the present. From the pulpit issues of how faith and life relate are regularly addressed. In addition, planning for church life and mission provide in-depth opportunities to assess and learn what it means to be the church and to be faithful witnesses and servants in the world. Special opportunities can also be provided for study and action at critical points in individuals' lives like confirmation, baptism, and the acceptance of leadership for the church. The Sunday school is a rich arena of broad popular education. As such it tends to be exploratory and introductory, but it nevertheless provides a foundation on which more systematic and cumulative settings of study can be built.

Within a broader concept of church education, the Sunday school has a crucial role. The task for educators is to be comprehensive in their visions and planning—not just criticizing the Sunday school for its limitations, but building on its strengths.

Conclusion

In 1890 William Reynolds, the chair of the Sixth International Sunday School Convention concluded that 83 percent of all new church members came directly through and because of the Sunday school.[44] Reynolds was convinced that the personal support and popular education received in the Sunday school were crucial for sharing the meaning of the faith and church membership with

43. For one attempt at a comprehensive reassessment see Jack L. Seymour, Robert T. O'Gorman, and Charles R. Foster, *The Church in the Education of the Public: Refocusing the Task of Religious Education* (Nashville: Abingdon, 1984).
44. William Reynolds, "Reports from the Field," in *Sixth International Sunday School Convention*, p. 28.

people. While the percentages have changed somewhat today, it is equally true that the Sunday school is crucial for church membership and understanding. For many Protestant denominations 65 percent of all members still come through the Sunday school. In some denominations like Southern Baptist, Nazarene, and Assemblies of God the percentage is over eighty.[45] The Sunday school is still a primary entry point into the church for many. Concomitantly, it is also the primary educational and support vehicle for many others.

To renew the Sunday school today is to take seriously its influence in people's lives and in the church. It is necessary to recognize that it functions typically at this *primary level*, providing an entry point into the faith, personal support in the quest for understanding, and a broad knowledge base. These functions have been true throughout its history and continue to be true. There is a need in present discussions to reclaim the heritage that birthed this institution and to build upon the accumulated past that fuels it in local churches. The past provides a wisdom which must not be lost in rhetoric or reformation.

A comprehensive and cumulative approach to education needs to be built that highlights the strengths of the Sunday school and expands the foundation it offers. It is very possible to be realistic about the Sunday school, understanding it as a strategy for popular education, while also building a more comprehensive program of Christian formation around it that takes life and decision making in the community of faith seriously, as well as other opportunities for more rigorous study. The challenge for Christian educators is to accept the past and present of the Sunday school to a sufficient degree to begin to think comprehensively about Christian religious education. A realistic celebration of the gifts of the Sunday school is a beginning to this effort.

---

45. See Warren J. Hartman, *A Study of the Church School in the United Methodist Church* (Nashville: General Board of Education, 1972); and Hartman's article in this book.

Chapter 2

The Confraternity of Christian Doctrine in the United States

MARY CHARLES BRYCE

The Confraternity of Christian Doctrine, known popularly as the "CCD," is an association of Roman Catholic individuals committed to the work of catechesis, religious education, among the faithful. The objective is to assist the latter, both children and adults, in deepening their faith through improved understanding and appreciation of doctrinal truths and of sacramental life. The Confraternity's apostolate extends also to inquirers interested in perceiving the commitment to Christianity according to Catholic tradition and practice.

The Confraternity dates its orgin from 1536 when an Italian priest in Milan, Castellino da Castelli (1476-1566), founded the first center for instructing children in Christian doctrine.[1] Castellino had discovered that most children and many adults were woefully ignorant of basic truths. Both groups needed guidance and instruction to help them live their baptismal commitment meaningfully.

From the beginning Castellino persuaded and trained selected members of the faithful to serve as instructors for the children and inquiring adults. He called the group of volunteer leaders-teachers by the descriptive title: *Compagnia della reformatione in carita,* "Society (company) of those (seeking) reformation in charity." That title caused uneasiness among some, and in 1564 the title was changed to *Compagnia dei servi de' puttini in car-*

1. See M. S. Conlan *"Castellino da Castelli," New Catholic Encyclopedia,* Vol. 3 p. 189. See also A. Tamvorini, *La Compagnia e le scuole della dottrina cristina* (Milan, 1939).

ita, "Society of servants of 'the little ones' in charity."[2]

Classes began to meet somewhat regularly and the practice was imitated by a few of the neighboring parishes. Slowly a wider number of communities followed suit. The availability of the smaller catechisms written by the Dutch Jesuit, Peter Canisius, assisted the cause.[3] Nevertheless Castellino had difficulty in getting the support of local bishops for the work.

It was St. Charles Borromeo (1538-1584), archbishop of Milan, who finally recognized the importance of the endeavor. In 1566, Borromeo formally established the newly named "Confraternity of Christian Doctrine" in his archdiocese. The practice then began to spread more easily to other dioceses in northern Italy and beyond.[4]

In its unique way the Confraternity predated and anticipated a decree promulgated by the Council of Trent (1545-1563) which stated that "people of all ages and degrees shall be nourished with solid doctrine in a manner that is in keeping with their capacity to understand and learn."[5] Trent also prescribed weekly catechesis sessions for the young.

Subsequent approval and implementation by local bishops and popes soon followed. Pope Pius V formally approved the Confraternity in 1571.[6] In 1607, Pope Paul V elevated the Confraternity to the status of an arch-confraternity in Rome for the purpose of widening the influence and effectiveness of weekly catechesis.[7] That fact served as an effective approbation of the practice and

2. Ibid., p. 189. See Joseph B. Collins, "The Beginnings of the CCD in Europe and Its Modern Revival," *American Ecclesiastical Review* (1973), p. 696.

3. Collins, "The Beginnings of the CCD," pp. 696-697. Canisius (1521-1597) had authored three catechisms. The last two, published in 1556 and 1558 respectively were more elementary and concise and became extremely popular among the people. During Canisius' lifetime they went through 200 editions. See "Canisius," by B. Schneider in *New Catholic Encyclopedia,* 3, pp. 24-26.

4. Collins, "The Beginnings of the CCD," p. 698. When Borromeo died in 1584 more than 40,000 adults and children were enrolled in the schools of the Confraternity. There were 3000 teachers and directors of the programs. See Cesare Orsenigo, *Life of St. Charles Borromeo* (St. Louis: B. Herder, 1943), p. 96.

5. Session 17 (1546). Cited in Collins, "The Beginnings of the CCD," p. 697.

6. *Fontes juris canonici,* I. No. 141, p. 248.

7. Collins, "The Beginnings of the CCD," p. 700.

encouraged emulation on a worldwide basis.

In the twentieth century it was Pope Pius X who brought the Confraternity into clear and significant focus. One of his earliest encyclicals, *Acerbo Nimis* (1905)—"On Teaching Christian Doctrine"—was devoted to the subject of catechizing.[8] According to Joseph Collins it earned the description of being "the Magna Carta of the Confraternity."[9] In that basically pastoral document Pius X prescribed the establishment of the CCD in every parish in order to counteract ignorance of the faith. He recognized the need that pastors had for assistance in that mission and urged them to call on devoted laity to assume some responsibility in the project. However, he cautioned all concerned that the ministry required them to take time and effort to study and prepare.

> No matter what facility from nature a person may have in ideas and language, let him always remember that he will never be able to teach Christian doctrine to children or to adults without first giving himself to very careful study and preparation. They are mistaken who think that because of the inexperience and lack of training of the people, the work of teaching religion can be performed in a slipshod manner. On the contrary, the less educated the hearers, the more zeal and diligence must be used to adapt the sublime truths to their untrained minds; these truths, indeed, far surpass the natural understanding of the people, yet must be known by all whether the cultured or the uncultured.[10]

Confraternity Beginnings in the United States

Studying the origins of the CCD in the United States against that brief historical overview one discovers a uniqueness and a similarity to the history just surveyed. One perceives a sort of "history repeating itself."

In the sixteenth century Castellino had recognized the need for formal study of Christian doctrine among the adults and children

---

8. *Acta Sedis Sanctae*, 37 (1905), 613-625. For a translation see Joseph B. Collins, ed., trans., *Catechetical Documents of P. Pius X* (Paterson, N.J.; St. Anthony Guild Press, 1946), pp. 13-27. Actually that was the first of twenty-one documents which Pius X wrote dealing with catechesial matters.

9. Collins, "The Beginnings of the CCD," p. 704.

10. Ibid.

he served. He did not inquire about the possible existence of a formal structure or of an official mandate. He responded to the existent needs according to what he considered a workable solution. Similarly, initial endeavors of people in this country arose out of the recognized need for serious and regular classes for children and grown-ups who were poorly or inadequately informed about Christian truth and their commitment to it.

The first gathering of what later became the "first established unit" of the Confraternity of Christian Doctrine originated as a volunteer body of people in the parish of Our Lady of Good Counsel in New York City in 1902. The "founding members," all laity, were concerned about the low level of Christian knowledge manifested by parish adults and children with regard to their faith.[11] They, the original founders of the group, had participated in a training program sponsored by a Catholic settlement house in the area. The program was held for catechists during the winter of 1901-02. The response in terms of attendance was moderate. In terms of enthusiasm the response was extraordinary.

During the course of the ensuing year the "founding" group asked Archbishop Michael A. Corrigan to recognize the organization as the Confraternity of Christian Doctrine and to request their affiliation with the Archconfraternity of Christian Doctrine in Rome. The request was granted and a certificate of affiliation, dated May 21, 1902, was received.[12]

The origins of the CCD in the United States were also rooted in the ministry to immigrants. In 1908 three lay teachers began providing Christian instruction for the mostly foreign-born Catholics in the mining districts around Pittsburgh. Their ministry mushroomed, and by 1919, 500 teachers were involved in 153 schools of religion in the area. More than 13,000 children and adolescents were enrolled in their classes.[13]

Having learned of the CCD apostolate in Pittsburgh, Verona Spellmire, a public school teacher and a volunteer in the Catholic Charities office in Los Angeles, initiated a project similar to the

11. Mary Charles Bryce, "The Confraternity of Christian Doctrine," in *Catholics in America 1776-1976*, ed. Robert Trisco (Washington, D.C.: National Conference of Catholic Bishops, 1976), pp. 149-153.

12. Joseph B. Collins, "Religious Education and CCD in the United States: Early Years (1902-1935)," *American Ecclesiastical Review* 169 (January, 1975).

13. Bryce, "The Confraternity of Christian Doctrine," p. 151.

one in Pittsburgh [14] The principal difference was that Spellmire's concern was for the Spanish-speaking inhabitants of her city. She encouraged others to join her efforts and the "idea" caught on. By the end of 1923, 150 teachers were involved and Bishop John J. Cantwell's hearty approval and blessing encouraged the movement. Cantwell officially established the Confraternity of Christian Doctrine there on March 11, 1922.[15]

From 1921 to 1930 parish and diocesan CCD units sprang up across the nation. Councils were established in the dioceses of Brooklyn (New York), Monterey-Fresno (California), Sante Fe (New Mexico), Boise (Idaho), Leavenworth (Kansas), Great Falls (Montana), Sioux City (Iowa), and others.

Meanwhile, the movement, which originated at Good Counsel in New York City, expanded beyond the few neighboring parishes. Catechists began collaborating with each other and by 1913 they created a vigorous foundation which named itself *Theta Phi Alpha*. John M. Farley (1842-1918), the Cardinal and fourth archbishop of New York, approved and encouraged the new society and its apostolate. Growing in number and activities, *Theta Phi Alpha* counted more than 3000 teachers among its members in 1929.[16]

Innovations and Expansion

In the early 1920s the CCD apostolate assumed more expansive and innovative dimensions. This was due to the interest and zeal of Edwin V. O'Hara (1881-1956), pastor of St. Mary's parish in Eugene, Oregon. In 1930 O'Hara became bishop of Great Falls,

14. Spellmire had first learned of the Pittsburgh CCD program through an article which appeared in a 1919 issue of the weekly periodical, *Our Sunday Visitor.* Collins, "Religious Education and CCD in the United States," p. 58. See also Dennis J. Burke, "The History of the Confraternity of Christian Doctrine in the Diocese of Los Angeles, 1923-1936" (M.A. dissertation. Washington, D.C.: The Catholic University of America, 1965), p. 19.

15. Collins, "Religious Education and CCD in the United States," p. 59.

16. They described themselves as "Workers for God and Country." Their membership consisted largely of Catholics who were teachers and/or principals in the public school system. They provided religious instruction for Catholic children attending public school. See Raymond J. G. Prindiville, *The Confraternity of Christian Doctrine* (Philadephia: American Ecclesiastical Review, 1932), pp. 14-17.

Montana. In 1939 he was transferred and consecrated bishop of Kansas City, Missouri. Throughout his pastoral life as both pastor and bishop his concern for the people in his parish and dioceses was paramount.[17] With regard to the CCD he was in his own unique way the Charles Borromeo of the church in the United States.

In Oregon O'Hara studied with keen interest the vast farm areas and the people living there. He came to recognize the situation of the parishioners in rural settings. Assessing their life he observed that "food commodities are not the chief thing the farm produces. People are."[18] And for him the rural people were the most important and the most neglected in the realm of social and spiritual endeavor. Studying the existing circumstances, O'Hara soon pinpointed the debilitating defect of rural life, namely, an absence of a cooperative community spirit. It was due, he explained, to "excessive individualism on the farm."[19] That in turn was due in some measure to the distances between family dwellings in farming regions. "Cooperative enterprises," on the other hand, "promise to build up real communities by creating common bonds of interest." "Cooperation is a Christian mode of industry," he maintained. "In removing destructive competition, mutual distrust, and individual selfishness, religion will have an effective aid in cooperative organization."[20]

Three things began to emerge as priorities for O'Hara. They were: 1) the need for rural religious leaders, lay and clerical, who not only knew the land and its people but identified with both; 2) further adult religious education—"A weakness of rural life in the past has been its intellectual poverty;"[21] and 3) the lack of opportunities for religious instruction for children—"The country Sunday school is universally conceded to be a failure."[22] From

17. Edwin V. O'Hara, *The Church and the Country* (New York: Macmillan & Co., 1927), p. 83. See James Gerard Shaw, *Edwin Vincent O'Hara, American Prelate* (New York: Farrar, Straus, and Cudahy, 1957), pp. 98-123. See also Mary Charles Bryce, "Pioneers of Religious Education in the 20th Century," *Religious Education* 73 (1978—Special Edition), pp. 51-57.

18. Shaw, *Edwin Vincent, O'Hara*, p. 65.

19. O'Hara, *The Church and The Country*, pp. 83-84.

20. Ibid., p. 83. See Bryce, "The Confraternity of Christian Doctrine," p. 151.

21. O'Hara, *The Church and the Country*, p. 83.

22. O'Hara, "The Rural Problem and Catholic Education," in *Catholic Educational Association Bulletin* 17 (1920), p. 235.

his youth he remembered his boyhood summers in Minneosta where he became acquainted with religious vacation schools sponsored by Lutherans. The summer school term there was from three to four weeks long and the children attended classes daily except on Sundays. The model seemed fitting.

O'Hara planned and organized a "vacation school" in the summer of 1921 in his parish in Eugene.[23] Actually three rural communities in the large parish participated in the project with sisters from the parish school at Eugene serving as instructors for one month at each of the three: Cottage Grove, Junction City, and Springfield. Teachers, pupils, and parents registered enthusiasm over the pioneer project and plans were made to repeat it the following and subsequent years. It was a program which "caught on" and "took off," netting interest and inquiries from other rural communities.[24] In honesty it must be pointed out that similar religious vacation schools under Catholic auspices had been held in isolated cases prior to the Oregon experiment. Bishop William Theodore Mulloy (1892-1959) told how as a seminarian he spent his summer vacations teaching in religious vacation schools.[25] Another priest related the existence of a similar school in Kansas in 1904. What O'Hara did, besides organizing those in his own area, was to promulgate the possibility of forming an organization of members of the farming community through which difficulties, issues, and "blessings" of rural life could be surfaced and assessed.

Seeking to share his perceptions, O'Hara began to confer with like-minded individuals. Through raising the consciousness of people in critical and political positions he was effective in persuading the Washington-based National Catholic Welfare Conference to set up a "Rural Life Bureau" as a part of its structure. That happened during a committee meeting of the Social Action Department of NCWC which convened in Chicago in Easter week, 1920. Peter James Muldoon (1862-1927), chairman of the Social Action Department and bishop of Rockford, Illinois, was favorably impressed with O'Hara's proposal and persuaded the com-

23. *The Confraternity Comes of Age—An Historical Symposium.* (Paterson, N.J.: Confraternity Publications, 1956), p. 42.

24. Shaw, *Edwin Vincent O'Hara,* pp. 77-79, 80. See Joseph P. Donovan, "Solving the Rural Problem in Missouri," *The Ecclesiastical Review* 71 (1924), pp. 590-598.

25. Raymond Philip Witte, *Twenty-five Years of Crusading* (Des Moines: The National Catholic Rural Life Conference, 1948), p. 142.

mittee as a whole to accept it. On October 1, 1921, O'Hara officially established local headquarters for the "Catholic Rural Life Bureau" in his parish rectory at St. Mary's Parish, Eugene, Oregon.[26] At the grass roots level he convened a meeting of eighty rural residents in November, 1923, at St. Louis, and with them pioneered and formed the National Catholic Rural Life Conference (NCRLC).[27]

Among other things the National Catholic Rural Life Conference held regular meetings which were open to all members of the farming communities. From 1930 to 1934, at each of those annual meetings one session featured talks and discussions on the work of the Confraternity of Christian Doctrine. "Stemming from an interest on the part of bishops and priests of rural areas, techniques were considered to bring the light of Christian doctrine to the families of those areas."[28] Those catechesis sessions soon became the highlight of the NCRLC gatherings as guest speakers presented inspiring and informative addresses to the participants.

Finally, during the NCRLC annual convention held in Rochester, New York, a full day, October 31, was devoted to CCD organization and activity. Meanwhile O'Hara had been consecrated bishop of Great Falls, Montana. He was one of the nine bishops and fifteen priests who made up the assembly of participants at the gathering. That one-day "first" Catechetical Congress was to be the forerunner of many successful congresses to come. An episcopal committee, including Bishop John T. McNicholas, Bishop John G. Murray, and Bishop O'Hara had been asked to serve as a guiding and consultative body for the CCD. They decided, in light of the success of the NCRLC one-day catechetics meeting, to sponsor an annual gathering of people involved in that ministry. The focus was not confined to people in rural settings but to the faithful at large. At the invitation of Patrick Cardinal Hays, the "second" National Catechetical Congress was held in New York City, October 3-6, 1936.[29] That "summons" brought to New York thousands of persons—priests, sisters, brothers, laymen and laywomen— "with one thought in mind: that they might learn how to teach

26. Report of Executive Secretary of the NCRLC, 1943. Bruce Files in Milwaukee.
27. Witte, *Twenty-five Years of Crusading,* p. 183.
28. Bernard J. Gulnerich, "Catechetical Congresses," in *The Confraternity Comes of Age,* pp. 221-222.
29. Ibid., p. 222.

Christian doctrine more effectively."[30]

From that time through 1941 the Catechetical Congresses sponsored by the CCD committee and its organized assistants were held annually. After World War II the congresses were resumed but with less regularity than before.[31]

Meanwhile another aspect of episcopal committee's responsibility was fulfilled. When a committee of the hierarchy had proposed an episcopal committee to serve as a directive and guiding body for CCD, they also formally requested that "a central office for the (national) exchange of information "be set up."[32] At their annual meeting in Washington, D.C., in November, 1934, the bishops, gathered in full assembly, approved both requests. The committee has already been referred to above. The central office, which became known as The National Center of the CCD, became a reality with Rev. Francis A. Walsh, OSB, a monk of St. Anselm's Abbey in Washington, D.C., named as acting director with offices on the campus of Catholic University. He held that position until his death in 1938. The offices however, were moved in May, 1935 to the National Catholic Welfare Conference headquarters at 1312 Massachusetts Avenue, N.W., in downtown Washington.[33]

The National Center

The concept and function of the Center was envisioned as being what its name implied:

> A center that would gather in and give out, for the service of the bishops and diocesan Confraternity directors, the fruits of the best thought and experience in the field of religious instruction for those outside of the Catholic school system.[34]

At the same time that Walsh was appointed national director, Mariam Marks was invited to be field representative, a position which she accepted. That move indicated clearly the intention of outreach and service to the numerous diocesan and parochial units across the country.

As time passed the CCD Center became a pulsating focus of

30. Ibid., p. 224.
31. Ibid., pp. 230-233.
32. Ruth Craven Rock, "The National Center of the CCD," in *The Confraternity Comes of Age*, pp. 148-150.
33. Ibid., p. 149.
34. Ibid., pp. 151-152.

service and activity. In 1935 O'Hara, lamenting the lack of an easily understandable English edition of the Bible for the people in the CCD-sponsored adult Study Clubs, proposed sponsoring the revision of the Challoner text of the Bible. That means "Americanizing" the centuries-old English version of the Latin vulgate.[35] The Center was charged with overseeing publication details of that project.

The Center was also the place where bishops, diocesan directors, and parish leaders could write for a variety of information and for assistance in needs or crises. The directorship changed periodically, but in general the ministry of the Center expanded steadily.

New ventures of the apostolate ultimately came back to the Center for clarification, approval, and in many cases promulgation. One such "new" enterprise had its initial start on the lawn in front of the country courthouse in Oklahoma City, Oklahoma. It was early evening on Monday, April 13, 1932, when a young priest stepped onto the grassy carpet and began to tell the loiterers and passersby about God's word and God's son, Jesus. The most startling thing about the event was that the loiterers interrupted their conversations or their naps and the strollers stopped their ambling. All listened. Furthermore that experience became a weekly event on Mondays through the spring and summer months of that year.

The speaker was twenty-seven-year-old Stephen A. Leven, assistant pastor at nearby St. Joseph Cathedral.[36] Accompanying him was a fellow priest, Victor J. Reed, who addressed the street congregation on alternate Mondays. It was a "first" in another way: the beginning of a twenty-seven-year apostolate of street preaching in the Southwest. Of particular interest here is that Leven became the National Director of the Center in 1948. Of further interest is that both men later became bishops: Leven,

35. The Latin Vulgate is associated with St. Jerome (d. 420) who served as translator, reviser, editor of existent manuscripts. The term "vulgate" indicates that the version was written for the poorly educated and not for the culturally elite. In 1593 a two-man team under the direction of Pope Clement VIII (1592-1605) edited, revised, and made mechanical improvements on the Jerome translation. Considered "official" the printings of that work appeared in 1593 and 1598. It is referred to as the "Clementine" text and/or the "Latin Vulgate." It was from the "Clementine" text that the U.S. translators worked in preparing the so-called "Confraternity edition" of 1941.

36. Rock, "The National Center of the CCD," p. 165.

bishop of San Angelo from 1969-1979 and Reed, bishop of Oklahoma, 1958-1971. The chief point here, is however, the broadening scope of the CCD and the role of the Center in that
expansion.[37]

Another figure and apostolate of the CCD and its Center
emerged in the person of Robert E. Lucey (1891-1977) who was
bishop of San Antonio from 1941-1977. The apostolate most associated with him with respect to the CCD was that of Spanish-
speaking people in the Southwest. His concern for them and
efforts to improve their understanding of Christianity and their
acceptance into the community were primary to him. The Center
in its turn "felt" this challenge and cooperated to work for the
immigrant church in whatever area it was necessary.

Because of his zeal and activity in the realm of the Confraternity it is important to consider some of the scope of his vision and
endeavors.

Though he is probably best remembered as a "champion of social justice"[38] with regard to the life and plight of Mexican-Ameri-
cans in his archdiocese and beyond, he was an innovator in the
sphere of catechesis on two scores: 1) the aspect of cultural differences and their influence in catechesis, and 2) the value of
modern communications media in transmitting the Christian message.

Regarding the first, he was largely responsible for the broadening out of this country's CCD movement to include ideas, practices, thrusts and exchanges from the church in other countries of
the Western Hemisphere. It was through his influence that the
first Regional Inter-American Catechetical Congress was held in
San Antonio, October 23-25, 1947. It was also through his influence that the 1961 Congress added a new dimension to its gatherings, an international quality which included contributions from
leaders in nations south of the Rio Grande.[39]

With farsightedness Lucey insisted on the merits of modern
technology in shaping and proclaiming the Good News. In June,

37. Ibid., pp. 167-168.
38. See "Archbishop Lucey . . . Champion of Social Justice." *Our Sunday Visitor* 66 (August 14, 1977), p. 1. See also "Justice for the Mexi-
cans," *Commonweal* 49 (November 12, 1948), p. 117.
39. See "Interest in Latin America," in Matthew F. Brady, "The Episcopal Committee of the Confraternity of Christian Doctrine," in *Confraternity Comes of Age*, pp. 121-122. See also *Proceedings of the Confraternity
of Christian Doctrine* (1961), pp. 333-340.

1969, he hosted an International Study Week of Mass Media and Catechetics in San Antonio.[40] Lucey seemed to exemplify the conviction that emerged, according to Alfonso Nebreda, from that Study Week:

> The Church must once again have recourse to the gift of tongues with this difference: in addition to Hebrew, Aramaic and Latin, it must master the language of the sound wave, the image and the computer.[41]

In that vein Lucey himself addressed the participants of the International Catechetical Congress in Rome on September 23, 1971.

> Religion must be actively associated with a worldwide satellite network. . . . Today, radio and TV programs are inferior. Tomorrow, a world network will provide programs of many kinds. The world audience will select the programs which please it best. Our script writers must give humanity the finest information and entertainment or lose the contest for men's minds. That would be a tragedy. Either we shall have trained men and women for religious education through the modern media of communication or the Church will face disaster.[42]

Whether or not Lucey placed exaggerated emphasis on the potential of electronic media may be questioned. One could justifiably argue that the person-to-person contact is of prime and irreplaceable importance. On the other hand, when one considers the extensive and persuasive media contacts made by contemporary fundamentalist evangelicals, one is forced to acknowledge the effectiveness of that means of communication. Undoubtedly it is not a matter of either-or but of the wise employment of both. What it does say in this context is that Lucey was a man of his own time with a "tomorrow" vision.

Actually, Lucey's catechesial concerns were comprehensive. The two-pronged innovative directions only partially conveyed his to-

40. The meeting dates were June 22-27. See Virgil Elizondo and Alan Oddie, "San Antonio International Study Week of Mass Media and Catechetics: A Report," *The Living Light* 6 (Winter, 1969), pp. 67-74.

41. Alfonso Nebreda, "Mass Media and Catechetics," *America* 121 (1969), p. 29.

42. See *International Catechetical Congress* (Rome), ed. William J. Tobin (Washington: United States Catholic Conference, 1971), p. 109. Pertinent to this in our own day is the recent publication sponsored by the NCDD: Angela Ann Zukowski, MHSH, *Cable Television*, National Conference of Diocesan Directors of Religious Education—CCD (1984).

tal conviction of the importance of catechesis. He took seriously Vatican II's statement addressed to bishops that "catechetical training is intended to make man's [sic] faith become living, conscious and active . . . [that] bishops should see to it that . . . children, adolescents, young adults and even grownups" should be provided catechetical opportunities. Furthermore, the bishops "should encourage institutes,"

> special meetings in which priests can gather . . . for the acquisition of deeper knowledge of ecclesiastical subjects especially scripture, theology, the social questions of major importance and new methods of pastoral activity.[43]

Lucey determined to implement those injunctions, and he did.

The Congresses

The Confraternity of Christian Doctrine became a forum for bishops, clergy, and others to emphasize and direct catechesial concerns, priorities, and approaches. The periodic congresses offered a platform for idea exchanges, inspiration, and encouragement that extended far beyond the assembly halls. For many, those congresses provided the arena for introducing fresh vigor, enthusiasm, and even pride in the church's life. Furthermore, the Confraternity welcomed apostolates related to, but not specifically, catechesis as such. Just as the CCD had hosted and made possible the more serious study of scripture through a new translation, so did it afford a setting and opportunity for better understanding and appreciation of the church's sacramental life and liturgical practice and the significance of culture and environment to valid expressions of Christian living.[44] The Confraternity

43. *Christus Dominus,* Decree on the Bishops' Pastoral Office in the Church, (October 28, 1965). See *The Documents of Vatican II,* ed., Walter Abbot (New York: Guild Press, 1966), #16d.

44. As chairman of the Episcopal Committee of the CCD, O'Hara had been called upon, in the Fall of 1951, to present a request to Rome for the optional use of English in connection with the rites of baptism, marriage, the sacrament of anointing and burial. He, in turn, called upon the expertise of at least two scholars dedicated to the promotion of the liturgical movement in this country. He asked Gerald Ellard, S.J. (1894-1963) and Godfrey Diekmann, O.S.B. (1908-   ) to undertake the preparation and presentation of the *Collectio Rituum.* He further sought their advice and direction in preparing congresses and programs. See Michael Mathis, "Collectio Rituum," in *The Confraternity Comes of Age,* pp. 301-310.

encouraged ecumenism, explored the relationship of findings in the human sciences toward realizing human potential, and emphasized the value of communication-media. All of those were presented in the overall perspective of one's growth in faith.

It was during the periodic CCD Congresses that these issues came into clear focus. The sessions provided opportunities for catechists to meet other catechists, to hear experts in different fields, to exchange views with their peers and with diocesan priests and leaders from other places. In retrospect it is possible to assess the congresses with quite positive acclaim. One of the most valuable merits of the periodic assemblies was the experience and image of "church" that they projected and realized. Gathered to celebrate the Eucharist together and reassembled alternately to address and listen to one another, they perceived and discovered anew that they were indeed the church alternately learning and teaching. As bishop so-and-so addressed the body—comprised of married and single people, sisters, brothers, priests and other bishops, all dedicated to promoting growth in understanding and in faith—one surveyed the listeners and was awed at that experience.

At the next session, several hours later, the presently speaking bishop would be among the attentive listeners as Mr. Craig or Miss Marks or Mrs. Tinney or Sr. Rosalia or Father Smith or another bishop addressed the gathering. It was a rare experience, that recognition of the church as a body of tacitly acknowledged "unfinished Christians" learning from each other. It was a realization of the fact which the early church knew and the late twentieth-century church is rediscovering—that indeed the *ecclesia*, the community of believers, is the primary catechist.

All were open to learn from, to share with, to search for the fullness of meaning in the reality of their being Christian. No one was "too big" in status or "too small" in importance to participate in those rally-like congresses. "The apostolate does not belong to bishops alone," someone observed.[45] It was evident that the bishops did not see themselves as "too magisterial" to learn from others. Nor did they, on the other hand, hesitate to fulfill their own role as formal catechists when the occasion arose.

An additional value of the congresses was the opportunity they provided for catechists in parochial schools to participate alongside those who, on a weekly basis, catechized children outside the

45. See *Confraternity Comes of Age*, p. 265.

parish school setting. Both groups profited from their informal exchanges with each other and the formal papers presented at the sessions.

Subsequent Events

In the early sixties a gradual sense of uneasiness with the Center developed in some of the outlying areas. Individual diocesan leaders and workers felt that some of their needs and inquiries were not adequately or wisely handled. There were at least two factors that undoubtedly contributed to that. One was due, in part, to overextension of responsibilities and work of those at the central office. Another was an increasing ideological "distance" that seemed to develop between some well-informed people "in the field" and those in the office. To a certain extent the latter was due to the progress of the so-called Catechetical Movement which was making strides in Europe and beginning to overflow into the United States. Those at the Center office were not always well-informed about it and were sometimes unable to respond knowledgeably to inquiries related to it.

The "movement" was usually associated with the work and writings of Josef A. Jungmann, S.J., of Innsbruck, but it was not confined to him. Jungmann was a guest lecturer at the University of Notre Dame during the summers in the mid-fifties. Others, such as Johannes Hofinger, S.J., followed him there.

In contrast to the usual dependency on the catechism, "modern catechetics," as it came to be called, relied more directly on scripture, especially under the concept of "salvation history," and the *"kerygmatic"* (good news) approach to Christian doctrine. It was *not* a total refutation of existing practice in the field of catechesis but a widening and expanding understanding of it.[46]

The staff at the Center made strides in keeping abreast of the progress. One major step was that of initiating the publication of a new journal, *The Living Light,* a quarterly described on its cover as "An International Review of Catholic Religious Education, Catechesis and Pastoral Ministry." The first issue appeared in

46. "The modern catechetical movement breathed new life into an old word. Catechesis becomes the focal point for a number of strategies aimed at revitalizing the Church and making its members more self-conscious of their identity as Christians." Berard L. Marthaler, "Introduction," *Sourcebook for Modern Catechetics,* ed. Michael Warren (Winona, Minn.: St. Mary's Press, 1983), p. 15.

1964 with Mary Perkins Ryan serving as editor. In 1972 she relinquished that position to Berard L. Marthaler, OFM, Conv., who continues to edit the periodical at the present time.

Another shift in direction for the Center and catechesis in this country took place in April, 1966, during a meeting of diocesan directors in New Orleans. At that gathering the directors felt the need for greater collaboration among themselves with regard to distinctive pastoral issues. They proposed the formation of an organized body from among their number. After serious deliberation the proposal carried and the National Conference of Diocesan Directors (NCDD) became a reality. Father John Russell was the first chairman.[47] Russell and his successors worked with the Center in serving the needs of the church in the sphere of catechesis-religious education. At their annual NCDD meetings the directors and fellow workers face and project issues and ideals pertinent to contemporary circumstances.

The year 1971 was full of events affecting the leadership and direction of catechesis in this country. Those events were not necessarily interrelated or resulting one from another. In June of that year the Sacred Congregation for the Clergy published the *Directorium Catechisticum Generale*[48] (The General Catechetical Directory), in fulfillment of the directive given by the Second Vatican Council.[49] In September of that year an International Catechetical Congress was held in Rome to put into clear perspective the ideals and principles of the Directory recently promulgated.[50] In October the last of the CCD Congresses was held in Miami, Florida. Finally, the National Center terminated its existence in Washington. Though the latter two had about them a nostalgic sense of sadness, the church's catechetical apostolate was not to suffer from them.

In 1979 the bishops of the church in the United States published their own directory under the title *Sharing the Light of Faith*.[51]

47. Robert Stamschor, "A Place of the NCDD in the Catechetical Movement," *The Living Light* 19 (1982), pp. 264-269.

48. *Directorium Catechisticum Generale* (Rome: Typis Polyglottis Vaticanis, 1971). English translation, *General Catechetical Directory* (Washington, D.C.: U.S. Catholic Conference, 1971).

49. *The Documents of Vatican II, Christus Dominus*, #44.

50. William J. Tobin, ed., *International Catechetical Congress. Selected Documentation* (Washington, D.C.: U.S. Catholic Conference, 1972).

51. *Sharing the Light of Faith* (Washington, D.C.: U.S. Catholic Conference, 1979).

The work was several years in process, involving countless persons—teachers, parents, pastors, and the faithful at large. Without in any way minimizing the role and leadership of the bishops it was a work of, for, and by the church in the United States.

Conclusion

References to the CCD are not used as frequently as they once were. That is not a rejection of an "out-dated" concept. There is a contemporaneity about the ideals and principles that the Confraternity has always maintained. More recent approaches, structures, and vocabulary build on the foundation laid by the wisdom and zeal of previous leaders and their experiences. But they do not necessarily contradict. That is verified when one examines selected conclusions from the greatly respected "International Conference" held in Eichstatt, Bavaria, in 1960.[52]

1. Catechesis carries out the command of Christ to proclaim God's message of salvation to all people.
2. Catechesis proclaims the merciful love of the Father for us and proclaims the Good News of God's Kingdom.
3. Catechesis is Christ-centered, reflecting the fufillment in and through the Christ of the Father's loving design.
4. Catechesis proclaims that Christ continues to live and work in his church through the Holy Spirit and the ministry of his shepherds.
5. Catechesis emphasizes that worship is the heart of community life.
6. Catechesis makes Christians aware of their responsibility for the world and betterment of its condition.[53]

Perhaps one participant in the 1971 Miami Congress expressed it best when he observed that there will always be the charge and the challenge of CCD, recognized as "continuing Christian development."

52. Those conclusions with commentary are cited in Warren, *Sourcebook for Modern Catechetics*, pp. 34-39.
53. The amplification of that principle deserves attention. It points out that "the Christian sees the world as the work and possession of the Father in heaven and feels responsible for it as 'son and heir.' What is called 'profane' or 'natural' order is no less from the hand of God. The Christian must value it in itself if he or she is to contribute to its sanctification in Christ." Ibid., p. 36.

Chapter 3

Research on the Sunday School Mosaic

WARREN J. HARTMAN

The Sunday school is a giant mosaic that spreads across the North American continent. It is found in the open country, in almost every village and hamlet, in every town and city, in every metropolitan area. Millions of children, youth, and adults meet together in Sunday schools for the purpose of studying the gospel and learning about the Christian faith and life in order that they might grow in faith and love.

The Sunday school movement is so massive that the exact number of schools and students is not known. Many are never reported. Other reports are not up-to-date. But of one thing we can be sure: the Sunday school movement is a giant enterprise.

The data in the *Yearbook of American and Canadian Churches* illustrate the fact.[1] Each annual *Yearbook* includes only the most recent data about the number of Sunday or Sabbath schools in each denomination along with their total enrollments. The Yearbooks do not include information that is out-of-date or non-current.

This practice, coupled with the fact that a number of denominations do not gather and report Sunday school data every year, means that the Yearbook reports do not represent the full strength and size of the Sunday school movement. Given those limitations, the Yearbooks still provide the most reliable long-term data available concerning the strength of and annual trends

---

1. *Yearbook of American and Canadian Churches*, ed. Constant H. Jacquet, Jr., (New York· Office of Research, Evaluation, and Planning of The National Council of Churches of Christ in the U.S.A.). Issued annually.

in the Sunday school and Sabbath school movement. We have
drawn heavily on the Yearbooks for much of what follows in this
chapter.

In order to examine some of the trends that have been developing the last ten years, we compared data from the *1974 Yearbook*
with those in the *1984 Yearbook.* Most of the reports in the Yearbooks are two years old. So, most of the data that we examined
were reported by the denominations in 1972 and 1982.

We found that both Yearbooks contain current Sunday and Sabbath school data for thirty-three denominations in the United
States and Canada that have an inclusive church membership of
100,000 or more. We chose the 100,000 membership figure as a
cut-off point in order to hold the number of cases to a more
manageable size. The decision was a pragmatic one and should not
be interpreted to mean that we consider the Sunday schools in
denominations with fewer than 100,000 members to be of lesser
importance or effectiveness.

The *1974 Yearbook* shows that the total Sunday and Sabbath
school enrollment in those thirty-three denominations stood at
25,293,833. Ten years later, the *1984 Yearbook* shows the total
enrollment in the same thirty-three denominations standing at
24,727,950. This represents a shrinkage of slightly more than
one-half million—565,883 students, or 2.2 percent in one decade.

Some Are Growing and Some Are Shrinking

On the surface it would appear that the Sunday schools in each
of the thirty-three denominations are relatively stable and most
have neither grown nor declined much during the last ten years.
However, an examination of the data on a denomination by denomination basis shows that there have been some very significant gains and losses within the churches.

Ten of the denominations reported Sunday or Sabbath school
gains over the last ten years that totaled 2.32 million students
That represents a percentage gain of 20.1 percent for the ten-year
period.

Table I lists the ten denominations with growing Sunday and
Sabbath schools and gives both the numerical and percentage
gains for each. Note that three of the ten denominations—The
Church of Jesus Christ of Latter Day Saints, the Assemblies of
God, and The Southern Baptist Convention—have a composite net
increase of 2.11 million enrollees. The gains in those three de-

Table I
SUNDAY SCHOOL GROWTH
1974-1984
DENOMINATIONS WITH 100,000 MEMBERS OR MORE

Denomination	1974	1984	# Gained	% Gain
Church of Jesus Christ of Latter-Day Saints Canada	53,205	96,000	42,795	80.4
The Christian Congregation, Inc.	33,960	57,998	24,038	70.8
The Church of Jesus Christ of Latter-Day Saints	2,023,287	3,298,000	1,274,713	63.0
Assemblies of God	1,078,332	1,421,924	343,592	31.9
Free Will Baptist	165,000	195,333	30,333	18.4
Seventh-Day Adventists	383,239	448,681	65,442	17.1
Southern Baptists	7,175,186	7,669,883	494,697	6.9
Church of God (Cleveland)	483,565	508,863	25,298	5.2
Mennonite Church	111,747	115,300	3,553	3.2
	11,507,521	13,811,982	2,304,461	20.0%

Source: Yearbooks of American and Canadian Churches 1974 and 1984

nominations account for 90.9 percent of the total gains reported by the ten denominations with growing Sunday and Sabbath schools!

During the same ten-year period, the remaining twenty-three denominations reported a net loss of 2.89 million Sunday school enrollees. That represents a percentage decrease of 21 percent.

The twenty-three denominations with shrinking Sunday schools are listed in Table II along with the numerical and percentage losses. Note that eight of the twenty-three denominations show losses in excess of 100,000 enrollees. The aggregate loss from those eight denominations was 2.51 million, or 87 percent of all the losses reported by the twenty-three denominations with declining Sunday schools.

The large gains among some churches and the equally large declines among other denominations during the same ten-year period raise several perplexing questions.

Since the increases in the growing Sunday and Sabbath schools totaled more than 2 million students and the losses in the declining Sunday schools were also in excess of 2 million, one might be inclined to ask how many of those gains and losses are due to

Table II
SUNDAY SCHOOL DECLINE
1974-1984
DENOMINATIONS WITH 100,000 MEMBERS OR MORE

Denomination	1974	1984	# Lost	% Loss
Baptist Missionary Assoc. of Amer.	102,479	101,613	(866)	−0.8
The Salvation Army	106,754	103,304	(3,450)	−3.2
The Episcopal Church	606,156	556,372	(49,784)	−8.2
The Christian & Miss. Alliance	180,745	165,491	(15,254)	−8.4
Church of God (Anderson, Ind)	244,921	221,130	(23,791)	−9.7
The American Lutheran Church	670,571	587,144	(83,407)	−12.4
Reformed Church in America	119,822	104,326	(15,492)	−12.9
United Church of Canada	293,990	252,237	(41,753)	−14.2
Wisc. Evangelical Lutheran Synod	56,527	47,208	(9,319)	−16.5
The Lutheran Church—Missouri	783,952	642,885	(141,067)	−18.0
Church of Nazarene	992,668	811,438	(181,230)	−18.3
Anglican Church of Canada	127,154	103,312	(23,842)	−18.7
Baptist General Conference	120,453	96,543	(23,910)	−19.8
Lutheran Church in America	844,195	670,578	(173,617)	−20.6
The United Methodist Church	5,380,147	4,201,400	(1,178,787)	−21.9
Presbyterian Church in the U.S.	489,050	375,256	(113,794)	−23.3
Church of the Brethren	80,077	61,067	(19,010)	−23.7
Lutheran Chu. in Amer-Canada Section	27,210	20,285	(6,925)	−25.5
United Presbyterian USA	1,109,570	803,386	(306,184)	−27.6
United Church of Christ	659,122	471,003	(188,119)	−28.5
Christian Church Disciples of Christ	580,503	349,715	(230,788)	−39.7

Christian Reformed Ch. in N. America	92,715	53,018	(39,697) −42.8
	13,668,781	10,798,711	(2,870,086) −21.0%

Source: Yearbooks of American and Canadian Churches 1974 and 1984

denominational switching. Roof and Hadaway[2] have found that an increasing number of persons are switching their church membership. While their studies focus primarily on church membership and not Sunday school enrollment, there is little evidence to indicate that the number who have switched from the denominations with shrinking Sunday schools to the three denominations with the fastest growing Sunday and Sabbath schools would be as great as two million. We therefore, are concluding that while some of the growth and shrinkage is undoubtedly due to switching, other factors probably contribute more to the growth and to the shrinkage.

A second question is prompted by the findings of the Gallup Organization in the 1978 study of "The Unchurched American."[3] In that study 95 percent of the churched parents and 74 percent of the unchurched parents said they wanted their children to receive religious instruction. Furthermore, three-fourths of those who want religious instruction for their children say that they want the Sunday school to provide that instruction. With that overwhelmingly expressed desire on the part of parents, both inside and outside the church, why are twenty-three denominations reporting such massive losses? One could speculate about a number of possible answers, but the persistently nagging question is: Do the parents not feel that the Sunday schools in those twenty-three denominations are offering the kind of quality of religious instruction that they want for their children?

One clue might be lodged in Hoge's rating of sixteen denominations.[4] He invited twenty-one experts to rate the churches in eight dimensions. Fifteen of the sixteen denominations are among the

2. Wade Clark Roof and Christopher Kirk Hadaway, "Denominational Switching in the Seventies: Going Beyond Stark and Glock," *Journal for the Scientific Study of Religion* 18, no. 4 (December, 1979), pp. 375-77.

3. *The Unchurched American* (Princeton: The Princeton Religion Research Center and The Gallup Organization, Inc., 1978), p. 47.

4. Dean R. Hoge *Understanding Church Growth and Decline, 1950-1978*, ed. Dean R. Hoge and Daird H. Roozen (New York/Philadelphia: The Pilgrim Press, 1979), pp. 183-86.

thirty-three in our investigation. Four of them have growing Sunday schools and eleven have declining Sunday schools.

All four of the growing Sunday and Sabbath schools are in denominations that, according to Hoge's ratings, place a heavier emphasis on local and community evangelism than any of the eleven churches that have declining Sunday schools.

Further, all four churches with growing Sunday or Sabbath schools are also judged to be more theologically conservative and less involved in social action than all but two of the eleven with shrinking Sunday schools. Those two are the Lutheran Church-Missouri Synod and the Church of the Nazarene.[5]

Those data suggest that the dominant theological position and the importance attached to local and community evangelism and to social action involvement may all affect the growth and decline of the Sunday school.

A third question has to do with the importance attached to the Sunday school as an organization or movement within the denomination as a whole. We have no solid documentation concerning this question. However, conversations with denominational headquarters personnel and a cursory review of denominational publications tend to support our belief that the health and effectiveness of the Sunday school is strongly affected by the place that it occupies in the bureaucratic and institutional life of the several denominations.

One example of this is found in a Southern Baptist list of characteristics of growing Southern Baptist churches. One characteristic is: "use of the Sunday school as the major growth outreach arm of the church."[6] As previously mentioned, we found little solid documentation to answer the three above questions or other

5. Although Sunday school enrollment has decreased in the Church of the Nazarene in the last decade, their Sunday school enrollment as a percentage of church membership stands at 162 percent. This is by far the highest among all thirty-three denominations. The average for the other ten dominations with growing Sunday schools is 80.6 percent and the overall average for the thirty-three denominations is 48.9 percent.

Undoubtedly, the high Sunday school enrollment contributed to the hefty 23 percent church membership gain that was reported by the Church of the Nazarene during the last decade.

6. In a research project to test the relevancy of the basics of Sunday School Growth, James E. Fitch quotes from a paper, "Growing Southern Baptist Churches," in which the presenters affirm "the use of the Sunday school as the major growth outreach arm of the Church." Fitch then shows how that statement is foundational to the Southern Baptist Sunday School Growth plan.

equally important ones that the data pose. The paucity of research that focuses sharply on the Sunday school suggests that future research might well probe into the dynamics that produce such opposite results among the different denominations.

As the Sunday School Goes, So Goes the Church

Through the years the Sunday school has had its detractors as well as its staunch supporters. In the earliest days, the relationship of the Sunday school to and its place in the larger church generated many fierce debates. In more recent years those debates have given way to discussions about the real value and worth of the Sunday school. Some have felt that the Sunday school has made its contribution and should either be replaced or radically altered. Others disagree and stoutly affirm its continued importance to the life of the church. We would now like to address that question, and we will do so by noting what we consider to be three strong pieces of evidence.

An analysis of the data from the thirty-three denominations shows that there is a definite relationship between changes in Sunday school enrollment and changes in church membership rolls.

When the percentage changes that have occurred in the Sunday school enrollment of the thirty-three denominations are compared with the percentage changes that have taken place in church membership during the last ten years, the correlation coefficient is a positive .83. The correlations between Sunday school and church membership changes in the twenty-seven denominations in the United States are an even higher positive .86!

That finding is consistent with those reported by Ruth T. Doyle and Sheila M. Kelly in "Understanding Church Growth and Decline."[7] When they analyzed data from ten denominations and allowed for a five-year time lag, they found positive correlations between Sunday school enrollment and church membership trends that ranged from .74 to .99. The five-year time lag was based on a United Methodist study which demonstrated that changes in church school enrollment are followed by corresponding changes in church membership within five years.[8]

The lag time may vary among denominations due primarily to

7. Ruth T. Doyle and Sheila M. Kelley, in *Understanding Church Growth and Decline*, p. 155.

8. Warren J. Hartman, *Membership Trends: A Study of Decline and Growth in The United Methodist Church, 1949-1975* (Nashville: Discipleship Resources, 1976).

different procedures that are followed by different churches
when adding or removing names from the Sunday school and
church membership rolls. However, even though the length of the
time lag may vary from church to church, changes in Sunday
school enrollment normally precede corresponding changes in
church membership totals.

That consistent sequence suggests that Sunday school enrollment trends may well be one of the most, if not *the* most, reliable
leading indicator of church membership trends.

Moreover, while we readily acknowledge that it is very difficult
to establish a definite cause-and-effect relationship between
factors within the life of the church, we will go a step farther and
offer the belief that the Sunday school is not only a predictor of
church membership trends but is a major determinant of church
membership trends.

Our rationale for the above assertion is as follows: The list of
thirty-three denominations in which we found a high positive
correlation between changes in Sunday school enrollment and
church membership totals includes some churches that are growing and some that are declining. In their study, Doyle and Kelly
also found consistently high positive correlations within growing
and declining churches.

Therefore, we conclude that there is a strong probability that a
definite cause-and-effect relationship does exist between both
positive and negative trends in Sunday school enrollment and
church membership totals.

Further, we noted that changes usually occur first in Sunday
school enrollment and then later, often as much as five years
later, corresponding changes occur in the church membership roll
totals. This sequence indicates that the Sunday school is the
cause agent in that relationship.

We conclude, therefore, that the dictum is true which states,
"As the Sunday school goes, so goes the church."

Two Keys to Two Doors

The foregoing discussion has focused on the total Sunday
school enrollment and the inclusive church membership of each
denomination and their interrelationships. Both are bottom-line
figures that can be separated into any number of distinct segments. For example: Sunday schools have traditionally been divided along age-group lines, but they can also be examined in
other ways. Church membership rolls can also be divided along

age-group lines, but for our purposes in this discussion we are examining church membership rolls from two other perspectives: those who are admitted to the church on confession of faith, and those who drop out of the church.

Our examination indicates that two age-level segments of the Sunday school are closely related to and probably affect the number of persons who are received on confession of faith, and the number of persons who drop-out of the church. Another way to say it is: There is some evidence that the Sunday school may be the principal keeper of the keys that unlock and lock the front and back doors of our churches.

The Front Door

In most denominations, persons are first received or admitted into church membership when they affirm their commitment in faith to Jesus Christ, declare their intention to be faithful to that commitment, and express their desire to unite with the church. The exact procedures, rituals, and symbols vary from church to church, but the intent and meaning are very similar. Every church follows an accepted plan for recognizing and celebrating the entrance of new Christians into the faith community.

There is considerable evidence which indicates that the Sunday school is a principal gateway through which many persons begin their faith journey that leads to the commitment described above.

We noted earlier that the Assemblies of God is one of the most rapidly growing denominations with an equally rapid growing Sunday school. A report from the denominational statistician shows that in 1982 the local congregations with an active Sunday school reported 31.2 percent more conversions than the churches without an active Sunday school.[9]

The Bureau of Research and Planning of the American Baptist Church, USA, has shared a report in which the correlation between percentage changes in church school enrollment and baptisms is a positive .87.[10]

Since 1974 United Methodist pastors have been asked to report the number of church school members who join the church on confession of faith each year. Those reports show that the church schools have supplied from 60 to 65 percent of those who have

9. From Sherri L. Doty in a letter to the author, dated August 20, 1984.
10. From data supplied by Dr. Richard K. Gladden, Director of Research and Planning, American Baptist Churches, September 10, 1984.

been received on confession of faith since 1974.[11]

Several other denominational leaders have reported that they are also operating on the assumption that the Sunday school is the source of as many or even a higher percentage of the new Christians who are received into church membership. However, their record systems are such that they cannot supply solid data to support that conviction. Undoubtedly, other explorations of the relationship of the Sunday school to other parts of congregational life have been conducted that have not come to our attention. For those omissions, we offer our apologies.

Because we have not located such other studies, the findings that follow are based largely on several long-term analyses of United Methodist data. We have included such supporting data from other sources that we been able to gather.

Not only do data show that a high percentage of those who are received on confession of faith come from the church school, but, more specifically, analyses indicate a strong positive correlation between the number of professions of faith and enrollment in the children's division of the Sunday school. Table III shows the correlations for the last ten years.

Table III
Correlations Between Children's Division Enrollment
and
The Number of Persons Received on Confession of Faith
The United Methodist Church
1974-1983[12]

Year	Correlation
1974	.90
1975	.93
1976	.90
1977	.88
1978	.93
1979	.90
1980	.94
1981	.94
1982	.85
1983	.94

11. *General Minutes of the Annual Conferences of the United Methodist Church* (Evanston: The General Council on Finance and Administration). Issued annually.

12. *General Minutes*, 1975-1984.

While the strength of the correlations varies slightly from year to year, the overall correlation is consistently positive and strong. We therefore have concluded that enrollment in the children's division in the Sunday schools is a reliable indicator of the number of persons that we can expect to receive into the United Methodist Church on confession of faith.

In light of the above data, who can deny the possibility that the Sunday school may well be the principal keeper of the key to the front door of the church through which new Christians enter into a life of faith and service?

And, the Back Door?

Just as one measure of the faithfulness of a congregation is the number of persons who are received on confession of faith, so another measure of faithfulness is the extent to which each person actually becomes a part of the congregation in such a way that his or her needs are satisfied. It is generally assumed that when the perceived needs of those in the congregation are being met the drop-out rate will be low. Conversely, when those perceived needs are not being met for one reason or another, the drop-rate will increase.

There is some evidence that adult Sunday school classes can provide the kind of acceptance, relationships, support, and faith nurture that adults want and need. When those needs are met, adults are more inclined to become assimilated and involved in the total life of the congregation on a consistent and continuing basis. When their perceived needs are not met, adults soon lose interest and are very likely to drop out altogether.

A comparison of enrollment in the adult division of United Methodist Sunday schools with the number of persons whose names are removed from the church membership rolls because they have dropped out shows a consistently strong negative correlation. Table IV gives the correlations for the last ten years. A stronger negative correlation indicates that as the enrollment increases, the number of drop-outs decreases. Conversely, a weaker negative correlation indicates either a decrease in enrollment or an increase in drop-outs, or possibly a combination of both.

The likelihood that fewer drop-outs will be found in churches where a larger percentage of adults are enrolled in the adult division of the Sunday school is probably related to several factors. We would like to offer two possibilities.

The first is related to the faith nurturing experience of adults

Table IV
Correlations of Adult Division Enrollment
with
The Number of Church Drop-Outs
The United Methodist Church
1974-1983[13]

Year	Correlation
1974	−.82
1975	−.84
1976	−.77
1977	−.77
1978	−.83
1979	−.77
1980	−.76
1981	−.70
1982	−.93
1983	−.68

who are enrolled in a Sunday school. A comparative study was made of the beliefs, attitudes, and practices of two groups of adults.[14] Those in one group were enrolled in a Sunday school and regularly attended worship services. Those in the other group were from the same congregations and regularly attended worship services, but did not attend Sunday school.

Significant differences between those in the two groups were found. Those who attended Sunday school and worship services were more regular in worship attendance, were more likely to invite others to enter into the fellowship of Christians, were much more inclined to believe that the church should be involved in the community and world, and read their Bibles and prayed more frequently.

Such data suggest that those who are in the Sunday school are less likely to drop out of the church because the Sunday school may be a means of nurturing them in ways that enhance their commitment to the church and all that it represents.

The second factor may be a psychosociological one. Several studies have shown that persons look on the Sunday school class as a place and setting in which they experience love and accept-

13. Ibid.
14. Warren J. Hartman, *A Study of the Church School in The United Methodist Church*, 1972 (Nashville: Board of Education).

ance and feel wanted and needed on a continuing basis.[15]

As might be expected, the study has also shown that the larger the congregation, the more importance persons attach to their Sunday school class and other settings that bring them into face-to-face relationships with those in the congregation.[16]

Richard A. Myers has also demonstrated that if a class or group is too large, the room is too crowded, or other conditions exist that cause persons to feel unwelcome, they will drop out or, at best, become quite irregular in attendance.[17]

This brings us to a disturbing observation: Just as the Sunday school is the gateway through which many persons begin their faith journey into the church, so also the Sunday school is the point from which many persons begin their exit from the church. Many church drop-outs tend to drop out gradually and often over an extended period of time. The first sign that a person is in the process of dropping out is irregular attendance and participation in the Sunday school or other small group of which he or she is a part. This is followed by increasingly irregular attendance in worship services and other congregational activities. Eventually, he or she stops attending altogether, or, at best, attendance is limited to special occasions.

We therefore have concluded that the above data, coupled with the all-too-familiar drop-out sequence, suggest the very strong possibility that the number of adults who are enrolled in the adult division of the Sunday school may be a good indicator of the number of church drop-outs that can be expected in the future.

So, perhaps the adult division may be one of the important keepers of the key that locks the back door of the church.

Five Audiences

Arnold Mitchell has identified nine distinct American life-styles.[18] His book is designed to help advertisers and marketing specialists understand and appeal to the various segments of their potential consumers.

15. Ibid.
16. Ibid.
17. Richard A. Myers, *Factors that Affect Church School Class Size*, Report No. 2 in the Church Development Series, 1969 (Indianapolis: Richard A. Myers).
18. Arnold Mitchell, *The Nine American Lifestyles*, (New York: Macmillan, 1983).

For too long Christian educators have tended to assume that all persons who attend and participate in the Sunday school want and need the same things. Of course, the educators have acknowledged developmental needs and have made provisions for age-level differences. But beyond that there has been a tendency to assume that a common organizational model, one or two styles of teaching, and one or two lines of curriculum resources would satisfy the needs of those in our Sunday schools.

Just as Mitchell has discovered that there are distinctively different American lifestyles, so we have found that there are at least five separate audience groups in most Sunday schools and congregations. Those in each audience group have characteristics and expectations that are unique to those in that group. They differ in their theological perspectives, personal characteristics, beliefs and attitudes; in their Sunday school and church expectations and participation patterns; as well in other ways.

The five audience groups were first identified in 1972 in a study that involved 1657 laypersons from 288 United Methodist congregations.[19] Subsequent investigations and tests with several thousand additional laypersons, pastors, professional educators, and others have helped to confirm the identity of the five groups and to flesh out the profiles. A more detailed discussion of the five audiences will appear in a forthcoming book.[20] In this chapter we will give only a very brief profile of those in each audience group and then identify three implications for Sunday school planners and administrators.

We have given labels to each audience group for identification purposes. The labels are not intended to be fully descriptive or definitive. We are listing the five audiences in the order of size, except for the last one which is made up of several different combinations.

Fellowship

Those in the fellowship group constitute the largest group. Theologically, they range from the very conservative to the very liberal. They are not inclined to attach strong importance to their theological position, nor to denominational labels. They have be-

19. Hartman, *A Study of the Church School in The United Methodist Church.*
20. The book, title to be determined, will be in Lyle Schaller's Creative Leadership Series and is scheduled for release in 1985.

longed to more different denominations than the majority of those in the congregation.

Two age-groups are dominant—young adults and those who are about fifty-five years of age and older. There are more men in this group. They report the highest level of income and the third highest level of education. Many are in vocations that call for frequent moves.

They look to the Sunday school and church for ready acceptance and a supportive group of friends. They maintain high records of attendance at informal and social activities in the church but have a poor record of worship attendance and are next to the lowest in regular Sunday school attendance.

They enjoy Sunday school classes that offer ample opportunity for informal conversation, that recognize and share in the joys as well as the concerns of others, and have social activities in addition to the more formal class sessions. They prefer teachers who function informally and encourage discussion. As a whole, those in this group are not particularly concerned about what kind of curriculum resources are used, providing they have ample opportunity to raise their questions, express their doubts, share their faith concerns, and experience the love and support of others.

Traditional

We have called the second audience group the traditionalists. Theologically, they are considerably more conservative than those in any other group and tend to look on others in the congregation, and often the pastor, as being quite liberal. Some listen regularly to radio and television religionists and occasionally have difficulty determining whether the theological positions of their pastor or those of the popular evangelists should be given the most credence.

As a group, they are older, and have the lowest level of education and income. They are fiercely loyal to their local congregation and have been members of the denomination and of their local congregation for a longer period of time than those in the other audiences. They are inclined to be less supportive of and interested in the cooperative or interdenominational activities beyond their immediate community.

They have the highest record of regular attendance in the worship services of their church and maintain the second highest record of Sunday school attendance. They prefer classes and groups that are organized and structured to do things about the same way each time they meet. They prefer curriculum resources that make heavy and consistent use of the Bible. Those in this group want teachers and leaders who are biblically oriented, who hold strong convictions about their own faith, and who are more inclined to lecture rather than lead discussions.

Study

The third audience group is made up of persons who place a high value on a faith pilgrimage that is informed by a broad understanding of the faith, the Bible, and the traditions of the church. They tend to hold theological positions that are just slightly to the left of center and are most accepting and tolerant of others whose theological position may differ from their own.

They are most likely to be older young adults or middle-aged persons who are in families where one or more persons follow a professional career, or hold a management or supervisory position. They have the highest level of education and report the third highest level of income.

They are strongly committed to the total ministry of the church through local, denominational, and ecumenical expressions. Many of those in this audience hold key positions in their local congregation, and are inclined to be willing to serve and give leadership to various forms of the church's ministry beyond the local congregation.

They have the highest record of regular attendance in Sunday school and are the second most regular in worship attendance.

Those in this study group prefer Sunday school classes that are rather loosely structured, flexible in their operation, and provide ample opportunities for discussion and dialogue. They like to study a wide range of subjects that contribute to their understanding of the Bible and the Christian faith. They tend to take such understandings seriously and will struggle with their implications for their daily lives and work.

Social Concerns

The fourth audience group is the smallest in number. Those in this group have a very deep concern about and commitment to the social expressions of the Christian faith. Theologically, they consider themselves to be the most liberal persons in the congregation, and they are inclined to believe that others in the congregation, and sometimes their pastor, are much more conservative than they are.

This group includes a larger percentage of women than any of the other groups. They have a high level of formal education and an income that is often above the average for the congregation.

They are strongly committed to the church as an agent for social change and are very supportive of those programs and activities that are designed to bring about those changes. At the same time, they are not inclined to give much attention to those ongoing activities of the church in which the social dimensions are not dominant or clearly visible.

They have the lowest record of Sunday school attendance and they have the third highest record of worship attendance.

They respond best to teachers and leaders who help them grow in their understanding of the Christian faith and life as it relates to the community and world in which they live. They do not attach much value to highly organized Sunday school classes or to groups lacking in a broad understanding of the faith and ministry of the church. They often look on the class as a launching pad or support base from which they might address the issues and concerns in their community and world.

Multiple Interests Group

The fifth and largest audience group is made up those whose characteristics include combinations of those which are found in the four more sharply defined groups described above. They fall almost at the mid-point mark in every characteristic that has been used as an indicator. For example, those in this group identify their theological position at a point that is about mid-way between the traditionalists and those in the social concern group. The levels of their formal education and income are usually just about average for the congregation.

Well over half of them tend to exhibit combinations of characteristics that define the fellowship group along with those of one or more of the other groups. Thus, the profiles of the majority of those in this group may be a combination of fellowship and traditional characteristics, fellowship and study characteristics, or fellowship and social concerns characteristics. Or perhaps they may indicate other combinations of any other two, or three, or even all four groups.

Generally they are interested in the total ministry of the church but are not inclined to take strong advocacy positions on issues and concerns that may arise from time to time. Most of them are cooperative and will adjust to and participate in the ongoing life

Figure I[21]
QUALITIES OF TEACHERS VALUED
—BY AUDIENCE GROUPS—

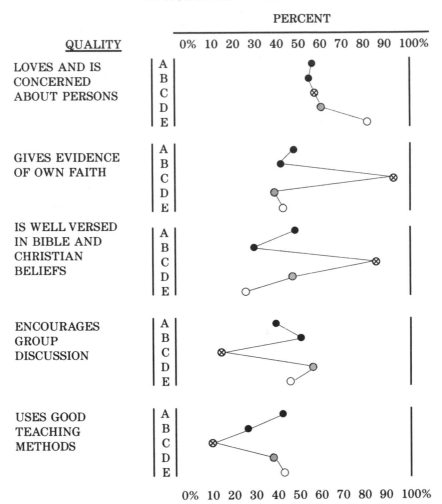

21. Hartman, *A Study of the Church School in The United Methodist Church.*

and activities of the Sunday school classes or groups to which they belong. They enjoy fellowship with others, and they also appreciate opportunities to explore the gospel and its meaning for their lives.

Teacher and Class Expectations

We have made brief references to the different expectations that those in each group hold concerning their Sunday school and their teacher. Figure I illustrates some of those expectations.

Figure I illustrates the amount of importance those in each audience group attach to five different qualities or characteristics of a Sunday school teacher. Note that the multiple interests group holds to the mid-point position in their rating of each of the teacher qualities just as they do in most other profile characteristics. While a few persons in the multiple interests group rate one or two of the values very high and a few say that some of the characteristics are of no importance, the majority tend to take a moderate position and are not overly anxious or disappointed when the teachers' characteristics or style of teaching are not entirely in accord with their expectations.

Since those in the fellowship group are looking for strong supportive relationships with others in the class, they are not overly concerned about the teacher's faith example, biblical knowledge, or teaching methodology. But they do want ample opportunity for discussion and interaction with others during the regular class session, as well as before and afterward. The traditionalists attach very high importance to the teacher's own personal faith example and his or her biblical and theological knowledge. They deplore group discussions and probably equate discussions with good teaching methods, which they also feel are worthless. The traditionalists want a teacher who lectures to them and is able to draw heavily on superior biblical and theological knowledge and understanding.

Those persons who have been identified as the study group tend to attach less importance to the teacher's own personal faith example than those in the other groups. However, they do want a teacher who is knowledgeable about the Bible and Christian beliefs and who uses good teaching methods. Above all, they feel that it is important to engage in discussion and dialogue with those in the class.

The social concerns group places an exceedingly high value on the importance of having a teacher who loves and shows concern for all persons. They seem to draw a distinction between loving and showing concern for others and giving evidence of personal faith, for they tend to attach only moderate importance to the latter. They do not feel that the teacher should be required to have a great deal of biblical and theological knowledge. It is, however, important for the teacher to use good teaching methods and to encourage group discussion.

Some Implications

The distinct differences among those in the five audience groups have a number of implications for those who would plan for and administer the Sunday school. Three of the most obvious implications are:

1. The diversity of theological perspectives, the wide range of expectations concerning the way the class should be conducted, and the different teacher characteristics and styles all suggest that deliberate efforts should be made to offer several different options in every congregation where that is possible.

2. The traditional manner of forming Sunday school classes and assigning persons to them on the basis of age, sex, or marital status is called into question by the above data. Perhaps other criteria such as teaching style, subject matter, and group life expectations should also be considered.

3. A wide variety of personal qualities and teaching styles (including the lecture) among the Sunday school teachers is affirmed. Such considerations should be taken into account when teachers are being recruited and trained.

Conclusion

The Sunday school is truly a massive mosaic within and among the different denominations. There is more than a little evidence that shows that the Sunday school occupies a very important place in many local congregations. However, the Sunday school, as a movement, has received only minimal attention from the religious research community. The few data that have been examined have generated findings that hint at much that is still not known or is awaiting rediscovery.

There are current signs that the Sunday school movement is experiencing both death and renewal. Hopefully, some of the foregoing data and discussion will enable us, as Christian educators, to become better diagnosticians of that which is not healthy, and better practitioners of that which will bring renewal of faith and life to the church through the Sunday school.

Chapter 4

Research on the CCD

ANDREW D. THOMPSON

This chapter presents empirical findings that describe the status and effectiveness of Roman Catholic parish religious education programs, most commonly called "CCD." The time-honored Catholic shorthand is used, despite the fact that this traditional title, Confraternity of Christian Doctrine, may give the false impression that such programs dwell primarily on doctrinal matters.

The traditional title "CCD" may also conjure up images of a monochromatic classroom approach that emphasizes the transfer of religious information, perhaps at the expense of a broad-minded spiritual formation and critical thinking. On the contrary, the goals of contemporary CCD programs are to foster Christian formation by expanding community awareness and include aspects of youth ministry, retreats, and other noninstructional approaches.[1] Many catechists prefer to identify the programs simply as parish religious education rather than as CCD.

In Catholic circles the term CCD refers primarily to parish-based religious education programs for elementary- and secondary-school-age youth. Programs for older parishioners are typically referred to as adult religious education. Official catechetical documents stress the necessity of seeing all catechesis as having as its goal the person's maturity of faith, that is, an adult orientation.[2] Although the primary focus here is CCD, there are important reasons for including references to adults as well. Cur-

1. *General Catechetical Directory,* articles 9, 38, and 39 (Washington, D.C.: United States Catholic Conference, 1971).
2. *Sharing the Light of Faith* (Washington, D.C.: NCEA, 1979), article 173ff.

rent research, for example, confirms the powerful influence that parents have on youths' approach to faith.[3] Even with the child-centered orientation of most contemporary CCD programs, research indicates, and diocesan leadership affirms, that any study of CCD must also include the contribution of CCD program directors, religion teachers, and parents. Diocesan CCD directors strongly advocate this life-span perspective.

Empirical Overview Requires Imagination

The assignment to summarize research pertinent to CCD is made difficult by the fact that nationwide and statistically representative empirical studies of CCD programs have been practically nonexistent. Yearly figures are available that provide ballpark national estimates of the number of CCD participants. But to date we have no empirical barometer for properly evaluating the CCD programs' quality and outcomes, which are the main focus of this book.

The absence of reliable national data leaves us two types of information for consideration: 1) a workable demographic overview of Catholic youths' participation in or absence from CCD programs; 2) a cluster of smaller, nonrepresentative but interesting studies of components of CCD programs. Accordingly, readers and writer alike need to use intuition and imagination to come up with a practical overview of the status of CCD programs and its implications for future directions in parish religious education.

CCD: An Alternative to Catholic Schools and "No Formal Training"

In order to understand the contribution CCD programs make to the religious development of Catholic youths it is necessary to examine CCD's contribution within a sufficiently broad context. Too frequently the results of CCD are compared unfavorably to the results of Catholic schools. Interesting as such comparison may be, from an empirical perspective it is unfair. Catholic schools typically have about four times the amount of time and greater financial resources than have the CCD programs. This results in Catholic school youths typically having more religious information than CCD youth. But adolescent participants in CCD programs are typically highly motivated and religiously more ac-

3. Andrew D. Thompson, *That They May Know You* (Washington, D.C.: NCEA, 1982), pp. 74-77.

tive than their average Catholic school counterpart. Because of these basic differences, further comparison here does not seem helpful.

The CCD program addresses the needs of roughly one in four Catholic youths.[4] Catholic schools address a second of the four while half of Catholic youths receive no formal religious instruction. Accordingly, the proper context for considering the contribution of CCD includes this major group who do not participate in any formal program, not in youth ministry programs nor in Catholic school programs.

The significance of this third type of Catholic youth, those receiving no formal training, grew between 1965 and 1974. The percentage of these Catholic youths receiving no formal religious instruction increased from 22.85 percent (1965) to 43.52 percent (1974) that is, from 3.1 to 6.6 million youths.[5] The obvious question this raises is the extent to which these youths will be socialized into their faith, be sensitive to the Catholic symbol system, religiously literate, and active in the parish community.

Again, because no such nationally representative study of CCD outcomes has been conducted, nor any in conjunction with Catholic school students, nor with youth receiving no formal instruction, we cannot answer this question. The best we can do is examine disparate studies that, when considered side-by-side, provide an impressionistic portrait, focused softly rather than with the exactness of statistical boundaries.

Participation: A Barometer of Priorities

The number of participants in CCD programs is one barometer of the importance that parish administrators, parents, and youths give the CCD programs. The number of CCD participants may also be an indicator of the quality of the CCD programs.

Examination of the number of CCD participants must be made within the context of the total number of Catholic children at the elementary and secondary age levels, as well as in comparison with the numbers of youths receiving Catholic education and those receiving no formal religious training.

The method of reporting the CCD participation figures in the *Official Catholic Directory* results in lower figures being reported

4. Andrew Thompson and Eugene Hemrick, *The Last Fifteen Years* (Washington, D.C.: USCC Publishers, 1982), p. 24.
5. Wilfrid Paradis and Andrew Thompson, *Where Are The 6.6 Million?* (Washington, D.C.: USCC, 1976), pp. 15-19.

for CCD attendance than are actually participating. In particular, the figures that parishes supply to dioceses, and that dioceses then pass along to the publisher, typically do not include a number of programs for sacramental preparation or for "youth ministry." One reason for this omission is that sometimes the same youth will participate in several different programs.

In a growing number of parish confirmation preparation programs, for example, youths, aged 12 to 16, enroll in an eighteen-month program of activities that includes retreats and community service projects. Because parish CCD programs were traditionally classroom centered rather than built around retreats, sacramental preparation, and community service, the number of confirmation, reconciliation, and Eucharist program participants are not necessarily included in the parish's count of CCD participants. So the officially reported number of CCD participants is probably lower than would be the case if "CCD participants" were understood broadly and included youth participating in non-classroom-centered programs.

The Scope of Catholic Religious Education and CCD

The Roman Catholic community in the United States consists of approximately 52 million persons. Based on extrapolation of baptismal records, there are approximately 12 million school-age Catholics in the U.S., that is, between grades one through twelve.

Records for participation in these parish-based programs, as explained above, are not kept as accurately as are Catholic school records. Therefore, exact figures for youths attending CCD programs are not available. Attendance varies during the course of the year, with high attendance in the fall and lower attendance in the late spring. Attendance also varies with age, with a greater percentage attending during the elementary grade levels and dropping dramatically after 10th grade.

The results of a study based on the only available CCD attendance figures and on extrapolation of the official church baptismal figures are presented in the demographic overview that follows.[6] The attendance figures are very important because they reflect *behavior* which may be a stronger indicator of how the community values the CCD programs than would be individuals' *verbal* evaluations.

6. Adapted from Thompson and Hemrick, *The Last Fifteen Years.*

Demographic Trends for Catholic Youth

Declining and Rising Population

The size of the U.S. youth population has declined over the last two decades. The number of children baptized Catholic during those years also declined, a trend that paralleled the declining national birth rate. The number of yearly baptisms identifies the downward trend, as evident from the figures for every fifth year.

1960	1,313,653
1965	1,274,939
1970	1,088,463
1975	894,992
1980	943,632

Since the 1974 low (876,306) in the number of infant baptisms, the number has been steadily rising. The most recently reported figures, for 1983, indicated there were 975,017 infant baptisms. This modest rise since 1974 is now evident at the elementary age level. But compared with the number of infant baptisms of the early 1960s, current figures still represent more than a 20 percent decline in the elementary-age Catholic population.

This precipitous decline is important. Parish catechetical leaders who see fewer children entering their programs may mistakenly believe parents and children are "voting with their feet," displeased with the quality of the program, and opting not to participate in the program.

The national demographic figures and the church baptismal statistics, however, provide a different picture. The fact of fewer CCD participants, in itself, does not cast a negative vote on the quality of the program, since the number of children in the Catholic school-age population is down from earlier years. When the decline in overall youth population is taken into consideration, it is clear that the *percentage* of Catholic children participating in CCD programs at the elementary level has actually risen. The reasons behind this percentage increase are many, and improvement in the quality of the programs should not be excluded from the list of influential factors.

Smaller Family Size

A second trend in the U.S. and Catholic population is toward smaller family size. The birthrate has declined dramatically from a high in the late fifties (approximately 250 births per thousand women aged 20-24) to a substantially lower figure in 1980 (approximately 115 births per thousand women aged 20-24).[7] This decline was offset somewhat by the post-World War II baby-boom, which resulted in greater numbers of couples of childbearing age during the decades of the sixties and seventies.

Today, although there are dramatically fewer children per household, there are significantly greater numbers of families. The result is that the number of children is higher than one would expect if one simply paid attention to the rapidly declining birth rate.

Are there any implications for CCD in the fact that Catholic children now seem to be coming from smaller families? To this author's knowledge, the point has not been researched. One might posit, however, that having fewer children would allow parents more time to be actively involved in the religious socialization of those children. Most Catholic dioceses presently require greater parental involvement in their children's sacramental preparation than was the case in previous decades.

The fact, then, that parents have been having fewer children would make for greater compliance with the church's request for greater parental involvement. Other factors, such as an increase in the number of parents working outside the home, greater numbers of single parents, and the feminization of poverty might militate against greater parental involvement. Without research, however, speculation has no solid base.

Single Parent Homes

A third major characteristic of Catholic children and therefore of many of those who attend Catholic CCD programs is they have grown up in and now live in families having a relatively high divorce rate. The Catholic divorce rate, it seems, parallels that of non-Catholics. According to demographer James McCarthy, while the research specifically about Catholic divorce rates is inadequate, what we do know gives strong indication that Catholics divorce at the same rate as the rest of the American population.[8]

Historically speaking, the annual rates of divorce for the gener-

7. See forthcoming publication of Department of Defense study of family trends, edited by Theodora Ooms et al., p. 3 ff.

8. Interview: July 1984, to be published in forthcoming study of Catholic marriages following divorce and annulment in the Catholic church, edited by Steven Preister and James Young.

al U.S. population have been steadily rising since 1860. They fell during the depression (1930s) and spiked dramatically after World War II. For the fifteen years between 1950 and 1965 the divorce rates leveled off until they again began a rapid rise. The divorce rate doubled between 1965 and 1979.[9] It reached a peak in the period from 1979 to 1981.

The point is that children attending CCD have grown up in and are products of this period of high divorce. Eventually, many of these children become part of a reconstituted family as the divorced parent who has custody remarries. Rarely is this pattern of experience (divorce, emotional restabilization, downward mobility, remarriage) smooth. Educational research, although not unanimous, suggests that children of divorced families have more difficulties with school achievement. This raises the question unanswered by current research: What influences do such experiences have on youths' religious education?

One might speculate that the fragmentation of the American Catholic family would result in a greater need for CCD programs to support the youth's Catholic identity. But at the same time, the fact of living in a single parent household, with its increased workloads for all members, might make it more difficult for the youth to attend such parish-based CCD programs.

It is with these three demographic trends in mind then—smaller youth population, smaller family size, and rising divorce rates—that one should review the following tables describing participation in CCD programs. Parish practitioners and diocesan leaders also need to keep these three trends in mind as they attempt to identify the strengths and weaknesses of their programs for religious education and catechesis.

Between 1965 and 1980, the highwater mark for the combined (elementary and secondary) number of CCD participants was 1971 (5,579,060). The most recent available figure for this combined group is 4,607,477 (1983). This decline is sharper than the decline in the elementary age youth population and indicates the ongoing difficulty of involving high-school youth in CCD programs (see Tables Two and Five). Without better figures, one can only hope some of these youths are participating in youth ministry programs whose numbers are not incorporated in CCD figures.

9. *Vital Statistics Report* 30, no. 2 (National Center for Health Statistics, 1981).

Table One
Formal Religious Instruction
of Catholic Elementary School-Age Children
[Grades 1-8] 1965-1980

Year	Total Catholic Elementary Population	In Parish CCD Programs	Attending Catholic School	Total Receiving Formal Instruction	Total Receiving No Formal Instruction
1965	9,656,607	3,486,902	4,491,953	7,978,855	1,677,752
1970	10,529,710	4,181,466	3,413,610	7,595,076	2,934,634
1975	9,742,070	3,892,457	2,576,856	6,469,313	3,272,757
1980	8,232,615	3,427,593	2,296,380	5,723,973	2,508,642

The highwater mark for the elementary level CCD population was 1972 when the number of participants reached 4,251,729 (40.59 percent). Since then, although the number of participants has declined to 3,106,281 (1983), this drop parallels the decline in the overall youth population. So CCD has continued to reach approximately four of every ten Catholic elementary age youths.

Table Two
Formal Religious Instruction
of Catholic
Secondary School-Age Children
[Grades 9-12] 1965-1980

Year	Total Catholic Secondary Population	In Parish CCD Programs	Attending Catholic School	Total Receiving Formal Instruction	Total Receiving No Formal Instruction
1965	3,872,498	1,369,751	1,090,401	2,460,152	1,412,346
1970	4,670,748	1,303,032	1,015,713	2,318,745	2,352,003
1975	5,318,266	1,013,198	895,845	1,909,043	3,409,223
1980	5,098,509	962,912	838,247	1,801,159	3,297,350

The decade and a half since 1965 witnessed the closing of a substantial number of Catholic schools. In addition, a significant number of Catholic schools increased their non-Catholic enrollment, especially in economically disadvantaged areas. So the decline from 41 percent of Catholic children attending Catholic schools in 1965 to 24 percent attending in 1980 probably cloaks a somewhat steeper decline. Catholic secondary-age youths' participation in CCD experienced a similarly steep decline from 35 percent in 1965 to 19 percent in 1980. The elementary age youths' participation in CCD, however, rose from 36 percent in 1965 to 42 percent in 1980. Research is needed to know whether this increase is due to greater organization of parish CCD programs,

Table Three
Formal Religious Instruction
of Combined Catholic Elementary and
Secondary School-Age Children and Youth
[Grades 1-12] 1965-1980

Year	Total Catholic School-Age Population	In Parish CCD Programs	Attending Catholic School	Total Receiving Formal Instruction	Total Receiving No Formal Instruction
1965	13,529,105	4,856,653	5,582,354	10,439,007	3,090,098
1970	15,200,458	5,484,498	4,429,323	9,913,821	5,286,637
1975	15,060,336	4,905,655	3,472,701	8,378,356	6,681,980
1980	13,331,124	4,390,505	3,134,627	7,525,132	5,805,992

Table Four
Formal Religious Instruction
of Catholic Elementary School-Age Children
[Grades 1-8] 1965-1980
Percentage Distribution

Year	In Parish Elementary CCD	Attending Catholic School	Total Receiving Formal Instruction	Total Receiving No Formal Instruction
1965	36.11	46.52	82.63	17.37
1970	39.71	32.42	72.13	27.87
1975	39.96	26.45	66.41	33.59
1980	41.63	27.89	69.53	30.47

Table Five
Formal Religious Instruction
of Catholic Secondary School-Age Youth
[Grades 9-12] 1965-1980
Percentage Distribution

Year	In Parish Secondary CCD	Attending Catholic School	Total Receiving Formal Instruction	Total Receiving No Formal Instruction
1965	35.37	28.16	63.53	36.47
1970	27.90	21.74	49.64	50.36
1975	19.50	16.84	35.89	64.10
1980	18.89	16.44	35.33	64.67

Table Six
Formal Religious Instruction
of Combined Catholic Elementary and
Secondary School-Age Children and Youth
[Grades 1-12] 1965-1980
Percentage Distribution

Year	In Parish CCD Programs	Attending Catholic School	Total Receiving Formal Instruction	Total Receiving No Formal Instruction
1965	35.89	41.26	77.15	22.85
1970	36.08	29.14	65.22	34.78
1975	32.57	23.06	55.63	44.37
1980	32.93	23.51	56.45	43.55

greater parental participation in sacramental programs, or other factors.

Key Indicator: Student Religious Beliefs and Values

One traditional approach to evaluating the strengths and weaknesses of religious programs is to survey youths' understandings, beliefs, attitudes, and behaviors. This approach provides an indicator of the religious topography of today's youth. The recent report on responses from 6,000 eighth and twelfth grade CCD and Catholic school youths, *That They May Know You*, identified several interesting patterns.

The findings indicated that today's youths have accepted much of Vatican II's emphasis on God loving and accepting them. They saw God as purposeful, personal, and generous to all people. Their responses indicated their faith was Christ-centered.

Two areas where youths showed a need for greater attention was in their approach to the church: strong on seeing church as community, but weak in seeing it as an historical institution. Second, few of today's youths understand traditional terms such as "incarnation" (27 percent), "revelation" (50 percent), "Paschal mystery" (54 percent), "infallibility" (38 percent), and "magisterium" (25 percent).

This National Catholic Education Association (NCEA) funded study called attention to a number of strengths and weaknesses found in many of today's Catholic school and parish CCD programs. Based on two survey inventory instruments, the student responses were intended primarily for analysis and study at the local level. Further, consideration of the percentage of correct responses to various questions in itself does not tell us how the broader systems of religion teachers, parents, pastors, and students are interacting. To get this type of information a different methodology is needed. One preliminary conclusion from an example of such an ongoing study will now be reviewed.

Key Indicator: How Parish Staff Responds to Crises

Researcher William McCready of the National Opinion Research Center recently reported preliminary results of an ongoing study that includes interviews with the catechetial staff of twenty successful CCD programs.[10] The primary characteristic of those programs, he said, was how the parish staff responded to crises. In particular, the staff used the crises to bring more adult participation and leadership into the program. For example, were a director of religious education (DRE) to leave the parish, the remaining parish catechetical leaders typically responded, not only by filling that position, but by increasing the number of other program supporters, whether salaried or volunteer.

By taking the parish program rather than the individual stu-

10. Preliminary report made at 1985 NCEA Annual Convention in St. Louis, April 10.

dent as the unit of research, this second NCEA-sponsored pilot study indirectly invites professionals and pastoral ministers to evaluate parish programs in accordance with the system's performance as a whole, rather than according to students' individual performance.

The following pages adapt Erik Erikson's patterns of tensions typically used to describe the individual's psycho-social development and apply them to this more systemic approach to the parish CCD program. For the past three decades, religious educators have made fruitful use of Erikson's stages.[11] Of particular help has been his description of the eight tensions that normally emerge as each person matures and meets the conflicts associated with the stages, ranging from the infant's struggle with trust/mistrust to the elderly person's struggle with hope/despair.

Family therapists have extended use of the stages by applying them to small groups such as families. Therapists have gained insight by noting how the stage of the parent(s) interfaces with those of the children.[12] Erikson's eight tensions are used here as a structure for the analysis of research findings within Roman Catholic parish-based religious education programs. Erikson's structure of eight developmental crises lends coherence to disparate and fragmentary empirical studies.

Findings Concerning Trust and Mistrust

Parish catechetics has made substantial strides toward professionalism in the past two decades. Since Vatican II, the rapid emergence of the full-time parish coordinator/director of religious education (DRE) has sounded a vote of confidence in these professionals. But in the view of Gabriel Moran, the role of the parish "coordinator/DRE remains in a precarious state."[13] Recent survey findings illustrate what is here interpreted as contributing to a trust/mistrust dialectic between the professional religious educator and the parish structure.

In this interesting study of parish catechetics (CCD), Thomas Walters surveyed 693 DREs who were nominated by their diocesan directors as professional. The sample was drawn from 143 dioceses, including large, middle-sized, and small dioceses. Al-

11. Erik Erikson, *Insight and Responsibility* (New York: Norton, 1964).

12. Elizabeth Carter and Monica McGoldrick, ed., *The Family Life-Cycle* (New York: Gardner Press, 1980).

13. Thomas P. Walters, ed., *DRE: Issues and Concerns for the 80s*, (Washington, D.C.: NCDD, 1983), pp. 5 and 18.

though almost all participants had an M.A. degree and an average of eight years of catechetical experience, 86 percent had but a one-year contract. Commenting on this, Moran drew a parallel between how the church treats DREs and how universities treat junior faculty. "The clergy are tenured for life and the coordinator/DRE is the instructor/adjunct who is hired for a year at a scandalously low rate."

According to Maria Harris, the insecurity caused by the low salaries results in DREs being a relatively silent group who keep a particularly low profile within the church system. The prevalence of the one-year contract raises a question about the level of trust between parish pastors and DREs. On the positive side, however, the substantial majority of DREs say they receive either total (48 percent) or adequate support (37 percent) from their pastor. Only 14 percent say they receive inadequate support.

The McCready-NCEA study of successful parish catechetical programs, in its preliminary report, judged that the presence of a full-time DRE was essential to each of the successful progams. So the presence of the professional DRE coordinating the parish catechetical program is a sign of both trust and mistrust within the pastoral context. This tension may be healthy, but the future of successful CCD programs requires all parties involved to build greater trust into their working relationships.

Findings Concerning Autonomy and Doubt

The terms "autonomy" and "doubt" are here applied to the affirmation or rejection of the worthwhileness of the parish catechetical programs. During the past two decades, CCD programs have suffered from naive comparison with Catholic school programs. Several NORC studies of Catholic adults, for example, concluded that attendance in Catholic schools is a strong factor contributing to the person's subsequent bonding as an adult with the Catholic community and Catholic institutions. Objective and important as that finding may be, lack of objectivity is evident in the studies' comparing the attitudes of adults who were trained respectively in Catholic schools and in CCD programs.

The *Young Catholics* study,[14] for example, found the following differences in the responses to several attitudinal questions asked of adults who attended either Catholic schools or CCD programs:

14. Andrew Greeley et al., *Young Catholics* (New York: William Sadlier, Inc., 1981), pp. 24 and 126.

	Catholic School	CCD
frequency of prayer	65%	55%
belief in infallibility	34%	20%
considered vocation	13%	2%
birth control wrong	5%	3%

The conclusion to this type of finding should not be, as Greeley has affirmed, that Catholic schools deserve additional support while CCD is comparatively worthless. Rather, one has to probe beyond these surface statistics and explore what role these beliefs may serve in the person's faith life. For example, a more recent analysis by John Convey, in working with 6,000 Catholic adolescents surveyed by NORC, found that Catholic males attending parochial schools actually rated the value of social justice *lower* in importance than did public school participants.[15] Further, senior females from parochial schools rated it lower than did senior females from nonparochial schools. When this Convey finding is compared with other studies, it suggests that caution needs to be exercised in interpreting what is at work in the respondents' answers.

Marianne Ferguson's dissertation research, for example, found Catholic school graduates' responses indicated they

> were more ready (than public school graduates) to acknowledge the influence of their religion on their personal moral attitudes and values. They were also more likely to say that their religious beliefs influenced their attitudes toward social justice.[16]

Given the Convey finding that Catholic youth expressed less concern for social justice, should one then conclude that participation in Catholic schools had a negative influence on the students' values of social justice? Probably not. But the irony of the Ferguson conclusion, when contrasted with Convey's finding, suggests that comparisons of the stated beliefs of graduates of Catholic schools and parish CCD programs are tenuous at best and need to be interpreted within a broad framework of how those beliefs operate in the rest of the person's belief system.

Parish-based CCD programs, however, do have advocates and

15. Summarized in *American Catholic Family* 1, no. 11 (June, 1983), p. 8.

16. See *Momentum* 14 (May, 1983), p. 12.

doubting Thomases within the ranks. The Walters survey of professional coordinators found that DREs gave CCD program components positive and negative evaluations at the same time. In particular, on the negative side, 36 percent of the DREs surveyed said the prevalent CCD structure for educating students in grades K-12 (75 minute sessions held weekly for 30 weeks) was basically ineffective. Yet, on the positive side, with regard to student participation, the overwhelming majority of DREs (over 95 percent) said they were successful in recruiting program participants at the elementary level. DREs also reported success in influencing youths' and adults' attitudes toward the church.

In their work with high-school students, some DREs reported having little (29 percent) or no (3 percent) success. Even more problematic, the DREs reported, was having little (53 percent) or no (19 percent) success working with young adults. The majority of DREs said they did not have moderate (62 percent) to high (13 percent) success involving adults in parish religious education programs. So one might tentatively conclude that the DREs' dissatisfaction with the CCD structure refers to ineffectiveness in involving older adolescents and young adults in programs. This probably has more to do with the DREs' time commitment to working with elementary age sacramental programs and the need for an expanded parish staff and volunteers to set up a youth ministry model to work with older adolescents and young adults.

Such research findings point to a growing need for CCD to develop greater autonomy from Catholic schools, as well as an increased doubt about the usefulness of traditional parish programs for older adolescents and young adults. Even with these tensions, the finding that the vast majority of professional DREs in the Walters' study said they had a high (52 percent) or moderate (40 percent) degree of satisfaction in their work suggests the surveyed DREs have established a certain degree of personal autonomy.

Findings Concerning Initiative and Guilt

The unresolved elements from the above tensions make evident what feeds and chokes the DREs' initiative. When the pastor encourages DREs by giving them sufficient autonomy and trust, the programs tend to be successful. A full 85 percent of these DREs indicated that their pastors gave them at least adequate or better support. However, when the DREs' employment depends so utterly on the will of the pastor, this invites coordinators to be overly cautious and hence short on initiative. Also, when the DREs' responsibilities cover the entire age spectrum of the parish, this lays a foundation for guilt.

The preliminary findings of the McCready-NCEA interviews of successful parish programs found one major vulnerability of CCD programs that erodes the DRE's initiative. McCready found the DREs' confidence decreased to the extent they saw weakness in the way their parish organization was structured. The Walters study illustrated what this could mean—36 percent of the professional DREs surveyed said the prevalent structure for educating nonparochial school students is basically ineffective.

The same study documented another organizational weakness. Seventy-two percent of the DREs reported directly to the pastor and few (10 percent) were responsible to an education commission, to a pastoral team (8 percent), or other individuals or groups (10 percent). Overdependence on a pastor invites a lack of due process and professional accountability.

Gabriel Moran summarized the negative resolution of this tension when he described DREs as "small in number and relatively powerless."[17] The positive resolution, Moran envisions, is that DREs are an advance guard of a different kind of church.

Findings Concerning Industry and Inferiority

Erikson explains that each person has a need for "being able to make things and make them well."[18] Available statistics indicate that DREs are extremely active workers. The average work week for professional DREs participating in the Walters survey was forty-eight hours. Fifty-two percent worked forty-eight hours or more each week. Another 32 percent worked forty to forty-five hours weekly. DREs are busy, but tension arises when they evaluate the results of this industry. The spiritual and educational nature of their goals, such as the spiritual formation of youth, is difficult to assess. The Walters National Profile found that the primary responsibilities for the majority of DREs are "the design, implementation and direction of educational or catechetical programs for children in grades K-8, particularly sacramental programs . . . (and) especially the training and recruiting of catechists."[19]

17. See Walters, *DRE: Issues and Concerns*, pp. 8, 19, and 83.
18. Erik Erikson, *Identity, Youth and Crisis* (New York: Norton, 1968), p. 123.
19. Walters, *DRE: Issues and Concerns*, p. 64.

The majority of DREs specify their responsibilities as follows:
1. Sacramental programs—for 29 percent of DREs, coordinating these programs occupies the majority of their attention.
2. Grades K-8—22 percent said coordinating the elementary-age level is their major concern.
3. Grades K-12—14 percent identified both elementary and secondary as their primary concern.
4. Grades 9-12—that the secondary was the DREs' primary responsibility was the case for only 8 percent.
5. Adult education—the primary focus for 14 percent of the DREs.

In addition, a major responsibility of 96 percent of professional DREs is the recruiting and training of teachers or catechists. On the elementary level, 76 percent of the DREs provide a monthly or bi-monthly training session. On the senior-high level, 55 percent provide training. Less training is provided for those working with young and older adults.

DREs said the major areas they were neglecting included: special education, preschool and family-based programing. So long as the DREs are expected to cover such a wide spectrum of parish needs, the tension between industry and inferiority will remain unnecessarily high and probably invite more "burnout" than positive development.

Findings Concerning Identity and Identity Confusion

One tension that has arisen in the emergence and professionalization of the parish coordinator is the DRE's identity as educator and/or minister. A major difference between the two roles is that the minister is an official or semi-official of the church, whereas the educator is not. Maria Harris sees the minister's work focusing on building the community's fellowship, service, and worship. In contrast, Harris sees the educator's work more concerned with examining and challenging the knowledge, values, attitudes, and traditions of the community.

The Walters study found that the majority of DREs defined their work more in educational than ministerial terms. Harris' fear is that many catechists will want to be identified as ministers and that the educational component and competence will be neglected. To the extent that the educational element is lost, a core element of the DRE's identity is missing.

The second major identity confusion arises when the DRE is viewed as a hybrid of the professional and the volunteer. Some professionals find this confusion particularly depressing.[20] One example of this ambiguity is exhibited in the 56 percent of DREs who said they should be working to put themselves out of a job. Romantic as the possibility of empowering others may be, it is naive to think the church community can do without the professional competencies of the trained DRE. Clearly, a balance is needed in shaping the DRE's identity both as educational and ministerial, as including professional self-development and empowering others.

Findings Concerning Intimacy and Isolation

The term "intimacy" is here used to refer to the extent to which the DRE plays a pivotal role in parish catechesis. The goal of catechesis, according to *Sharing the Light of Faith*, is the development of living, conscious, and active faith life through the light of instruction.[21]

One indicator of the DRE's "intimacy," in the sense of being integral to parish catechesis, is the extent to which he or she is supported by the central decision-making figures in the parish. The 1978 National Conference of Diocesan Directors (NCDD) survey of parish coordinators and diocesan directors, *Survey of Needs and Actions Regarding Recognition/Support of Parish Coordinators/Directors*, found that there was a great lack of personal and professional support for DREs. In exploring this point, respondents to the subsequent Walters survey indicated the sources and extent of their support. The DREs practically unanimously said they received either total (62 percent) or adequate (37 percent) support from the parish catechists. DREs said they received either total (48 percent) or adequate (37 percent) support from pastors. They said they received similar levels of support from the parish's grade school principal and associate pastor.

Intimacy, in the sense of felt support from DREs in other parishes, was quite strong. Four out of five DREs said such support was either total or adequate. But one in five said they did not relate to other DREs enough to rate the degree of support realistically. If such isolation is present among the professional DREs, one must be concerned about those DREs who are less professionally trained.

20. Ibid., p. 22.
21. Articles 5 and 221.

Another indicator of "intimacy" is the effectiveness of the DRE's work, a variable which, as indicated above, remains difficult to assess.

Findings Concerning Generativity and Stagnation

One of the signs of an individual's generativity is the extent to which he or she works cooperatively with key people both inside and outside the immediate system. One of the major benefits the advent of DREs has brought to parish catechetical programs is the expansion of out of school sacramental preparation programs, typically including parent involvement.

That sacramental preparation programs are a primary focus of the DREs' generativity is evident from the fact that DREs said they gave sacramental programs more attention than any other programs.[22] By giving sacramental catechesis their highest priority, DREs are actually fulfilling the two highest priorities Catholic parents and religion teachers give to their children's religious education, namely moral maturity and sacraments.[23]

In addition, 80 percent of the DREs said that in conjunction with sacramental preparation for the children, they hold special meetings for the parents. So the DREs' generativity is actually rooted in a form of "intimacy" with the parents, who are key figures in the youths' religious formation.[24]

As Erikson wisely pointed out, however, the shadow side of generativity is stagnation. Some religious educators have raised concerns that despite the benefits of strong sacramental preparation programs, they have blossomed at the expense of other underdeveloped areas such as social justice and knowledge of the church's history.[25]

Findings Concerning Hope and Despair

The tension concerning the future of Catholic parish-based programs is closely tied to the growth of the professionalization of the coordinator/DRE. Again, Moran's summary of this tension bears repeating: "The coordinator/DRE is either the advance

22. See Walters, *DRE: Issues and Concerns*, table 8, p. 26.
23. D. Hoge, P. Philibert, and A. Thompson, *Review of Religious Research: Adolescent Religious Socialization* 23, no. 3 (March, 1982), p. 241.
24. See Thompson, *That They May Know You*, p. 75.
25. James DeBoy, in Walters, *DRE: Issues and Concerns*, p. 50.

guard of a different kind of church or else a grim sign of the institution's erosion."[26]

During the past two decades, since the renewal fostered by Vatican II, Roman Catholicism has experienced a rapid expansion of ministries. This growth coincided with a shift of Catholicism's lay and religious professional personnel, who in the 1950s were concentrated in the Catholic schools. Just when the youth population declined and many Catholic schools closed or consolidated in the late sixties and early seventies, many church professionals began applying their talents to developing parish CCD and programs for adults.

The Catholic parishes and dioceses of the 1980s now include a growing cadre of professionals in relatively new ministries such as marriage preparation, separated and divorced, youth, social justice, family, young adult, elderly, prayer, healing, lectoring, and distributing eucharist. These ministries form an environment with which CCD programs need to interact and to which they can contribute. The key for such a fruitful interaction is a shared parish vision, a recognition and agreement on the parish programs' goals and objectives.

The *National Catechetical Directory* (SLF) affirms that catechesis needs to implement this comprehensive overview.

> Every parish needs a coherent, well-integrated catechetical plan which provides opportunities for all parishioners to encounter the gospel message and respond by fostering community and giving service.[27]

The Walters' survey asked DREs to indicate the degree to which their programs reflected a common parish vision. Thirty-five percent said their programs "very much" reflected a common parish vision while 53 percent said their programs reflected a common vision "somewhat."[28]

The term "common vision" does not of itself convey the sense of close cooperation among the various ministries. So we cannot be certain what the DREs were affirming. But the survey suggests that a wholistic or parish-wide vision is being promoted among DREs. The hope is that in time it will take root in a larger population of professional and volunteer catechists, lend coherence to

26. Ibid., p. 5.
27. *National Catholic Directory,* article 224.
28. Walters, *DRE: Issues and Concerns,* p. 42.

their programs, and overshadow the shortcomings of existing programs.

A Core Tension for CCD: Balancing Individuality and Togetherness

A powerful principle that family researchers and therapists have articulated in recent decades is that the healthy family is characterized by enabling people "to be separate together."[29] When this principle is applied to the health of the CCD program and the eight tensions explained above, interesting possibilities surface:

1. Does the DRE's dependence on the pastor stem from the parish structure, putting the pastor on a pedestal and insulating him from accountability to a parish council or education committee? If there is too much individualism in the parish system, the CCD program will have to expend energy to cope with it and be distracted from its primary mission, that of promoting maturity of faith within the community.

2. Although research has found Catholic youth to have a strong concern for family togetherness,[30] there seem to be some shortcomings in the way youth extend that solidarity to those suffering from social and economic inequalities. In 1980 the National Opinion Research Center conducted a study of 58,000 youths to identify trends in their values and work expectations.[31] This "High School and Beyond" (HSB) research, originally commissioned by the National Center for Education Statistics, was reanalyzed to study the responses of Catholic youths. John Convey found that high-school male Catholics attending Catholic schools rated the value of correcting social and economic inequalities lower in importance than did the entire HSB sample.[32]

Although this HSB secondary analysis did not compare CCD and Catholic school students, it did confirm that many students receiving religious instruction in Catholic schools were strong on family togetherness but weak on extending the value of togetherness to the disadvantaged. It will be very interesting to see if the media's portrayal of the suffering caused by the African drought fosters in Catholic youth a greater sense of missionary awareness

29. Herbert Anderson, *The Family and Pastoral Care* (Philadelphia: Fortress Press, 1984).
30. Summarized in *American Catholic Family* 1, no. 11, p. 8.
31. Coleman, Hoffer and Kilgore, *Public and Private Schools*, 1981.
32. *American Catholic Family* 1 no. 11 (June, 1983), pp. 8-9.

and a togetherness that manifests itself in helping their peers in underdeveloped nations. The outpouring of concern demonstrated by donations offered to date through the Propagation of the Faith, Catholic Relief Services, and the Holy Childhood Association have been impressive. But the future of mission education and education for social justice remains uncertain.

3. A third manifestation of the need to balance "togetherness" and "individuality" is found in CCD teachers' efforts to balance a content-centered pedagogy with an experience-centered pedagogy. A substantial part of the content of Catholic catechesis includes cognitive aspects such as knowledge of the biblical, sacramental, moral, and ecclesial traditions. By emphasizing such content, CCD programs, in effect, stress the individual's togetherness with the Catholic tradition. By emphasizing the importance of the individual's faith experiences, CCD programs, in effect, promote either the student's individuality before God or solidarity with the community.

One study of several hundred Catholic religious educators found that a substantial majority prioritized their concerns as though they were striving for a balance of both the cognitive and the experiential components of catechesis. The same study showed that only a few religion teachers emphasized either content or experience (process) while showing little concern for the other.[33]

Catholic religious education, whether in the form of parish CCD, youth ministry, family-centered catechesis, or private Catholic schooling has the goal of sharing a Catholic identity. This implies sharing some cognitive information about the Catholic community such as its beliefs, history, and liturgy. Beyond this cognitive element, teachers and parents are concerned about the extent to which youth and the adults themselves synthesize their faith and their daily experience. By paying greater attention to the tensions parish DREs experience in operating the CCD program and by discerning the forces operating in the youths' changing family settings, the Catholic parish community will enhance the integration of faith with daily life and thereby foster the goal of CCD, the maturity of faith.

33. "Experience and Knowledge: A Study of Theological Understandings and Pedagogical Priorities," in *Character Potential* IX, no. 4 (November, 1981), pp. 193-202.

Recommendations for Improving CCD Programs

- Establishment of an information clearinghouse for research statistics, personnel, and resources for supporting CCD and youth ministry.
- Systematic collaboration by diocesan and parish catechetical leaders to discover ways of balancing creatively the major parish and family tensions and issues pertaining to CCD programs.
- More equitable distribution of parish funds and personnel to tap the potential of the CCD and youth ministry programs.
- Greater attention to the missionary component of youth's religious development and spirituality.
- Greater collaboration at the national, regional, and parish levels between CCD coordinators and youth ministers.

Chapter 5

Analysis and Assessment: The General Protestant Sunday School

LOCKE E. BOWMAN, JR.

Sunday schools in the general Protestant churches present a confusing picture. Here and there one finds a lively Sunday morning enterprise that looks very much like the school of a generation or more ago. Often one encounters a dispirited group attempting to carry on, lamenting difficulties that seem to prevent liveliness or growth. The majority of the churches' programs lie somewhere between these extremes—neither thriving nor foundering, but marked by a certain wistful yearning for a better day ahead.

The Sunday school is probably the best example of disparity these days between the thought patterns of clergy and laity. Lay persons know what they mean when they say "Sunday school." They have a concept of children and young people, men and women, engaged in organized study on Sunday mornings. The subject matter is the Bible, teachers are lay volunteers working under the leadership of lay superintendents, and the learners are the church's people and others to whom they reach out with an invitation to hear the good news of Jesus Christ.

The clergy, on the other hand, have learned to question the validity of "Sunday school as usual." They tend to be impatient with the details of keeping it in operation, wonder about the value of "an hour a week," doubt the abilities of the lay leadership, and fear that this well-rooted American tradition deserves the epithetical rejection symbolized by the term "Sunday school religion" (meaning superficial theology and ethical insensitivity).

Lay leaders in congregations tend to worry when Sunday schools decline in vitality and size. They wonder whether this signifies a sickness in the church's sense of mission. The clergy, so it appears, rarely worry aloud about such matters; they tend to say, if pressed, that the Sunday school has "had its day," and we are now challenged to find new forms and approaches to the education and evangelization of people.

To this writer's knowledge, no vital forums exist today in which laity and clergy together can assess the strengths and weaknesses of the Sunday school. Until such discussions can occur, with positive and constructive planning for the future, the churches' ministry of teaching will continue to languish for much-needed attention.

To focus on the laity-clergy perceptions of the issues in general Protestant education seems absolutely essential. Where a Sunday school, for good or ill, is a "going concern," you can count on it that the church's minister (and especially the "senior minister," in the larger congregation) is 100 percent "for it," encouraging the teachers and lending much personal and moral support. And where a Sunday school is in the death throes, you can ordinarily trace a direct correlation to the lack of clergy support through the years.

Curiously, the very term "Sunday school" is both a strength and a weakness. It communicates well to both its supporters and its detractors. For longer than two generations now, the professional educators of Protestantism have written and spoken at length in an effort to substitute "religious education program," or "Christian education program" or "church school," or even "Sunday church school," for what happens in a congregation's formalized teaching. But the laity persist in using the simple words, Sunday school; they say what is meant—that there is a school available on Sunday in which people of all ages can meet to enjoy fellowship as well as learning.

The laity often point to these strengths of the Sunday school:

—It provides an orientation to the structure and content of the Bible—the stories of the Judeo-Christian heritage and the development of the Christian church.
—It fosters a climate of caring and friendship among its pupils.
—It helps children, youth, and adults to reaffirm their moral values and to support one another in the Christian life.
—It supplements and supports the family in its teaching tasks.
—It is a means of evangelizing—reaching out to the non-churched with the good news of the gospel.

While no Sunday school is able to do all these things effectively all the time, countless persons can cite instances from their own lives, and the experience of their faith communities, to support the claim that faithful attendance in a smoothly functioning school of the church is a positive and desirable factor.

It remains for the professional educators and ordained leadership of the church to raise the flags of caution about Sunday school. They single out such weaknesses as the following:

—That lifelong attendance in such a school is no guarantee that essential data of the faith will be communicated; most people have large gaps in their religious knowledge.

—That Sunday school actually separates family members and fosters the idea that age-level groupings are to be valued over togetherness.

—That Sunday school teaching and curricular resources are seldom of adequate quality to be called "educational."

—That evangelization is not a proper complement to the work of teaching.

—That the church functioned well for centuries without a Sunday school and could do so again.

—That the times call for an emphasis upon adult education; parents and not the organized church are primarily responsible for children's induction into the faith community and its subject matter.

—That Sunday schools tend to be pedestrian in character, slow to promote social consciousness and aggressive social action.

While there is obviously much evidence to support these assertions, none of them can be the basis for wiping out an effort that has commanded so much attention from so many of the churches' most talented leadership in the last century.

It seems apparent that the time is right for bringing clergy and laity together for sustained and genuine dialogue about the best means for teaching and learning in the church. The general Protestant clientele includes a large percentage of the intelligentsia in our society; they need to think seriously about the state of church education and to chart a course for the coming decades.

Who will take the lead to encourage such dialogue? Who will follow up on the discussions and implement better communication about Sunday school and its strengths and weaknesses? The answers to these questions are not immediately apparent.

Strong educational effort, and better schools, would require all the following "ingredients" at the same time:

1. A firm sense of purpose and mission—"goal statements." At

present these are either lacking in denominational judicatories or poorly communicated to the churches' constituencies.

2. Appropriate organizational structures for maintaining order and communication. Where these existed in judicatories as recently as two decades ago, they are greatly weakened or nonexistent at the present time. The denominations have allowed the nomenclature of the Sunday school (terms like superintendent, department, secretary, etc.), and also the language of the Christian education movement (such as Christian education committee, curriculum servicing, laboratory school, etc.), to be divested of their power to communicate. It is difficult to find either a local Sunday school or a church judicatory in which, for instance, the role of a "superintendent" is clearly defined or even greatly valued.

3. Teacher training—to help laity catch a vision of what is possible in a classroom setting at the various age levels and to use the published resources to advantage. Teacher training requires vigilance, persistence, and the tedious business of repetition, year after year. The majority of Sunday school teachers are still offered little or no help in their specific tasks, much less a chance to consider innovative approaches.

4. Good teaching materials—published guides for teachers, attractive items for pupils, and a general design for their use in a sustained fashion over a period of years. The remarkably high-quality curricular resources that emerged after World War II have been unexcelled in the history of the Sunday school movement. That they have ceased to be published, declined in quality, or lost their verve is the tragedy of our era in the churches' history.

5. Adequate physical facilities for teaching/learning. Buildings have been constructed in abundance during the last quarter of a century. Many are under-utilized, inadequately maintained, and used without sufficient attention to the importance of a clean, attractive environment.

These five factors must all be present at the same time in order to have a strong school. To them must be added the spiritual dimension of Christian commitment and prayerful dedication to the ministry of teaching in the name of the Lord.

Only if the clergy as spiritual leaders and directors, and the laity as the "movers and doers," can be united in pursuing all these ingredients at the same time, can we expect the future to bring a genuine resurgence of strong and effective teaching.

One who observes the scene in general Protestant churches for a period of decades is struck by the fact that we seem able to do only one thing at a time. We work hard at curriculum production, only to neglect the teacher training. We turn our attention to facilities and teacher education, and the curriculum falters or dies. We move to strengthen the judicatories' staffs for education and to set up adequate regional structures, only to discover that our goals are not clear and inadequately communicated. We improve the technical language of education, and the language of the Spirit is allowed to recede (to our great detriment).

A longtime church educator said recently, to this writer, "There has to be something demonic at work in our history as Christian teachers. We cannot seem to 'get it together' and move ahead vigorously to teach the life-giving gospel as we surely know how to do it!"

Certainly, when one surveys the wholly significant role the general Protestant churches played in the civil rights movement, and in protesting the Vietnam War, we can applaud a prophetic stance that was backed with social action. But was it necessary to neglect the essential work of the Sunday school while being engaged in these activities? Many clergy persons might say that there was no other choice; many concerned lay persons would see it differently, insisting that the teaching ministry and the prophetic ministry are both required at every period in the churches' life.

All these matters have been addressed in scholarly gatherings of the remaining denominational leaders in Christian (or religious) education. They have yet to be discussed broadly with the laity fully involved and articulating a point of view for the years ahead.

It has come to be a truism that local congregations, when evaluating program at the time of a search for new clerical leadership, tend to place a very high priority on such items as "better church school classes" or "Christian education leadership." Questionnaires and surveys almost without fail will turn up a strong demand for ministers who can teach and support other teachers.

But the candidates who apply for new positions in the churches seem to find ways of circumventing this area of concern. The result is an undercurrent of uneasiness or dissatisfaction. While there may be no overt voicing of complaint, there is an air of anxiety: How will the people be taught? How will the traditions of the faith be understood? What must be done to assure more knowledge and understanding among the people of God?

To restate the obvious, we are in need of clergy-laity conferences on these questions—not in isolated little klatches but in widespread and deliberate encounters that will attract public attention. Out of such a groundswell could emerge the impetus for taking all the knowledge and experience we have gleaned in the Sunday school movement and forging a healthier climate in general Protestant churches.

Observable Changes

The Professionals
At the risk of seeming to be anti-intellectual, one can note with some justification that the more sophisticated the churches' efforts at the preparation of professional educators to guide Christian education programs, the weaker the schools become. Why is this apparently the case?

Listen to the conversations of the employed directors of education in churches when they gather for professional meetings. They discuss their interests in educational psychology, in theological developments, in current ethical dilemmas, and the like. But the day-to-day issues of helping lay teachers to do a better job, of administering a school efficiently, of helping to implement learning at all age levels, and of the pastoral duties incumbent on someone who facilitates the work of a staff of volunteers—all these matters do seem to have taken a secondary role in recent years. We need hardly point out the results—many churches have simply decided they can eliminate the directors' jobs. Many seek other employment.

Putting theory into practice, balancing the scholarly and professional role with the work of being a Sunday school teacher and advocate—this is not easily learned or achieved. Attesting to the difficulty of bringing the everyday work of parish teaching into focus, in ways that are intellectually respectable and "worthy," is the current situation in the general Protestant theological institutions for training clergy. In seminary after seminary, the departments of Christian education have been canceled out or greatly reduced in their influence. It is entirely possible for clergy to be ordained in their denominations without ever having learned in any formal way about the history and development of church education, curricula, and teaching techniques. Indeed, many candidates for ministry appear to have learned that it is chic to denigrate all such courses!

When one looks about to see who is making the strongest impact on the conduct of Christian education and Sunday schools, it is fairly clear that the best work is being done these days by part-time "paraprofessionals." These are lay persons who have taught Sunday school, caught a vision of the possibilities for classroom learning, and accepted positions as coordinators or enablers in the parishes. They organize materials, help to spruce up the environment, work individually at training teachers, and generally provide heroic effort for which they are underpaid. But they would not abandon the cause for anything—they believe in teachers and learners, and they know how important the school of the church can be in a person's life.

Regrettably, these lay persons are considered second-class citizens in the work of the professional organizations; their lack of degrees from graduate school denies them admission to the inner circle.

If this seems to be too harsh an indictment, the writer is willing to stand corrected. But there is a mountain of evidence to suggest that something has gone awry with our approach to training of educational leadership. The chasm widens between professionals and laity; it should be quite the opposite, for only when there is a bonding of commitment and mutual respect between the scholarly leaders and the practicing teachers can there be hope for better morale and stronger sense of purpose in the Sunday school.

Resource "Centers"

The denominations have been cooperating, locally and regionally, in the establishment of resource centers—places where parish planners and teachers can go to examine publications and media for their schools and classes. Such centers have sprung up all around the country, funded cooperatively and staffed with both trained and volunteer consultants.

The purpose of a center is to offer, in one location, the opportunity to explore a variety of materials, from a range of publishers and producers, that would not be available for examination in the local congregation.

But it is very easy for denominational executives to be deluded by the notion that a resource center means wider knowledge and greater usage of the available materials. The number of teachers who actually visit the centers and dig into the materials is minimal at best. The fact remains that people get excited about, and really use, only those items that have been introduced to them in a hands-on kind of situation. If another teacher, in a situation similar to one's own, has found a book or guide helpful, that recommendation is likely to be heard and acted upon much more readily than any other. The resource centers, to be truly effective, should have fulltime, adequately-compensated consultants who will work aggressively to make items known and available to the teaching staffs of the Sunday schools. An abstract "newsletter" is not enough, nor an announced "workshop" to which only a few persons respond. Ways need to be found to put the contents of resource centers into broader circulation.

A center is hardly a "center" if it remains peripheral to the operation of the Sunday school.

The churches doing the best job of orienting teachers to the many helps available have found means of communicating steadily with each staff member. Having a central supply area, attractively kept and maintained with an inviting atmosphere, can work wonders in a Sunday school building. It is comparable to the "teachers' lounge" area, with comfortable seating and a place to browse through the organized and labeled displays of books and other items. Such an area can quickly become the parish "center."

If regional resource centers could become advocates for such local parish centers, there could be a networking plan to circulate items among the member churches. (And with the coming of the computer for indexing resources, there should be no such thing as an unanswered teacher's question, "Where can I find. . . ?" Finding things to teach with and from should be the easiest task of all.)

Still, it is surprising beyond description to learn that many clergy and laity alike are totally unaware of most of the available resources produced by the denominations and independent publishers. The busyness of their lives has not allowed them to become knowledgeable of the field, and no one has undertaken to educate them by placing items into their hands for examination at moments of their greatest "readiness."

Curricular Choices

The curriculum picture in the denominations is variegated, to say the least. As recently as fifteen years ago, one could expect that most congregations would adopt, in principle, a general system of curricular resources in a fairly consistent pattern for across-the-board teaching. The Presbyterians, for example, would be using either *Covenant Life* or *Christian Faith and Action* materials—from preschool through adulthood. The United Methodists had their *Wesley Series* that was thorough and comprehensive. The Episcopalians were still publishing the *Seabury Series* for recommended use in parishes. The United Church of Christ had pioneered a splendid array of materials, and the Disciples of Christ had introduced the *Christian Life Series*. We could cite various other publishing programs; these are sufficient to stress that the denominations offered *norm-setting* guides for teachers and pupils. It was assumed that, in practice, most congregations would adopt these as their own and set about "making them work."

Millions of dollars of denominational budgets went into the research and development essential to producing these materials. Local planners and curriculum choosers looked to "headquarters" for previews of curriculum offerings and waited for new publications to reflect changes based on broad denominational usage and evaluation.

Peter Drucker, the secular authority on management and administration in business, himself a devoted Christian layman, has focused for decades on a primary issue in American life—what he terms the strong tension between centralized and localized planning. The special trick for effectiveness in any enterprise (educational, industrial, governmental) is to achieve a delicate balance between local and central planning, he believes.

The denominations of general Protestant persuasion have apparently struggled for too long now at achieving that delicate balance. The largely successful curriculum publishing efforts of the '50s and '60s were an example of centralized planning. In the '70s, as the total society came to grips with protest movements and an unraveling of traditions, accompanied by distrust of "institutional" leadership, the central boards and agencies in denominations came upon hard times. Their personnel lost touch with the laity; funds dwindled, and staffs were cut. The National Council of Churches, which had provided such creative leadership for education through its Division of Christian Education, became a shadow of its former self.

So what was the effect upon the Sunday schools in local communities throughout the country? Slowly their leaders came to recognize that something had happened to "headquarters." They began to turn in every conceivable direction for supplemental teaching materials—to independent, "nondenominational" publishers, to items from other denominations, and also to the practice of "writing their own" curricula.

Localized planning took over, for there was little choice. The regional field staffs of the denominations had been eliminated in budget cuts. It was hard to find a denominational consultant who could offer authoritative guidance on what to do about teaching resources.

Children, young people, and adults are being taught from a "smorgasbord" of resources. It is not at all unusual to find, in a single Sunday school, that teachers in various departments are unaware of what is being taught in classes other than their own. There is no overall scheme readily apparent either to teachers or pupils. This writer has visited parishes where the curriculum has been changed every year for five or more successive years; the very concept of a sense of unity, articulation, and orderly progression in the exploration of the Bible has virtually disappeared in such congregations.

The Joint Educational Development group of nine or more denominations, representing a large proportion of the general Protestant scene, promised, in the mid-70s, that a series of four *Shared Approaches* would offer to local planners a variety of options for building sensible teaching programs. "Knowing the Word" would continue the style of the *Cooperative Uniform Lesson Series* (reminiscent of the older Sunday school patterns of covering the Bible in a cycle over a period of years). "Interpreting the Word" would provide a more critical type of biblical study; the "reconstructed" biblical stories would reflect the insights of modern Scripture studies. "Living the Word" would focus upon the concept of "community" and the integration of Bible study with social responsibility. And "Doing the Word" would be an innovative, nonuniform collection of resources to focus upon social action and awareness of contemporary ethical issues.

The original promotion of the JED resources encouraged congregations to use "planning kits" for the sake of evaluating the theological stance of a church and selecting materials best suited to each community—its age groups, socio-economic setting, and the like. A principle of "mixing and matching" would be encouraged; local planners could choose from different approaches at different departmental levels if they so elected.

But at this writing it has become apparent that the *Shared Approaches* were less effective than the denominational programs they superseded. The lack of staff and money for developing materials of higher quality, together with the difficulties of editing and producing items jointly when so many different faith traditions are represented, have worked against the achievement of the original concept. Congregations seldom exhibit the same loyalty to *Shared Approaches* that they once mustered for their centrally planned denominational resources.

One can only view with sorrow some of the local experimentation in which congregations have floundered in efforts to produce their "own" materials. Weak theology, faulty Bible scholarship, and ill-conceived approaches to the teaching of children and youth, have characterized many of these attempts. The absence of norms provided by personnel who have expert knowledge is reflected over and over again in the classes where poor resources are employed.

Some churches, without serious reflection on their professed faith and theology, actually choose published resources that subvert their own orthodoxies. But this is a consequence where the delicate balance between centralized and localized planning has eluded us.

Teacher Training

Few of the general Protestant churches reach the ideal of thorough teacher training for everyone who works in the Sunday school. Recruiting practices vary widely; some congregations seek only qualified teachers willing to give time and effort to their tasks commensurate with the high calling of communicating the Christian faith, while others appear to "take anyone they can get" for the Sunday school teaching staff.

In the years when curricular resources were aggressively promoted by denominational leaders, the training of teachers was more often than not related specifically to the use of the materials. In quarterly preview sessions, teachers were assisted in getting a precis of the lessons just ahead. In many congregations, these previews were augmented by weekly planning sessions—all of which added up to a considerable amount of teacher education.

Field personnel of the denominations conducted events for teachers as well, again usually related to the actual materials for the Sunday school.

The breakdown in the systems of curricular development left the churches locally at sea in the area of teacher preparation. The result has been a spottiness in such offerings. A common pattern is for a local congregation to get exercised by the lack of teacher training; its leaders seek out others in the community feeling the same frustration. Then some kind of Saturday event, or even a two-day clinic for teachers will be planned and led by an expert from outside. Free-lance teacher educators have found a ready market for their services, and they are called on by local planners willing to pay fees and travel expenses in order to fill the vacuum in teacher training.

Certain well-established facts about the society have profoundly affected the work of Sunday school teachers as well as others who volunteer in churches or other agencies:

—A much larger percentage of women (traditionally the principal church teachers) are now employed outside the home; they have less time to give to meetings and special events.

—Fewer persons are available in the "pool" of potential teachers; the percentage of our population between the ages of thirty-five to fifty, from whom we have tended to obtain most of our volunteer workers, is lower proportionately than at other periods in our history.

—The "liberation" of women from serving in traditional roles has caused many of them to resist saying yes to requests to teach in the Sunday school.

—People generally do not read as much as they formerly did, preferring television and other pursuits. This means that Sunday school teaching materials are not examined with the same thoroughness the teachers once gave to them.

—A lowered birth rate in the population served by the general Protestant sector has led to lower enrollments in Sunday classes that formerly required more teachers and aides. This had led many persons to feel that Sunday school teaching is not so urgently needed in their particular communities.

Despite all these factors, one can still locate congregations in which the leaders have placed a high priority on providing specialized training for Sunday school personnel. Teachers have been sent to special week-long institutes and other events, to get a new view of what is possible in church teaching. Videotaped segments of teaching have been used for sharing with teachers in local meetings. Demonstration and practice teaching sessions have continued to attract larger numbers of observer/participants than other forms of teacher training events.

One gets the general impression, from visiting Sunday school sessions, that teachers would benefit greatly from seeing and meeting other teachers who are having more successes in their work—and that the denominational structures would be wise to

72125

foster much more by way of inter-parish exchanges devoted to quality in teaching.

Teachers seem especially to need more insight into age level "stages of development" and other data regarding how people learn; having greater knowledge of what it is possible to accomplish at the various age levels would help to counter most of the "discipline" problems of which Sunday school teachers frequently complain.

Some Promising Innovations

Lesson Planning Format

Sunday school teachers hunger for lesson plans that are more easily grasped and executed—not necessarily in order to shortcut essential study and preparation but rather to increase their efficiency when time is at a premium. A frequent complaint about published materials has been that the extensive prose surrounding the "steps" of a lesson plan is hard to wade through. The complaint seems warranted if one takes the time to go through an extensive number of curricular publications. The various writers and editors have their individual styles, and it takes time to "get the hang" of each one's approach to lesson format.

In recent years a more standardized format for lesson planning has shown promise. It consists of the following elements:

a. A clear summation of each major concept to be explored in class (whatever the age level being taught). A concept is a general idea, a manageable block of thought to be considered before moving on to another. Some concepts are global and abstract; others are narrower and more concrete.

b. Carefully formulated goals and objectives for lessons. Goals are the general aims and purposes, stated in terms of students' understandings, knowledge, realization, appreciation, and the like. Objectives, on the other hand, are specific and observable—the kinds of actions on the part of students that are a local outcome of a period of teaching/learning; collectively they add up to the attainment of goals. Objectives are stated through the use of active verbs like "state," "demonstrate," "make," "describe," and "identify."

c. Suggested strategies for teaching—methods of attack, possible ways of approaching learning tasks, lists of media that may be employed, and means of evaluating whether students can in fact accomplish the stated objectives.

Teachers' efficiency is greatly enhanced if they can be provided with planning sheets that encourage them to ask a series of inter-related questions: What is the main idea to be explored in the class session? What are the hoped-for objectives, and how do they "fit in" with the larger goals of education in the church? What are some likely strategies to be employed in class? Which is the best way for us to begin our teaching, given our particular group of students and their interests, needs, and abilities?

The relative simplicity of this "C-O-S" format (Concepts, Objectives, Strategies), when it is kept in mind every week as one plans for Sunday teaching, enables a teaching staff to plan much more quickly and to feel less "snowed" by the page-upon-page suggestions of teachers' guides. Experience shows that it is an innovative theory for instruction and classroom practice.

Curriculum producers could do much to encourage better and more consistent planning and evaluation by individual Sunday school teachers if they would standardize their formats along the lines suggested above. It is discouraging to find inconsistent usage of the terms "goals" and "objectives," inadequate attention to making key concepts stand out plainly, and limited effort on the printed page to explain simply and clearly just what some of the possible strategies might be.

Variety in Media

The use of the term "media" to describe all the kinds of materials teachers may use to appeal to the five senses—so that students may see, hear, taste, smell, and feel as they enter into learning tasks—has proven useful.

When Sunday school teachers are sensitized to the fact that it really matters how their classrooms look and feel to the learners, a new quality of openness to variety in method begins to show up week by week. It is not essential that teachers strive for elaborateness; it is, however, a matter of being considerate of learners when they are provided with attractive bulletin board displays, enjoyable activities that enhance the concepts being explored, and opportunities to be genuinely creative in the expression of ideas.

The right brain/left brain research has demonstrated conclusively that learners bring varied styles to their learning tasks. Some are more oriented to analytical thought, and they learn by listening and reading; others learn by participating in movement, art, and creative expression. Teachers need to provide for both right and left brain, and a variety of media will assure that such provision is being made.

We have learned that long filmstrips with carefully programed text to accompany a series of frames may not be the best way to combine image and sound. Sometimes a single frame, accompanied by a series of well-phrased questions, will serve just as well.

Motion pictures have given way to the easy-to-use video cassette. A cassette can be stopped and started, replayed with ease, and discussed much more easily.

Audio tapes have the advantage of being used by individual students (with or without headsets), and students themselves may make tapes for use in the classroom—as a means of demonstrating knowledge or as a way of sharing creative ideas.

These are only a few of the hints gleaned for innovative use of media in Sunday teaching. Media are not a substitute for "teaching"—they are the tools employed by teachers and learners to provide, in the classroom, simulated experiences and opportunities for creative reflection.

Sunday school teachers will tend to shy away from the use of any medium that is new or unfamiliar. They need hands-on experience in order to gain a sense of comfort and satisfaction with a medium. The overhead projector is a good example. Developed in the '60s, during the height of the innovative period in public education, this piece of hardware has proved an enduring vehicle for classroom communication. It is surprisingly versatile. Teachers may make transparencies ahead of class time, utilizing color and overlays and various means of revealing images progressively to the learners. Or the students themselves may be provided with transparencies and pens to produce reports, artistic presentations, and the like.

But if a teacher has never had a chance to experiment with the overhead and learn how to use it with ease, the instrument is likely to find itself in a closet gathering dust instead of becoming the indispensable medium it is meant to be.

Churches with first-rate Sunday schools will have a common storage area for the hardware like tape recorders, video recorders, projectors, etc. Someone on the staff will be in charge of seeing to it that the use of these items is scheduled with care and that each piece is kept in good repair—always clean and ready for the classroom, with spare bulbs and parts on hand.

Electives for Adults

One promising result of localized planning has been the emerging pattern of planning adult classes in the general Protestant churches around a system of electives, lasting anywhere from four to ten weeks.

Perhaps unconsciously taking their cue from the community college movement, with its emphasis upon lifelong learning for adults, many churches have come forth with impressive offerings of options for adult study.

Teachers/leaders of elective groups are chosen on the basis of their subject matter competencies. A professor of Bible at a nearby college or seminary will be asked to teach a course on a scripture theme; a specialist in the problems of hunger in the world will agree to teach a course on that topic . . . and so it goes. Teachers' interests and abilities sometimes become the determining factor in defining the course offerings. At other times, surveys/questionnaires circulated among adults will disclose a keen interest (such as a course on sexism in the church), and local planners will set about locating a leader and making the course available.

The approach works best when adults have a choice from among several courses (even in the smaller congregation where class size is a concern). Adults respond more readily to a course that has been described ahead of time in writing, so that they know just what they will be learning. And any kind of prerequisite (such as reading a text or doing special preparation for each class session) seems to increase the interest rather than discouraging participation.

Courses in the Bethel Bible Series, the kerygma approach to scripture study, and other sustained programs like these—intended to involve the laity in systematic examination of the Bible—appear to work better when there are planned vacation periods within the schedule and when additional opportunities for study are supplied alongside them in the calendar. Forum-type studies, with a presenter followed by discussion, prove to be a popular format for class sessions.

In response to the electives idea, more curricula for adult Sunday school classes are appearing in clearly separate "units of study." Teachers can work toward terminal points along the way, so that learners have a feeling of accomplishment and "credit for having learned." This moves the Sunday classes away from the steady stream into which people may enter or from which they may drop out at will, without appreciable effect.

Participation in elective courses spaced out through the year makes it possible for conscientious parents to have their own Sunday school experience interspersed with times for being with their children in intergenerational learning as well. The liturgical year lends itself to schedule adaptations where adult electives are provided. Intergenerational or family activity can occur during Advent and in the season from Easter through Pentecost; adult electives can be pursued during Lent and at other times between Pentecost and the following Advent.

Some of the larger churches publish "catalog-type" descriptions of their adult course offerings, and provision is made for pre-registration, and for the purchasing of texts and other preparation. Sunday morning still affords some of the best opportunities for such a program to succeed.

Learning Centers

Another innovation that has the possibility of being more than a mere fad is the use of "learning centers" in the Sunday school. It is a development stemming from the open classroom movement that received so much attention in the '70s in public education. The churches are possibly in a better position to make such an approach work effectively than a public school, for a variety of reasons, but chiefly because teachers are not planning for week-long activities; they plan only for short periods of weekly gathering.

A learning center, as the term is used here, refers to a small segment of subject matter treated in a particular way that is manageable by an individual learner (or small group) for a limited period of time. Typically, a classroom will be set up with a collection of these learning centers to be visited by the students in an order of their own choosing. The activities to be accomplished in each one will be described in printed or taped directions. Learners go to the centers, find out what is required, and set about the tasks as directed.

The method is most effective when the following points are kept in mind:

a. A careful introduction to the centers should be provided for the class members; it can take the form of a short presentation or a "tour" of the centers conducted by the teacher(s), or both.

b. Ground rules need to be provided for the learners, such as
guidance on how many persons may work in a given center
at one time; what kinds of talking and sharing are encouraged, and how learners are to keep records of their choices
and what they have learned.

c. Provision needs to be made for "closure" after learners have
explored a group of centers. This can be a discussion period
for the whole class, led by a teacher. Or it can be a prayer
service incorporating some of the insights gleaned in the
centers. Or it can be a sharing of products completed in the
centers. The point is that the learners should not simply
work individually in centers and then leave the classroom;
this works against the preservation of a sense of community,
and it dissipates the values that are potentially present in
having done the learning tasks.

d. Learning centers need to be well-planned and tested out be-
forehand. Are the directions clear and not too complicated
for younger learners? Are the centers devoted to central
concepts that fall together logically for learners? Are the
activities likely to appeal to a variety of learning styles—
employing variety in media, method, and sensory stimuli?

Much work is required for teachers to adapt curricular resources prepared for the self-contained classroom to the open
classroom style. Denominational publishers have been slow to
produce learning center materials, knowing that only a minority
of the churches will be purchasers and users. So, an innovation
that has strong possibilities for making Sunday school more interesting to learners has had to be primarily a method dependent
upon skilled local planning.

Teachers who have worked hard to master the skills needed,
and who have practiced with care the principles noted above, are
reluctant to go back to traditional forms of teaching after they
have "tested" the learning center approach. Vacation church
schools and other groups have also found it to be a valid way to
involve learners.

A special advantage of learning centers is that they permit the
combining of age levels, particularly in small churches where
there are not enough children or youth to make the usual grade
groupings possible.

Learning centers work especially well for intergenerational
learning. Grandparents, parents, adolescents, and younger learners, even preschoolers, can gather in an open classroom and work
in learning centers. Teachers who plan something especially for

adults to do in the centers are often surprised to find those activities appealing to brighter children as well. Centers planned for young children (such as a "fishing well" with magnets for hooks and questions attached to paper clips, to be "caught" by the magnets on the lines) will inevitably delight some of the adults! Cross word puzzles seem to appeal to all age groups. A bit of practice with the learning centers in open classrooms will provide keen insights for Sunday school teachers—into the learning styles and preferences of individual members of the groups involved.

This whole process does not lend itself readily to description in curriculum manuals. Teachers who have not experienced learning centers for themselves have a difficult time visualizing what is meant by the terminology. Virtually the only workable method for teaching teachers to use and design learning centers is to provide for them a time when they become learners themselves in an open classroom. Out of the experience of trying out the concept, teachers grasp the concepts quickly and become creative planners of this type of individualized learning.

The Common Lectionary

The interest in liturgical renewal is widespread among the general Protestant churches. New worshipbooks and hymnals have appeared in all the denominations, and a strong ecumenical dimension is apparent as the results of liturgical studies in this century become more widely known.

When the *Common Lectionary*, consisting of a three-year cycle of Sunday Scripture readings, was adopted after Vatican II, the framers of it had no idea that it would provide such impetus for Christian unity and parish studies. But that has been a happy by-product. Not only the clergy find the *Lectionary* to be a meeting ground for mutual exchange of insight about scripture and the rhythm of the church year; the laity as well have learned to focus on the readings and their theological themes in preparation for worship and in family devotional practice.

A prime example of the *Lectionary*-oriented approach to the Sunday school curriculum has been the Concordia Series of the Lutheran Church (Missouri Synod). A local effort that has gained national attention is the *Living the Good News* series produced by the Episcopal Diocese of Colorado.

The weekly readings focus on the Gospels of Matthew, Mark, and Luke (with additional pasages from John now and then). These gospel readings are correlated with selected Old Testament passages in the cycle. The Epistles, Acts, and Revelation are read in sequence; these readings may or may not relate directly to the other two passages.

Two difficulties emerge in the forming of a church-wide curriculum based on the Lectionary:

a. The cycle assumes that readers/listeners have a general background in the Old Testament and know the "story" of the patriarchs, the covenants, and the people of Israel and their prophets. This assumption must be questioned, for many adults are not that familiar with the Bible and our faith history. Children and young people need to learn the story in its broad outline, through a much more systematic study than the cycle of readings will permit. There is so much skipping around in the Sunday readings that it is very difficult to teach Old Testament meaningfully.

b. The *Lectionary* is adult-oriented. Many of the passages are beyond the capacity of children to understand. And as curriculum writers attempt to handle the three readings week after week, they find themselves struggling mightily to connect the readings with the lives of younger learners.

The interest of educational planners in *Lectionary*-based curricula stems from a concern for bringing about intergenerational learning, family study, and a sense of genuine community. It also reflects a perceived need to relate what happens educationally to the central act of the people, the worship of God. The lines of reasoning are that it should be possible for the whole parish/congregation to study the same thing each week—thus fostering family conversation and community-wide focusing upon central biblical/liturgical themes, and that it should also be possible for the churches to gain a stronger understanding of the Christian faith through observance of the seasons of the church year.

Teachers of youth and adults generally express satisfaction with the *Lectionary*-oriented studies. Teachers of children express their reservations, as they face the weekly task of selecting *which* reading to focus on and often feeling that none is quite appropriate for their pupils.

The use of learning centers related broadly to the seasons of Lent, Christmas and Epiphany, Lent and Easter, and the feast of Pentecost, seems a practical way for Sunday teaching to relate meaningfully to the church year. But that leaves the larger question of how to "cover" the essential subject matter of Old and New

Testaments, together with denominational heritage materials.

When listening to the aims of the *Lectionary*-based curriculum (to reach all age levels in all churches with the same biblical themes each week), an old-timer who attended Sunday school fifty years ago is reminded of the way in which the curriculum was organized at that time. The Bible was treated in a seven-year cycle, with all age levels studying the same selected text each week, fifty-two Sundays a year. The only interruptions were the quarterly Temperance Sunday lessons, tucked into the cycle for the purpose of involving the whole church in considering the problems of alcohol abuse.

That system of study had its shortcomings, too—the same as the ones now encountered by planners of *Lectionary*-based materials. But the problems were not quite identical, at least the Sunday school lessons did not attempt to deal weekly with Old Testament, Epistle, and Gospel, all three!

Still, it is important, and worthy of our concentration, to think through how our programs of Sunday teaching are related conceptually to the worship life of the congregations. Anything that can be done to help learners in a secularized society to sense the interrelationship of biblical and theological themes, and their connectedness to daily living, is to be applauded—and if the *Lectionary* proves a suitable vehicle for making these connections possible, it will be all to the good.

Future Prospects

Hardly any generalization about Sunday school in the general Protestant churches can be offered without inviting serious debate. Reactions to the Sunday school run all the way from surprise that anyone would even question its value to vehement attacks upon it as a classic "mistake."

This writer holds to a set of biases born out of a lifetime of participation in the churches' educational programs; he favors renewal of Sunday school, believing that such a strategy has the best chance of helping the churches of our time to offer a strong and much-needed ministry of teaching for the people of God. It has a checkered history, and some of the Sunday school stereotypes are all too telling. Still, it persists as a concept—and it seems both sensible and possible that people could gather for meaningful study on Sundays and learn much that is needful for the living of Christian faith.

The future of the whole movement will hinge on the following key factors:

1. The leadership provided by clergy and professional Christian/religious educators.

Whereas Sunday schools of the past were a lay movement and derived their vitality from heavy involvement of lay persons in the decision making, it is a fact that in general Protestant churches these days the key personnel are the ordained and professionally trained leaders. They are the ones who support or demoralize the laity. They decide when, where, and how education will be offered in the congregations. They determine the curricula. They are responsible, ultimately, for the denominational structures.

If the clergy and other professionals were to decide that Sunday school needed to be renewed, and if they empowered the laity to devote talent and energy to the task, then nothing could stop the renewal from beginning. We wait for articulate pastors and Christian educators to sound the call.

2. The stress placed upon what it means to teach and learn.

In the last quarter of a century, we have learned very, very much about the nature of human growth and development. The data are still coming in, and much work needs to be done to relate the insights of Piaget, Erikson, and the other giants in the field to the everyday tasks of teachers and pupils. Sunday schools cannot ignore all these valuable contributions; it is the general Protestant churches where the finest opportunities exist for developing programs of learning that take all such knowledge into account.

The laity include the teachers, educators, and administrators who know a vast amount about teaching and learning. Their talents could be tapped. Most of them know little about Sunday school education since their own childhood experiences of it; they would welcome being brought abreast of the issues and involved in developing local, regional, and national strategies for renewal.

3. Fearless emphasis upon sharing biblical and theological scholarship.

We know more about the scriptures than we have ever known before. Newly discovered manuscripts, archaeological data, cultural and anthropological evidence—all point the way to a rich unfolding of our faith history. People in the churches are largely unaware of this world of knowledge contained chiefly in journals and in seminary and university libraries. The Sunday schools could be enriched immeasurably by renewed depth in the process of teaching.

To face unflinchingly the rise of literalism and fundamentalism, with their outright rejection of scholarly Scripture study, is a mission that can best be undertaken by leaders of the general Protestant sector.

Just after World War I, as the continental theologies were making their way into the consciousness of American church leaders, the curricula of the denominations reflected a genuine seriousness about sharing biblical knowledge and neo-Reformation theology with both adults and youth in the churches. To compare the content of Sunday school materials in those years with that of the present time is to be struck by the fact that the editors and writers have backed away from forthright and thorough scholarship of this sort.

There is no time like these closing decades of the millenium for recovering a sense of mission in congregational teaching programs. One has a hunch that the laity are ready to hear and ponder; it is up to the scholars and clergy to take the lead in restoring real depth.

4. Redefinition of "school" and administrative policy.

School does not need to be a negative word; it means only the gathering of persons in convenient settings for the purpose of teaching/learning.

The operation of a Sunday school requires attention to recruitment of good teachers, training them for their tasks, and supporting them with adequate resources, equipment, facilities, and budget.

Much more can be done by the denominations to define once again, in contemporary prose, just what is needed for the smooth operation of a church's school. The laity are best able to see that the tasks are accomplished, and they would do it if their jobs were clearly defined.

The assistance of computers now makes it possible to carry on administration in efficient ways. Records of students' interests and abilities, enrollment and attendance data, and logs of accomplishments at the various age levels—all these can be organized and made readily available through existing computer programs. Even lesson planning can be aided by the use of computers.

Far better than attempting computer-aided instruction would be the use of these machines for helpful administrative and planning.

5. Achieving an optimal balance between local and centralized planning.

As noted earlier, the denominational structures play a vital role in norm-setting for Sunday school education. To lose sight of this, leaving most of the curricular decision making up to each congregation, is to lose the connectional strengths of Protestant churches.

Beginning with regional denominational structures and personnel, the churches should address themselves to the task of rebuilding widespread support for strong educational programs in the congregations. Laity must play a significant role in this kind of reassessment and this new beginning, if progress is to be made.

6. *Most importantly, a prayerful sense of openness to the leading of the Spirit.*

There should be no sense of dichotomy between education and spirituality. Our spiritual formation requires the disciplines of study and learning. To be "born again," as Christians understand this, is to become children of God, open to learning and discovering.

Sunday schools and their teachers should be able to combine the language systems of Bible and theology with the technical and altogether useful languages of human psychology, pedagogy, and the like. It is in the general Protestant sector that some of the finest work can be done to demonstrate the unity of spirit, mind, and body under the compelling direction of the Holy Spirit. In prayerful approaches to our work, we become open to God's leading and sensitive to all that we have yet to learn from the ageless and life-giving gospel.

Chapter 6

Traditional Can Be Good: The Evangelical Sunday School

ROBERT J. DEAN

One of the basic premises of this book is that the Sunday school has a future. Evangelicals are among those who do not seriously question the continuing potential of the Sunday school in Christian education. As active participants in Sunday school work, evangelicals are well aware of the weaknesses of today's Sunday schools and the inadequacy of the Sunday school to do the total work of Christian education. Most evangelicals, therefore, are anxious to renew the Sunday school and to complement it with other educational activities. However, evangelicals are not searching for alternatives to replace the Sunday school.

"Evangelicals see the Sunday school as a divine institution with divine oversight, a divine mission and a divine program."[1] Although some evangelicals would be more restrained in how they state it, most would basically agree with this description. They are aware that Sunday schools are a fairly recent phenomenon, but they feel that the Sunday school provides a way to fulfill many biblical mandates for Christians and churches.

Evangelical Distinctives

When some people hear the words *evangelical Sunday schools*, they think of the Sunday schools of the late nineteenth century; but this chapter deals with Sunday schools in contemporary evangelical Protestant churches. When the editor of this book planned separate chapters on general and evangelical Protestant

1. James DeForest Murch, *Teach or Perish!* (Grand Rapids, Mich.: Eerdmans, 1961), p. 52.

113

Sunday schools, the purpose was not to split theological hairs, but to include any distinctive perspectives.

A broad definition of *evangelical*, therefore, is in order. Richard Quebedeaux paints with broad strokes when he defines an evangelical as "a person who attests to the truth of, and acts upon, three theological principles: (1) the full authority of Scriptures in matters of faith and practice; (2) the necessity of personal faith in Jesus Christ as Savior and Lord (conversion); and (3) the urgency of seeking the conversion of sinful men and women to Christ (evangelism)."[2] Quebedeaux identifies three highly visible subcultures within this broad spectrum: Fundamentalists, Charismatics, and Neo-evangelicals. He points out that a number of Christians of evangelical sentiment are in many Christian groups; but most are in independent churches or in one of several denominations, the largest of which is Southern Baptists.[3]

Although there is considerable diversity in such a broad spectrum of churches and groups, evangelical Sunday schools have some common distinctives; and these distinctives of contemporary evangelical Sunday schools are basically the same distinctives that characterized nineteenth-century evangelical Sunday schools.

Historians debate the degree of continuity and discontinuity between the Sunday schools of that period and the Sunday schools of today's general Protestant churches.[4] There is little doubt, however, that considerable continuity exists between the evangelical Sunday schools of the nineteenth and twentieth centuries.[5] A national Sunday school movement is a thing of the past, and some of the old approaches have been replaced; however, many of the basic tenets remain.

---

2. *The Worldly Evangelicals* (San Francisco: Harper & Row, 1978), p. 7.

3. Ibid., p. 36. Some Southern Baptists prefer not to be called "evangelicals." Cf. diverse answers to the question *Are Southern Baptists Evangelicals?* by three Southern Baptist historians (Macon, Ga.: Mercer University Press, 1983). Some fundamentalists make a clear distinction between themselves and evangelicals. See Elmer L. Towns, *America's Fastest Growing Churches: Why 10 Sunday Schools Are Growing* (Nashville: Impact Books, 1972), pp. 158-176.

4. Jack L. Seymour argues for considerable continuity in *From Sunday School to Church School: Continuities in Protestant Church Education in the United States, 1860-1929* (Washington, D.C.: University Press of America, 1982).

5. For a history of the Sunday school from an evangelical perspective, see Wesley R. Willis, *200 Years—and Still Counting: Past, Present, and Future of the Sunday School* (Wheaton, Ill.: Victor Books, 1980).

The Bible as Textbook

Although evangelicals do not all use the same words to describe their view of biblical authority, all of them consider the Bible to be authoritative and trustworthy in matters of faith and practice. Bernard Ramm defines this evangelical distinctive in terms of the objective and subjective dimensions of faith. Evangelicals tend to emphasize the objective reality of divine revelation as separate from and prior to the human response of faith, and they view the Bible as the authoritative record of this divinely revealed truth.[6]

One noted evangelical Christian educator defines the core of the Christian faith as "the confidence that our Creator God is, that He has acted in Christ Jesus to redeem, and that He has revealed both Himself and Truth to us in the written Word."[7]

Not surprisingly, therefore, evangelicals consider the Bible as the textbook for the Sunday school. Curriculum plans and materials are viewed as aids in studying the Bible and in drawing from it lessons for life. Many evangelicals prefer an approach that moves through an entire Bible book, making applications to life that grow out of the text and context. Others like a variety of approaches to Bible study: book studies, personality studies, topical studies. All evangelicals agree that the Bible must be the textbook used in Sunday school.

Evangelicals are generally agreed that the Bible is the textbook not only for adults but also for younger age-groups in Sunday school; however, this presents a challenge. We struggle, for example, with such questions as: What parts of the Bible are appropriate for children of various ages? How can the Bible be used as the text in trying to deal with the developmental tasks of learners as they move from one stage to another?

Emphasis on Conversion

Whereas some groups emphasize the Sunday school primarily as a school for nurturing and instructing Christians, evangelical Sunday schools emphasize evangelism as well as education. Evangelicals have always held that one objective of the Sunday school is to lead children, youth, and adults to personal faith in Jesus Christ.

This emphasis on conversion is consistent with the history and

6. Bernard Ramm, *The Evangelical Heritage* (Waco, Tex.: Word Books, 1973), p. 13.
7. Lawrence O. Richards, *A Theology of Christian Education* (Grand Rapids, Mich.: Zondervan, 1975), p. 309.

beliefs of evangelicals. Most evangelicals have their roots in the sectarian rather than the churchly tradition. In this tradition, church membership is reserved for persons who have experienced conversion through personal faith in Christ. In most cases, even the children of believers do not become church members until they make a profession of faith.

Although church membership in most evangelical churches is only for professing Christians, the Sunday school is for everyone. Preschool children are enrolled in Sunday school at an early age. Children from Christian and non-Christian homes are taught the Bible; and when they are old enough, they are encouraged to experience personal salvation. Likewise, non-Christian youth and adults are enrolled in Sunday school with the prayerful expectation that they may be led to personal faith in Christ.

Child evangelization is a lively topic among evangelicals—not *that* it should be done but *when* and *how* it should be done. Most evangelicals would agree with Edward L. Hayes: "There are two simple demands of the gospel—renunciation of sin and trust in Jesus. A child can meet both of these demands."[8]

Emphasis on Outreach

One of the impressive distinctives about evangelical churches is that they have continued to grow at a time when attendance in many other groups has declined. This is due primarily to the aggressive spirit of outreach practiced by many evangelical Sunday schools. Is the Sunday school exclusively the school of the church to teach church members and their children, or is it also the outreach arm of the church to reach the unchurched and non-Christians? The basic tenets of evangelicals predetermine their answer to this question.

One of the reasons for evangelicals' enthusiasm about Sunday schools is the Sunday school's proven effectiveness as the outreach arm of the church. Throughout a lifetime of work in Southern Baptist Sunday schools, John T. Sisemore has emphasized the outreach potential of the Sunday school. In an obvious response to the variety of strategies of the church growth movement, Sisemore has written *Church Growth Through the Sunday School*, in which he maintains that the Sunday school continues to be the

8. Edward L. Hayes, "Evangelization of Children," in *Childhood Education in the Church*, ed. Roy B. Zuck and Robert E. Clark (Chicago: Moody Press, 1975), p. 164.

key to the most balanced and most effective kind of church growth. The grading by ages into small classes with lay leaders makes the Sunday school a ready-made organization for outreach.[9]

Arthur Flake identified five steps in effective Sunday school outreach: (1) find the people, (2) provide space, (3) enlarge the organization, (4) train the workers, and (5) maintain systematic visitation.[10] This formula for growth has been successfully used by many evangelical Sunday schools. The secret to the success of this formula is a spirit of evangelism that pervades growing Sunday schools.

Some of the fastest-growing churches are large fundamentalist churches. They often have an aggressive program of bus outreach, although this is less prevalent now than during the 1970s. The growth strategy of many of these large churches is growth of their own congregation rather than growth through establishing missions and new churches. A charismatic pastor is a key factor in the growth of these churches.[11]

The growth strategy of Sunday schools in these churches is modeled after the growth strategy of the church. That is, whereas the traditional evangelical approach is to divide into smaller classes and to enlist and train more teachers, the large fundamentalist churches often encourage large classes with a gifted master teacher. Many assistants help with the administration, fellowship, outreach, and ministry of the class; but the master teacher is considered the key.[12]

This points up another dimension of evangelical outreach—an emphasis on reaching adults. Whether in small classes or in large classes, evangelicals see reaching adults as the key to reaching entire families.[13] This was the pattern of New Testament evangelism, and it is particularly effective in a day when adult education is big business and the adult population is growing. Classes of young adults, often couples classes, are reaching young families.

9. John T. Sisemore, *Church Growth Through the Sunday School* (Nashville: Broadman Press, 1983).

10. Arthur Flake, *The True Functions of the Sunday School* (Nashville: Convention Press, 1955).

11. Towns, *America's Fastest Growing Churches*, pp. 193-218.

12. Elmer Towns, "The Aggressive Sunday School," *Journal of Christian Education* III, no. 1 (1982) pp. 30-31.

13. See Gene Getz, "The Renewal Sunday School," *Journal of Christian Education* III, no. 1 (1982) pp. 16-17.

And Sunday schools that reach out to singles usually find another group of responsive adults.

Weaknesses and Strengths

In an article on "The Traditional Sunday School," Sherman Williams attacks the mind-set against anything called "traditional." Anything old is assumed to be bad; and anything new, good. New concepts and approaches have the advantage of being untried; history has not had time to record their failures or weaknesses. Because we see the well-known faults of something traditional, we may overlook its inherent strengths.[14]

Because the Sunday school has been around for so long, its faults are well-known. The Sunday school has been a favorite whipping boy for groups ranging all the way from the secular press to religious education professionals. In their history of *The Big Little School*, Robert W. Lynn and Elliott Wright wrote: "Criticism of all schools is a recurring American pastime, but none has been so savagely attacked since 1900 as the Sunday school."[15] Some people feel that the faults of the Sunday school are so serious that it has no viable future. Some professional religious educators even recommend that Christian education alternatives be sought.[16]

Certainly no one is more aware of the weaknesses of the Sunday school than those who spend their lives working on it. Evangelicals, therefore, are aware of the shortcomings of their Sunday schools. Some of these are inherent weaknesses growing out of the nature of the Sunday school; others are areas that can be (and in some churches have been) improved. These weaknesses, therefore, are not fatal flaws that cause evangelicals to give up on the Sunday school. Rather they point up areas for renewal.

Quality of Teaching

Wesley Shrader's famous article, "Our Troubled Sunday Schools," is often remembered by its opening story, in which a

14. Sherman Williams, "The Traditional Sunday School," *Journal of Christian Education* III, no. 1 (1982), pp. 10-11.

15. Robert W. Lynn and Elliott Wright, *The Big Little School*, 2nd ed. rev. (Birmingham and Nashville: Religious Education Press and Abingdon Press, 1980), p. 118.

16. John H. Westerhoff III, *Values for Tomorrow's Children* (Boston: Pilgrim Press, 1970), p. 89.

fourteen-year-old referred to "the most wasted hour of the week."[17] The article effectively exposed the Sunday school's failures, especially poor teaching. In fact, Shrader was so effective in making this point that few people remember that his purpose was to show how churches could use new methods to redeem the Sunday school.

The Sunday school has been operated primarily by lay people. This accounts for the Sunday school's greatest weakness and one of its greatest strengths. The weakness is the poor quality of teaching. The strength is that the Sunday school has involved laypeople in the church's ministry.

No one denies the poor quality of much of the teaching in evangelical Sunday schools. The most ardent Sunday school supporters concede this fact. Instead of vibrating with life, Sunday school is too often a dull, boring experience.[18]

A multitude of problems affect the quality of teaching in the Sunday school.

1. Some teachers' lack of interest is apparent in frequent absenteeism, lack of preparation, and humdrum class sessions.
2. Other teachers have good intentions, but they are hampered by lack of training for their task and lack of time for adequate preparation.
3. Still other teachers have "taught" for years, but the quality of their teaching leaves much to be desired.

On the positive side, however, not all of the teaching in Sunday school is so poor as to be of no value. Little of it would meet professional standards, but this does not mean that all of the quality is poor or that the quality cannot be improved.

Keep in mind also that effective teaching is much more than communicating cognitive skills. Many lay teachers have a love for people that is expressed in their Sunday school work. Lynn and Wright record this observation about the "amateur" status of Sunday school workers: "To speak of Sunday school workers as amateurs is not to depreciate them. One root meaning of 'amateur' points toward caring and intelligent love. An amateur is not a person who does things poorly; rather, one who cares about an

17. Wesley Shrader, "Our Troubled Sunday Schools," *Life* XLII (11 February 1957), p. 100.

18. Lois E. LeBar, *Education That Is Christian*, rev. ed. (Old Tappan, N.J.: Fleming H. Revell 1981), p. 15.

activity and is intelligent in the way he or she cares."[19]

Many amateur Sunday school teachers have succeeded in communicating a sense of caring to their pupils. As my own church prepared to observe "Teacher Appreciation Day," our pastor invited me to preach. During the several weeks before the day, I conducted a kind of straw poll. I asked a number of people to describe what makes a good Sunday school teacher. In nearly every case, the first thing mentioned was a person who genuinely cares for the pupils.

Most Sunday school teachers could never meet professional educational standards. They should not be expected to become professionals. On the other hand, they can become better Sunday school teachers through training designed for them. The training can encourage them to share their faith and love with their pupils, and it can sharpen the basic skills that enable teachers to do this as effectively as possible.

Since the early days of the Sunday school movement, teacher training has been the most important strategy for improving Sunday schools. Effective teacher training includes not only orientation training but ongoing training. The most effective teacher training is a weekly workshop in which preparation for next Sunday is combined with evaluation and improvement of the time spent in Sunday school. Even in small churches a pastor or an experienced teacher can render invaluable help by working with teachers in this kind of setting.

Depth of Study

A consistent criticism of the evangelical Sunday school is that it does not achieve the minimum it sets out to do—to teach the Bible. The criticism often comes from parents who complain that their children have received only a smattering of Bible knowledge in Sunday school. They know several Bible stories, but they lack basic Bible skills and they have little sense of the sweep and flow of the Bible's meaning and message.

Pastors and seminary professors often are appalled at the biblical and theological shallowness of Sunday school. They want Sunday school pupils—particularly young people and adults—to demonstrate that they are skilled biblical interpreters and thoroughly grounded in the faith. Instead they encounter young people and adults whose biblical and theological perceptions are

---

19. Lynn and Wright, *The Big Little School*, p. 155.

shallow at best. This is particularly disturbing to evangelicals, who emphasize the Bible as the Sunday school's textbook and objective truth as something to be taught and learned.

Anyone who evaluates the effectiveness of the Sunday school by these standards is bound to be discouraged at the findings. Many factors explain it: inadequately trained teachers, shortness of time, absenteeism of learners and sometimes of leaders, lack of motivation, etc.

Two observations are in order. First of all, many Sunday schools do teach basic Bible skills. Many people were first introduced to the Bible in Sunday school. We may pay so much attention to Sunday school pupils who learn almost nothing that we overlook others who do develop some Bible skills. Rather than lamenting how little Bible insight many people get in Sunday school, why not recognize how much less there would be without Sunday schools?

The other observation is that the Sunday school should not be expected to provide educational experiences that require a specially trained professional. Rather than focusing on what the Sunday school cannot do, why not be grateful for what it does accomplish: lay involvement in Bible study, fellowship, ministry, and evangelism? And why not complement Sunday school with educational activities designed to achieve other goals of Christian education?

The most striking recent example of this in evangelical churches is the phenomenon of Christian schools. During the 1970s these were established at the rate of three per day.[20] Analyzing the factors in this amazing growth is beyond the scope of this book; however, one factor obviously is the desire of parents to provide a Christian education of more depth, scope, and intensity than is available in Sunday school.

What will be the ultimate impact of Christian schools on the Sunday school? Because of the newness of the phenomenon, research has revealed no clear conclusions. Few evangelicals expect Christian schools to replace Sunday schools, but nearly everyone recognizes that they introduce a new dynamic into Sunday school.[21]

A children's curriculum editor teaches third graders in Sunday

20. Kenneth O. Gangel, *Building Leaders for Church Education* (Chicago: Moody Press, 1970, 1974, 1981), p. 415.

21. Ibid., p. 418.

school. In his department are three boys who attend Christian
schools. These boys have much more factual Bible knowledge than
the other children, although their grasp of its meaning and relevance is about the same. The teacher, therefore, tries to involve
the three boys in getting factual data before the entire department. This helps to involve them and to keep them from getting
bored. The teacher, however, involves the boys on the same level
as the other children when dealing with insights, feelings, and
activities that grow out of the lesson.

Most churches have a number of Christian educational activities to complement the foundation laid by the Sunday school.
Vacation Bible School, for example, provides a more intensive
learning opportunity because of spending several hours on con-
secutive days. Many churches also have regular study groups that
deal with a variety of subjects. Southern Baptists, for example,
use Sunday night to teach such areas of scope as ethics, doctrine,
history, polity, and discipleship. On Wednesday night, other
groups study music and missions. Many churches also have special study and training opportunities, often led by a trained specialist. Conferences or workshops are led by a member of the
church staff or by an outside specialist.

Transmitting Values

Moral development has always been an important part of Christian education and one of the objectives of the Sunday school, but
critics charge that the Sunday school has been unsuccessful in
transmitting genuine Christian values. At best, they say, the Sunday school has only succeeded in transmitting cultural values
mixed with popular piety.

This criticism is particularly serious to evangelicals for at least
two reasons: For one thing, evangelicals are disturbed by the
erosion of traditional values in contemporary society. Whatever
one may think of the Moral Majority—and even evangelicals are
not agreed about it—the movement reflects the frustration felt by
many conservative Christians. Hedonism, secularism, pluralism,
and relativism have played havoc with traditional moral values.
Evangelicals, therefore, are determined to find ways to defend
and transmit traditional values.

The other reason for evangelical concern is that they believe
certain basic moral values are absolute and eternal because they
grow out of the character of God, who created us in his image.
The biblical commandments about justice and mercy, for example,

reflect the expectations of a just and merciful God. Biblical standards of morality, therefore, are not arbitrary; rather they reflect life as it was intended to be lived, life at its fullest and best. Based on this presupposition, moral failures are sinful because they deny God and undermine human welfare.[22]

What about the charge that the Sunday school transmits only cultural values and popular piety? This is basically accurate, but it is a worthwhile function. Transmitting cultural values is a role of institutions in any culture. The younger generation must learn the values of the culture in order to function in society. The Sunday school has been one of the institutions that transmits cultural values in our society. This is potentially a strength that becomes a weakness when the Sunday school denies its own biblical heritage by an uncritical transmission of cultural values.

Many cultural values are good, but others are not. An uncritical acceptance of cultural values, for example, sometimes equates provincial prejudices with Christian truth. Sadly, evangelical Sunday schools at times have been guilty; and ironically, by committing this sin, they have denied their own biblical heritage.

"Popular piety," like "cultural values," is another ambiguous phrase. The phrases are similar in meaning, but popular piety often connotes an emphasis on personal morality that excludes any broader social dimensions. Evangelical Sunday schools have stressed such things as industry, honesty, purity, and temperance; and they have played a positive role in transmitting these values, especially when reinforcing training received at home. In a study of youth in eleven major denominational groups, Merton Strommen found less premarital sex and alcohol and drug abuse among youth with a strong personal faith, one of the traditional emphases of Sunday schools.[29]

Evangelicals—with the exception of blacks—do not have an enviable record for dealing with social issues. Lynn and Wright point out that too many evangelicals seem unaware that the Sunday school movement began as a social reform movement and that many earlier evangelicals combined evangelism and social concern.[24] A resurgence of social concern among evangelicals is taking place, but there are differences of opinion about what the key

22. See Donald M. Joy, "Moral Development: Evangelical Perspectives," *Religious Education* 75, no. 2 (March-April 1980), pp. 142-151.

23. Merton Strommen, "The Future of the Sunday School: A Researcher's Reflections," *Religious Education* 78, no. 3 (Summer, 1983), p. 343.

24. Lynn and Wright, *The Big Little School*, p. 157.,

issues are and how to deal with them. Many evangelicals consider
the key issues to be such things as abortion, crime, and pornogra-
phy; but a growing number are focusing more attention on such
issues as nuclear war, hunger, and racism. Publishers of Sunday
school curriculum materials for evangelical Sunday schools are
caught in the middle of this continuing tension.[25]

Given the make-up of the Sunday school, it cannot be expected
to deal with moral issues in the depth and breadth that is needed.
However, a church can *complement* what the Sunday school does
by planning special opportunities to deal with moral issues; and it
can *improve* what the Sunday school does by an effective program of teacher training.

Unresolved Tensions

Earlier parts of this chapter have hinted at some unresolved
tensions in evangelical Sunday schools. Anyone who is interested
in improving these Sunday schools must come to grips with these
tensions.

Reach or Teach?

Is the primary objective of the Sunday school to reach or to
teach? Is it designed primarily to reach non-Christians and unchurched people or to teach and nurture believers? Evangelical
Sunday schools are committed to doing both, but maintaining the
proper balance between the two is not easy. Sunday schools often
emphasize one to the neglect of the other, with resultant side
effects.

Sometimes a Sunday school will devote all its efforts to outreach and neglect the life of the group. One such church promoted
a high-attendance day in Sunday school. They were more successful than they had expected. The excited Sunday school superintendent shared this glowing report: "We had people everywhere.
Every chair was filled and we had people sitting on window sills.
In fact, we had so many people we couldn't even teach them!"

He did not seem to recognize the irony of having too many
people for an effective class session. Outreach without Bible
study and fellowship misses the point of the outreach. The people
who are brought to Sunday school need to have a good experi-

25. See Marlene LeFever, "Is Sunday School Losing Its Punch?" *Christianity Today* 23 (September 21, 1979), pp. 17-19.

ence, or most will not return. Crowded conditions and poor teaching will eventually defeat the purpose of any outreach program, no matter how successful initially.

The other extreme is equally bad. A high quality of teaching and fellowship will not compensate for a neglect of outreach. An unevangelistic spirit has two serious side effects. For one thing, it leaves unreached the multitude of people who need Christ and the fellowship and nurture of the Sunday school. Neglect of outreach also affects the spirit of the group that participates in Sunday school.

Bruce Powers points out that churches often go through a life cycle of birth, development, peak ministry, plateau, decline, and struggle to survive. One of the characteristics of the decline stage of the cycle is a shift in focus from mission and ministry to maintenance: "The teaching ministry, formerly devoted to a balanced emphasis on instruction, nurture, and outreach, usually now emphasizes nurture and neglects the other areas."[26]

The best resolution of this particular tension is to strive to maintain the proper balance between enriching the life of the group and bringing new people into the group. This ought not to be a matter of "either . . . or," but "both . . . and." Many of the biblical models of church life show that *koinonia* and evangelization are not enemies, but allies. The inner life was strong and supportive, and much of its vitality was that new people were continually being drawn into the fellowship.

The most successful Sunday schools are those that have followed this model. An adult Sunday school class should be a caring-and-sharing fellowship that continually integrates new people into the class. Too many classes do not reflect biblical *koinonia*. People relate to one another on the most superficial level. Their conversations are on a casual level. They seldom reveal anything of themselves or deal with the real issues of life. Such classes also seldom reach and hold any new people. People attend because of habit, duty, or pressure.

Other classes, however, do deal with real issues. People care and share with one another. They may even enjoy being together so much that they are tempted to become a kind of closed sharing group; but if they resist this fatal temptation, they can successfully bring new people into the group.

26. Bruce P. Powers, ed./comp., *Christian Education Handbook* (Nashville: Broadman Press, 1981), p. 20. See also Getz, "The Renewal Sunday School," pp. 20-21.

Nurture or Convert Children?

As noted earlier, evangelicals are in general agreement that children should be converted, but they sometimes disagree about the most appropriate age for conversion and the best approach for Sunday school teachers to use.

In an article on "Child Evangelization" in the *Journal of Christian Education*, Perry G. Downs critiques five different approaches.[27] The approaches range all the way from the revivalist approach, which seeks to convince children they are terrible sinners, to the nurturing approach associated with Horace Bushnell. One of the mediating approaches is a kind of modified revivalist approach. It does not spend as much time emphasizing the terrible sins of children as did some of the old-time revivalists, but it does expect a memorable conversion experience. That is, the converted person should be able to identify the exact time and place at which the person was born again.

Downs himself favors a modified nurturing approach. A pure nurturing approach might assume that children never need to confess their sins and claim Jesus as their personal Savior. As an evangelical, Downs believes repentance and faith are conditions for salvation; however, he believes a nurturing approach provides the best context for children to repent and believe. On the other hand, Downs does not believe that persons converted as children can always recall the time and place when they were converted.

Each of these approaches is practiced by some evangelicals. Some type of revivalist approach is favored by many, but some form of nurturing model also has its advocates. Many evangelicals, and nearly all professional Christian educators, favor an approach similar to the one proposed by Downs. They advocate nurturing children from their earliest years to develop a sense of God's love and care and to trust in and pray to God. As children grow older, Sunday school teachers and parents try to be sensitive to a developing sense of moral and spiritual accountability. When children begin to show signs of concern, they are encouraged to confess their sins to God and to entrust themselves to Jesus Christ as personal Savior.

Those who follow the nurturing model are reluctant to put outside pressure on a child. They are hesitant about adults—parents, teachers, or preachers—using their adult authority to

27. Perry G. Downs, "Child Evangelization," *Journal of Christian Education* III, no. 2 (1982), pp. 5-13.

overinfluence children who are not ready to make their own commitments. A nurturing approach, therefore, focuses its evangelistic expectations on older children and youth rather than younger children.

Those who rely on a revivalistic approach often encourage professions of faith by younger children. Some leaders are aware of the risks, but they would rather risk a child making an unreal profession than risk a child missing an opportunity to be saved.

This tension has existed since the earliest days of the Sunday school movement, and it will probably continue for years to come. Advocates of the revivalist approach sometimes feel that the other group is not genuinely concerned about the spiritual welfare of children. Advocates of the nurturing approach sometimes feel that well-intentioned revivalists do more harm than good by influencing impressionable children to make "decisions" that are not real decisions for Christ.

Teach the Bible or Teach People?

When conducting a training conference for Sunday school teachers, I have sometimes used this multiple-choice question as a basis for discussion: "In your opinion, a teacher's goal should be: (a) to do the job assigned by the church, (b) to cover the material each week, (c) to teach the Bible, (d) to help people meet life needs through Bible study."

Given all the choices, most teachers select the right one; however, if they were simply asked, "What is your goal as a Sunday school teacher?" some would say, "To teach the Bible." This is understandable since evangelicals view the Bible as the textbook of the Sunday school. Only an insensitive teacher, however, would fail to recognize that the class session must address the interests and needs of the people. One of the continuing tensions for evangelicals is how to achieve this objective.

For example, how can we use the Bible in teaching children, especially younger children and preschoolers? Evangelicals are aware the Bible was written for adults, but we do not agree with those who conclude from this that the Bible is inappropriate for use with children of varying stages of development.

On one side are those who strongly emphasize a developmental approach. They tend to be more selective in use of biblical material for children of varying ages. They also tend to prefer an approach to Bible study that begins with and focuses on the child's interests and needs rather than on the biblical text.

On the other side are those who feel that the content of the
Bible considered appropriate for children is too restricted if it is
determined primarily by the findings of developmental psychology. Teachers of younger children, for example, sometimes complain that curriculum materials repeat only a few Bible stories
and never deal with other Bible stories and teachings. Many of
them would concede that parts of the Bible are inappropriate for
younger children, but they feel that the children should begin to
be exposed to a much broader biblical and theological scope.

Another aspect of this tension centers around the relevance of
the Bible for the lives of Sunday school pupils. Some Sunday
school teaching does little to relate the biblical text to life. This is
often done by default. A teacher spends so much time on biblical
background and interpretation that no time is left for anything
else. Many teachers are much more comfortable dealing with biblical content than with its contemporary relevance.

Other teachers do an effective job of using Bible study as a
setting in which to help people live as Christians. Such teachers
have found ways to make Bible study come alive. Here is one
formula:

1. Draw from the life-centered message of the Bible. The scriptures are concrete, not abstract. The truth is personified in
   the lives of human beings, supremely in the Incarnate Son of
   God.
2. Focus on the lives of people in the Sunday school class. What
   are their interests, dreams, needs, questions, struggles, and
   problems? How does the biblical message speak to these
   areas of concern?
3. Put your life into it. Fully share in the Bible study as a fellow
   Christian pilgrim and fellow learner.

Indoctrinate or Involve?

What is the proper role of the teacher and the learners in a
Sunday school class? Is the teacher an authority who indoctrinates pupils, or is the teacher a facilitator who involves learners
in activities through which they grow? Each of these approaches
has advocates and practitioners in evangelical Sunday schools.

Some evangelicals assume that an authoritative teacher is the
only model consistent with evangelical presuppositions about authoritative scripture, objective truth, and absolute moral values.
The model for this kind of teaching is a combination of a preach-

er's sermon and a professor's lecture. According to this model, the teacher proclaims the truth to the class or lectures about the content of the Bible. The role of the pupils is to be quiet and to listen. Little advantage is taken of the small-group setting; and even when pupils are allowed to participate by asking questions or sharing ideas, the teacher is expected to give the correct, authoritative answer to all questions.

An increasing number of evangelicals are aware that this model is not the only one consistent with the objectives of the Sunday school. Not only professional Christian educators but also many teachers and learners are concerned about more effective and more challenging approaches to Bible study in Sunday school.

Can I Help It If They Don't Learn? is the title of a book by Howard Mayes and James Long. The title reflects the frustration felt by lecturers who recognize the ineffectiveness of their approach but who seem unaware of alternate methods of teaching. Some teachers tend to excuse themselves, but Mayes and Long point out: "When students are not learning, it not only means *they* are failing to learn; it also means that the *teacher* is failing to teach."[28]

Lecturing, of course, is a time-honored teaching method that has continued validity under certain circumstances. (The teacher has access to information or insights that pupils need, and the size of the group and/or the shortness of time make lecturing the best way to share it.) Most of us can learn by listening to a good lecture, but we also learn by activities that involve us in more than listening and thinking.

Teaching methodology, then, is an area of continuing tension among evangelicals. At one extreme are those who are suspicious of "newfangled" methods; however, an increasing number of teachers are aware of the need to take advantage of group dynamics by involving class members in learning from one another. Many of these teachers seldom go beyond such bread-and-butter approaches as questions and discussion, but others use a wide variety of other methods.

Larry Richards feels that the problem is larger than a debate about methods. The basic problem is a "schooling" approach to communicating the Christian life and faith. This approach emphasizes one teacher instructing a class of pupils in content they

28. Howard Mayes and James Long, *Can I Help It If They Don't Learn?* (Wheaton, Ill.: Victor Books, 1977), p. 6.

need to know. Richards feels that the biblical model is the communication of life through the mutual ministry of the body of Christ—all its members, not just through the pastor and a staff of teachers. Richards does not advocate replacing the Sunday school, but he does advocate magnifying the home and church as primary in Christian education. In order for the Sunday school to be effective in this context, it must replace its educational approach with a socialization approach that emphasizes informal sharing with one another rather than formal instruction.[29]

Richards developed an approach called *Sunday School, PLUS*, which was "not to attack the Sunday school, but rather to attempt to go beyond what the Sunday school is doing, and to integrate the Sunday learning time with a more significant weekday process of learning faith."[30] The approach attempted to train Christian parents to fulfill their role at home and to retrain Sunday school teachers as faith-sharers rather than as teachers of content. After two years of testing, Richards reported more success in retaining teachers than in training parents.[31]

Sunday School, PLUS materials are no longer in production.[32] We lament the failure to continue a curriculum that links the home and the church as partners in Christian education. Given the situation in today's homes, this is regrettable but understandable. On the other hand, we can take heart from Richard's success in retraining Sunday school teachers to emphasize the informal approaches of modeling, caring, and sharing, not to the exclusion of some instruction in the content, but as the primary setting in which nurture takes place.

Many other programs of teacher training have met with similar success. Those who want to renew the Sunday school must give priority to teacher training, and the heart of teacher training should be the role of teacher as facilitator, guide, and fellow learner.

Conclusions

1. The basic distinctives of today's evangelical Sunday schools were the distinctives of nineteenth-century evangelical Sunday schools: the Bible, conversion, and outreach.

29. See Richards, *A Theology of Christian Education*, pp. 46-47.
30. Ibid., p. 206.
31. Ibid., pp. 216-217.
32. LeFever, "Is the Sunday School Losing Its Punch?" p. 20.

2. Maintaining a balanced emphasis on outreach, Bible study, and fellowship is a key to the continuing vitality of evangelical Sunday schools.
3. The Sunday school has certain inherent strengths and continues to make contributions in such areas as lay involvement, Bible study, fellowship, ministry, and outreach.
4. None of the Sunday school's well-known faults is such a fatal flaw that the Sunday school should be replaced.
5. The Sunday school should not be expected to provide educational opportunities beyond the capacity of its lay teachers; instead, the church should complement the Sunday school experience with other Christian educational opportunities.
6. The poor quality of teaching is the Sunday school's basic weakness and effective teacher training its most hopeful strategy for improving the Sunday school.
7. The goal of teacher training is not to equip teachers to be professional educators but to encourage them to make Sunday school a time for mutual sharing of faith and love within the context of Bible study.

Chapter 7

Reclaiming and Re-Visioning Catechesis

NATHAN W. JONES

By virtually any yardstick Roman Catholic religious education has come full circle. During the past twenty years we have been gradually liberated from a stifling system of bad theology, a uniform question-and-answer method of classroom instruction, an overemphasis on guilt and punishment, an authoritative church leadership on doctrinal and moral issues, a fixed Latin liturgy, and the obsession with introverted, exclusivist politics.

This chapter attempts to explore and assess some of the more outstanding feature of renewal in American Catholic religious education and the Confraternity of Christian Doctrine (CCD). I will attempt to reflect on the strengths and weaknesses, while identifying developing issues and concerns, as well as promising innovations. Such an enormous task makes me a little fearful of betrayal. I fear that my personal issues and prejudices will be revealed. So I approach this task with a reasonable hesitation and care, yet with confidence (Heb. 13:21).

"Catechetics doesn't move through history in a straight line. It zigs and zags. It curves; it wanders around a bit; it veers in one direction for a while, then swings off at an angle along a different way which promises to be better."[1] These lines written by John S. Nelson of Fordham University poetically chart the course of this article, its tides and currents.

General Observations

Generally, the state of religious education in the American Catholic community is healthy. No longer is religious education

1. John S. Nelson, "The Zig and Zags of Catechetics," *New Catholic World* (January/February, 1981), p. 4.

perceived as the exclusive responsibility of a few church professionals and volunteers, but as *a mission at the very core of the church's life involving a broad spectrum of persons and gifts.*

Like the Protestant Sunday school, Confraternity of Christian Doctrine (CCD) programs and schools of religion, as well as Catholic schools, are battered survivors. Those who have participated in these institutions and "movements" whether as students or teachers, probably can remember how they were shaped or, sometimes, misshaped by them. While church educators and churchgoers debate the enduring value of these protean institutions, cartoonists and movie screen writers tell a different story. Sunday schools, referred to as "the children's weekly spiritual pit stop," by Martin Marty,[2] and the origin of the legendary ban on patent leather shoes in Catholic schools have been sources of recollection, but also humor and scorn.

In the past, many CCD schools of religion have frightfully resembled a Saturday version of the traditional Protestant Sunday school. Like our Protestant brothers and sisters who have consistently added new coats of paint to a rotting superstructure, Catholics have continually propped up what has proved to be a failed and ineffective concept for faith education. We are learning from one another's mistakes. Grassroots ecumenism!

One of the most important breakthroughs for Catholic religious education has been the sobering realization that education cannot answer all church problems. Setting the direction in American catechetical renewal, the bishops of the church released the *General Catechetical Directory* in 1971. In that noteworthy document we read the following statement: "Renewal in the ministry of the Word, especially in catechesis, can in no way be separated from general pastoral renewal."[3] The failure of many parishes to provide *a vital ecclesial life—community, education, worship, and service*—signals that something has been missing in the way the parish community gathers and in what happens when and after it does. This has been cited as one of the principal stumbling blocks to effective Christian education.[4]

A leading Catholic religious education theorist, Gabriel Moran,

2. Martin Marty, "The Sunday School: Battered Survivor," *The Christian Century* (June 4-11, 1980), p. 636.

3. *General Catechetical Directory* (Washington, D.C.: United States Catholic Conference, 1971), p. 12.

4. Michael Warren, "The Catechetical Ministry of the Church," *New Catholic World* (March/April, 1977), p. 67.

expressed this position well when he wrote that we have suddenly discovered that *religious education is not coextensive* with either Catholic schools or CCD programs (italics mine).[5] This is a major breakthrough in understanding and practice for a formerly immigrant church that placed serious value on its schools and alternative approaches to Christian formation, such as CCD.

A Teaching and Learning Church

Eminent Catholic theologian Karl Rahner (d. 1984) once observed that the church itself is changing from a Western institution basically identified with European culture into *a world church* (italics mine). In past years, he tells us, we emphasized uniformity rather than unity. Now in this world church we are going to have as much of a change as when the first generation following Christ changed from an exclusively Jewish church to one which responded to the whole people of the world, Jew and Gentile.[6]

There has been *a full-blown educational revolution.* The good old days are gone for good. The Second Vatican Council (1962-1965, a.k.a. Vatican II) brought sweeping changes during the past two decades in every aspect of church life and practice. Catechetical renewal movements in Vienna and Munich, begun in the early decades of this century, and the international catechetical congresses in Europe and the Third World were vindicated in principle by Vatican II.

Aquinas with great insight indicated that *the church is always a teaching and a learning community.* Christian faith—and Catholic tradition—is not frozen but must be rephrased and reinterpreted. The foundational symbols of faith (God, Jesus, church, Bible, eucharist) are changeless. However, like the householder in Matthew's gospel, the church and its educational ministry must always bring out of the storeroom new things as well as old. If the Christian story is to find meaning for a new generation, catechetical ministers must *uncover fresh understandings in old symbols while discovering new ones.*

5. Gabriel Moran, *Vision and Tactics* (New York: Herder and Herder, 1968), p. 74.
6. Karl Rahner, *Concern for the Church* (New York: Crossroad Press, 1982), p. 85.

In theological language it is a question of *hermeneutics*—how to translate the Christian story into a language that can speak for a new day.[7] The historian of religion Raimundo Panikkar, a Catholic priest of Hindu heritage, offers a definition of hermeneutics as "the art . . . of interpretation, of bringing forth significance, of conveying meaning, of restoring symbols to life and eventually of letting new symbols emerge. (It is) the method of overcoming the distance between a knowing subject and an object to be known."[8]

A question that is shaping discussions, innovations, and future directions is: *"How will a growing American Catholic community with upwards of 50 million members enable one another to live as Christians?"* Moran has pointed out that "American Catholicism may be in a position to assume a key leadership role in the coming era of church education. Certainly, the characteristics of pluralism in unity, empiricism and practicality, freedom with organization, will be those in need in the new era of religious education. Instead of looking to Europe, as we have in the past, we might have more confidence in American style and experimentation."[9]

The church has increasingly become aware of the *necessity to peel away layers of influences that have contaminated and adulterated its catechesis,* such as outdated cultural practices, a static European worldview, racism, sexism, and doctrinal defensiveness. Bernard Lonergan has suggested that the obvious conclusion to draw from the call for *aggiornamento* ("bringing things up to date") by the late beloved Pope John XXIII is that the church must have been behind the times and was in need of being renewed or made new.[10]

The church envisioned by Vatican II is a *pluralistic* church open to pluralism; a *modern* church open to modernity; an *ecumenical* church open to the whole wide world; a *living* church open to new life and to the change it brings and requires; a *catholic* church open in principle to all truth and to every value.[11]

7. Berard Marthaler, "Handing on the Symbols of Faith," *Chicago Studies* 19, no. 1 (Spring, 1980), p. 30.

8. Raimundo Panikkar, *Myth, Faith and Hermeneutics* (New York: Paulist Press, 1979), p. 8.

9. Moran, *Vision and Tactics*, pp. 58-59.

10. Bernard Lonergan, *Theology of Renewal* (New York: Herder and Herder, 1968), p. 34.

11. Richard McBrien, *Catholicism: A Study Edition* (Minneapolis: Winston Press, 1981), p. 1175.

Certainly, one can give credit to our Protestant brothers and sisters who anticipated by four centuries many outstanding new directions taken by Roman Catholic reform.

Undoubtedly there have been times when religious education in Catholic settings has been rambling, vague, and trendy. We could characterize this as an age of mediocrity. Such approaches have proved not to foster a firm commitment in faith. Well-intentioned progressives themselves determined that these methods were inadequate and did not fully serve the passing on of Christian faith and Catholic tradition. But we have paid a high price: the leakage of young people from active church participation and practice; widespread biblical and religious illiteracy; and growth in the numbers of "communal Catholics" who, according to Andrew Greeley, are religiously concerned, acknowledging their roots in the Catholic tradition, but with a studied indifference to institutional structure.

Illustrative of this point, William McCready, Study Director at Chicago's National Opinion Research Center, conducted a survey about the religious attitudes and practices of young Catholics. Among the findings the survey revealed a change in the attitude of Catholic youth toward the Sunday eucharist. "I think one of the most important questions that we asked on the survey was the reason why they missed Mass, and if they did go to Mass, why? We asked the same question on surveys in '64 and '76. Over that time the changes were quite dramatic. In the '60s, people overwhelmingly would say, 'because it's a sin to miss Mass.' Overwhelmingly in the '80s they're saying, 'We go to Mass to worship God; we go to Mass because we love God.' No mention of sin. Now it's also true that about half as many of them are going. But of those that go, the reasons are much less rule-oriented and much more for reasons of devotion or worship."[12]

On the other hand, today there is evidence that a conservative backlash and retrenchment is underway promising to retard mature faith among Catholics. The mounting crisis confronting today's church has placed us at a crossroad. We are entering a new epoch in the history of the church and we're faced with choices: *Will we make the quantum leaps which will move us into the twenty-first century or will we continue to limp along as a divided, damaged, and neurotic church?*

12. Quoted in *Overview: A Continuing Survey of Issues Affecting Catholics* 16, no. 1 (July/August, 1983), pp. 1-2.

The Work of Restoration

Catholics are reclaiming the word "catechesis," that comes from the Greek verb *katechein*, meaning "to resound," "to echo," or "to hand down." This esteemed word from our Christian roots is finding wider appreciation among Catholics, and it is receiving renewed attention from Protestants. The truth is, catechesis embodies a venerable tradition much older in the church than religious education.

While a variety of terms are used to denote this broadly conceived pastoral activity of making "faith become living, conscious, and active through the light of instruction,"[13] (including religious education, Christian education, CCD, etc.) "catechesis" serves to link us with the universal church and a rich heritage of the past. Moran has stressed that "change of language is at the center of institutional change."[14] While words help us to be more concrete, they can also contribute to the danger of parochialism.

Pope John Paul II has taken a leading pastoral role in defining the nature and task of catechesis. His *Catechesi Tradendae: The Apostolic Exhortation on Catechetics*, defines catechesis as "an education of children, young people, and adults in the faith which includes especially the teaching of Christian doctrine imparted, generally speaking, in an organic and systematic way, with a view to initiating the hearers into a fullness of Christian life."[15] Continuing he wrote, "Hence also, in its endeavor to educate faith, the concern of catechesis is not to omit, but to clarify proper reality such as man's activity for his integral liberation, the search for a society with greater solidarity and fraternity, the fight for justice and the building of peace."[16]

Finally, the Pope emphasized, "the age and the intellectual development of Christians, their decree of ecclesial and spiritual maturity, and many other personal circumstances demand that catechesis should adopt widely differing methods for the attainment of its specific aim: education in the faith."[17]

---

13. *Sharing the Light of Faith, The National Catechetical Directory for the U.S.* (Washington, D.C.: United States Catholic Conference, 1979), #32.

14. Gabriel Moran, "Two Languages of Religious Education," *The Living Light* 14, no. 1 (Spring, 1977), p. 7.

15. Pope John Paul II, *Catechesi Tradendae* (Washington, D.C.: National Catholic News Service, 1979), #21, p. 334.

16. Ibid., p. 337.

17. Ibid., p. 341.

American Catholics have proposed a meaning for catechesis as a form of the ministry of the word (that) flows from the ministry of worship and supports the ministry of service. The fundamental tasks of Christian educators or catechists are to proclaim Christ's message, to participate in efforts to develop community, to lead people in worship and prayer, and to motivate them to serve others in love.

New Passageways

Seven perspectives surface as significant strengths of present-day Catholic religious education. These are by no means exhaustive, and there is no "grand design" to their arrangement. In the evolving body of professional literature, at the level of diocesan religious education offices, and the local congregation, these themes rise as clear signs of renewal and re-vision.

1. *The local church is the primary evangelizing and nurturing community.*
2. *Catechetical renewal has paralleled theological, liturgical, and spiritual renewal.*
3. *Adult education is at the center of the church's educational mission.*
4. *There are emerging roles for the laity as educational leaders.*
5. *There is an essential link between Christian faith and justice.*
6. *Changes in U.S. social and cultural patterns have increased awareness that the church is multicultural.*
7. *There is a "new" model, methodology, and approach for education in faith.*

Summarily, while these are signs reflecting a marvelous evidence of grace, there exist varied degrees of flaws and weaknesses in each as is essentially characteristic of the developmental nature of pastoral life.

New passageways are being explored here. Ancient understandings are being revitalized. Old symbols are being infused with fresh meaning.

The local church is the primary evangelizing and nurturing community.

Catholicism, like all of Christianity, is a community event. Catholic parishes are buzzing with the activity of renewal. Occasioned by Vatican II, the local parish experience has been filled with experimentation. New programs and renewal movements have prospered such as Marriage Encounter, Renew, Charismatic Renewal, Christ Renews His Parish, small base Christian communities, and retreats and have made a significant impact on total pastoral renewal in the American Catholic community. However, these programs and movements have often provided experiences of conversion and community *outside* the local worshiping community. That is, every renewal movement has pointed up the sad condition of most parishes. Parishioners had to leave their parish to have their hearts touched by an experience of genuine community.[18] In addition, the most creative leaders among the laity were using their energies elsewhere than the parish.

Such a situation could possibly exist as an interim stage in the renewal process, but if the local congregation is to serve as the primary evangelizing and nurturing community, it is critical that *the parish itself be restructured, remodeled, and re-visioned.*

First, the traditional parish structure has proven to be too institutional, too authoritarian, and too impersonal. One bishop noted that the symbol of the church as a triangle with the pope at the top, the bishops in the middle, and the people at the bottom was pleasing to the eye, but did nothing for the heart. He has suggested a new symbol, the circle, where all work and pray together in communion.[19] Clearly there has been a tragic gap between our religious rhetoric and our practical experience.

Without question there is a need for a parish model more adequate to our times and to the vision of Vatican II. Patterns of paternalism/ maternalism ("Father/Sister-know-best!") continue to be operative with tacit acceptance by a laity accustomed to being spoon-fed. Ministry is what professionals do *for* the laity. Since the priest is responsible for ministry, the people don't have to be.

In parishes of racial minorities, these attitudes are frequently judged to be racist and unacceptable. In suburban, rural, urban, and ethnic churches there is a growing dissatisfaction with these traditional approaches. Many good Catholics painfully learned that their own churches could not provide the experience of living

18. Bishop Albert Ottenweller, "Parish Ministry: The Old and the New," *The Parish in Community and Ministry,* ed. Evelyn Eaton Whitehead (New York: Paulist Press, 1978), pp. 15-17.

19. Ibid., p. 19.

Christian community that had been tasted on a weekend retreat, for instance. As a result, some people withdrew from regular parish participation and substituted movements and programs for a parish congregation. The most fertile minds and Spirit-led people, due to frustration, have largely abandoned the parish as a source of conversion, community, and ministry.

The ideals of mutuality, the "people of God" ecclesiology, shared decision making, collegiality, and collaboration espoused by the waves of renewal have become stumbling blocks. Our expectations became much too removed from our experience and a crisis has developed.

The result of this ferment is a promising though gradual shift from a *managerial style of pastoral leadership* ("officially designated ministers") to *ministering communities* (members ministering to one another).

A second result of changing attitudes and practices toward local church life is the vast number of parishes engaged in some kind of ongoing self-renewal and periodic review of their life together. Congregations are writing mission statements, setting goals and, in some places, slowly moving toward a sense of ownership of the church, its mission and ministry.

Among the questions being raised are: How deeply do people feel the need that parishes are established to meet? What does the parish add to family and civic life? How might the parish facilitate ongoing growth in faith for new members and the already baptized?

Third, with a reassessment of the role of Catholic schools we are beginning to channel more of our resources into alternate educational and pastoral ministries. The need for evangelization has never been greater. Local congregations, inspired by the call of the American bishops, have made modest attempts to reclaim "retired" Catholics while inviting others to come and see. Black Catholics have pioneered a Catholic version of the evangelical revival, while door-to-door neighborhood canvassing, evangelism training events, and Bible sharing groups are no longer uncommon in the average parish.

The overhaul in Catholic baptismal practice for adults mandated by Vatican II was accomplished with the 1972 publication of *The Rite of Christian Initiation of Adults* (RCIA). The RCIA restores the integrity of the Christian initiation rite: baptism-confirmation-eucharist. A period of careful preparation for those seeking baptism is accomplished through the restoration of the ancient catechumenate. The *rite* is not simply for adult converts but speaks of conversion as a spiritual journey, an ever-deepening, lifelong process for individuals and the whole assembly. Parishes are nowadays involving their members in faith-sharing with baptismal candidates, and a whole new way of convert-making and disciple-making is developing. As evidence of the Spirit of God moving among us, parishes themselves are creatively endeavoring to harmonize what they say with what they do. But this has consistently brought us full circle to the necessity for new models of Christian community.

Catechetical renewal has paralleled theological, liturgical, and spiritual renewal.

Theology is the setting where historical tradition, present experience, and future hope coexist. Given this definition, perhaps Dickens' phrase "the best of times, the worst of times" provides an apt description of the theological developments since the Council. At the outset it must be stressed that *pluralism characterizes Catholic theology today.* Catholic theologians are not of a single mind with regard to all issues or strategies. Characteristic of Catholicism is its capacity for open-endedness—a both/and rather than an either/or approach. "At such turning points as these," writes Father Richard McBrien, "the church needs to be in touch with its own roots, needs to see with clear, unbiased vision the whole sweep of Catholic tradition, needs to see the interrelationships among all the elements of its doctrine and practice. Only by understanding its own past can it understand what it is now. Then, and only then, can it press forward with confidence and hope."[20]

Sharing the Light of Faith points to the relationship between theology and religious education. "Catechesis draws on theology, and theology draws in turn on the richness of the church's catechetical experience. Both must be at the service of the church."[21] The role of theology, according to Anselm of Canterbury's well-worn phrase *fides quaerens intellectum* ("faith seeking understanding"), is to feed into, deepen, clarify, and express our appreciation of the Christian story.

Theologians are charged to help each succeeding generation rethink and reappropriate the tradition. Hence *the theological*

20. McBrien, *Catholicism: Study Edition*, p. 20.
21. *Sharing the Light of Faith*, #37.

task is never finished, but is always active and creative. The scope of Catholic theology—and therefore the scope of religious education—includes the whole experience and reflection of the community throughout the ages in all its many expressions.

Theological presuppositions provide the shape, content, and support for our understanding of religious education theory and praxis. That is, religious education does not function removed from the ongoing self-reflection and self-criticism of the church. D. Campbell Wyckoff has noted that "questions of objective, scope, context, process, personnel, and timing" in church education are ultimately theological questions.[22] Both liturgy and Christian education, broadly conceived, are the primary channels through which most Catholics are instructed in their faith.

In the 1930s Josef Jungmann, professor of pastoral theology at Innsbruck, pointed out that most catechisms used in religion teaching were written at a time when Catholic theology was at a low ebb. As a consequence, many of the shortcomings and inadequacies of the theological texts are also found in catechetical materials inherited from the last century. It was Jungmann, who has perhaps been the most influential European religious education theorist in this century, who sparked a renewal of catechesis with the advance of the kerygmatic revival and the liturgical movement.[23]

The radical changes in church life and practice have caused many adults to seek clarity regarding the so-called "new theology" through religious education programs. A number of promising new developments in theology are having a significant impact on educational ministry at every level.

Among the most popular of these new theological developments is the emergence of narrative or story theology espoused by such fertile minds as John Shea[24] and David Tracy[25] (both Catholics and priests), and the earlier work of Amos Wilder,[26] a Protestant

22. D. Campbell Wyckoff, "Religious Education as a Discipline: Toward a Definition of Religious Education as a Discipline," *Religious Education* LXII (September/October, 1967), p. 393.

23. Berard Marthaler, *Catechetics in Context* (Huntington, Ind.: Our Sunday Visitor, Inc., 1973), p. 29.

24. John Shea, *Stories of God: An Unauthorized Biography* (Chicago: The Thomas More Press, 1978).

25. David Tracy, *Blessed Rage for Order: The New Pluralism in Theology* (New York: Seabury 1975).

26. Amos Niven Wilder, *Theopoetic* (Philadelphia: Fortress, 1976).

New Testament scholar. These theologians are highlighting that all religious symbols are implicitly narrative and tell a story. The stories of our faith-tradition intersect with our personal stories giving us identity, purpose, and direction.

A religious educator, Thomas Groome, whose seminal work *Christian Religious Education*[27] is taking the continent by storm, had admittedly been influenced by story theology. His dialogical model of Christian religious education is termed "critical reflection on shared praxis." Groome's emphasis on dialogue and on the unity of reflection and action is drawn from the work of Brazilian educator, Paulo Freire.[28] Persons are invited to reflect on their lived experience in light of the Christian community's tradition or Story and its Vision of the Kingdom of God. The community's Story and Vision serve as a critique of one's present experience and serve as a guide for future action. Conversely, the present experience of persons serves as a critique of the community's story and can foster its re-vision.

On the local parish level there is another exciting development: lay people are learning how to theologize. Due to increased efforts to upgrade the quality of Sunday preaching and adult education opportunities along with the emergence of prayer groups, base communities, etc., persons are discovering that it is of the very nature of faith that it be formed and reformed in the light of past, present, and future experience. Religious education as a pastoral necessity has been well established.

Adult education is at the center of the church's
educational mission.

Suddenly church educators have realized what psychologists have been saying all along: we spend the bulk of our lives as adults. In a popular culture hostile to Christian values, there has been a renewed interest in adult-centered catechesis. *To Teach As Jesus Did*, a statement of the American bishops on Christian education put it this way: "The continuing education of adults is situated not at the periphery of the church's educational mission but at its center."[29]

Carl Jung was the first psychologist to explicitly treat the sec-

27. Thomas Groome, *Christian Religious Education* (San Francisco: Harper & Row, 1980).
28. Paulo Freire, *Pedagogy of the Oppressed* (New York: Herder and Herder, 1970).
29. National Conference of Catholic Bishops, *To Teach As Jesus Did* (Washington, D.C.: United States Catholic Conference, 1971), p. 21.

ond half of a person's life. He discovered clear evidence of religious needs, concerns, and questions during this period of life. Religion continues to play a key role in the socialization and lifelong development of adults. Erikson, building on Freud's insights, delineated a theory of human development. More recently, empirical studies by Levinson and Gould on adult development have enriched many, while the pioneering work of James and Evelyn Whitehead link adult psychological growth with life's religious challenges and invitations.

For nearly five hundred years Catholics, like other Christians, have educated children and played with the adults! While this was not always the case, we have been greatly influenced by the child-centeredness of the larger society. On another note, it is not uncommon to find large segments of Catholic adults who still do not know and feel that they are indeed the church. With 60-90 percent of the total budget of some parishes designated for the education of children and youth, there is little hope that there will be a radical shift in local practice in the near future.

Adults have been induced to passivity, minimal involvement, content with the religious education of their childhood, and quick to expect priests and sisters to take care of the religious formation of their children.[30] We've paid a high price for this child-centered approach with many adults failing to appreciate the implications of the Word of God for their lives.

Prior to the watershed event of Vatican II, there was only a limited awareness of the importance and place of adult education. Today, most diocesan religious education offices have one or more staff persons who are responsible for adult education ministry. Parishes have undertaken programing for adults and some have hired specialized professionals. Major church education organizations, such as the National Catholic Education Association (NCEA) and the National Conference of Diocesan Directors of Religious Education-CCD (NCDD), have devoted considerable energy to adult learning and have produced well-researched documents. Publishers have produced quality resources for educators and learners.[31]

James Schaefer, writing on the role of adult education consul-

30. Kevin Coughlin, *Motivating Adults for Religious Education* (Washington, D.C.: National Conference of Diocesan Directors of Religious Education-CCD, 1976), p. 3.
31. *Christian Adulthood: A Catechetical Resource 1982* (Washington, D.C.: United States Catholic Conference, Department of Education, 1982), p. 1.

tants, states that there exists a task to "develop the stimuli, challenges and climates by which adult Catholics . . . will want freely to accept personal responsibility for their religious growth individually and for the growth of the church corporately."[32]

Malcolm Knowles, a pioneer adult education theorist, charted a course for future directions when he wrote: "The choice facing Christian adult educators is between producing 'dependent believers,' adults whose intellectual understanding of religion is derived from others, and producing 'mature believers,' adults whose intellectual understanding of religion is the result of guided self-inquiry."[33]

The 1980s challenge us more clearly to define the *kinds of persons* and *what kind of faith community* religious education should produce. Wrestling with this question necessarily precedes any meaningful discussion of methodology.

A second challenge for adult educators is to explore ways to satisfy the critical need for lifelong conversion and growth in faith among the already baptized.

Lastly, an engaging question has been raised by James Schaefer in an important article entitled, "Tensions Between Adult Growth and Church Authority." The author unflinchingly recognizes that there exists a "conflict between contemporary principles of adult learning and growth on the one hand, and habits of exercising church authority on the other. Bluntly put, the question is: 'Can the Roman Catholic Church tolerate the emergence of mature believers?' "[34] I am reminded of Whitehead's enormously significant argument that "the dominant note of education at its beginning and at its end is *freedom* (italics mine)."[35]

There are emerging roles for the laity as educational leaders.

"Ministry" has been a popular term among Catholics as we have progressed from a church in which everything was done by the clergy to one in which the laity, religious, and clergy all share mission and ministry in common.

In many ways the professional role of the Director of Religious

32. From an unpublished report of adult education consultants edited by Thomas Tewey of the USCC, Nov. 1977. Quoted in Thomas Downs, *The Parish as Learning Community* (New York: Paulist Press, 1979), p. 110.
33. *Christian Adulthood*, p. 10.
34. Ibid., p. 21.
35. Alfred North Whitehead, *Aims of Education and Other Essays* (New York: The Free Press, 1929), p. 31.

Education (DRE)—begun c. 1967 in Catholic parishes[36]—could be termed American Catholicism's first nonordained ministry. DREs (a.k.a. Religious Education Coordinators, Ministers of Education, etc.) serve as a vital part of many parish staffs with no sacramental designation other than his or her baptism. Youth and campus ministers, music ministers, liturgical ministers, and parish council members are rarely ordained either. *Ministry has been opened in principle to every baptized Christian.* An abiding concern, of course, is that those chosen for ministry will be competent and committed Christians. The church has suffered enough in history from well-meaning but inept ministers.

The laity are assuming new ministerial roles as catechists, liturgists, family ministers, certified lay ministers, youth ministers, social advocates, and pastoral associates. New names seem to appear on the front of the Sunday bulletin each week! Through participation in specialized training programs, men and women are becoming equipped with competencies and professional ministry skills.

While the ministry of the laity even when successful is not fully accepted, one thing is certain: *there will be no return to the ministerial clericalism of the past.* There exists no unanimity among theologians, or even among ministers themselves, regarding the nature and purpose of ministry; a number of questions continue to remain. The two most pressing questions are: "Does ministry require official authorization, like ordination? Can lay people, especially women, exercise ministry?"[37]

As a consequence of the emergence of a plurality of ministries, the role of the ordained priest is receiving renewed attention. Vatican II's *Dogmatic Constitution on the Church* put it this way: "Pastors also know that they themselves were not meant by Christ to shoulder alone the entire saving mission of the Church toward the world. On the contrary, they understand that it is their noble duty so to shepherd the faithful and recognize their services and charismatic gifts that all according to their proper role may cooperate in this common undertaking with one heart."[38]

36. Joseph C. Neiman, "The Religious Education Profession: Parish Coordinators," *Religious Education* LXVIII, no. 2 (March/April, 1973), pp. 264-265.

37. Richard P. McBrien, "Service + Mission = Ministry," *Today's Parish* (October, 1979), p. 43.

38. *The Documents of Vatican II,* Walter M. Abbott, S.J., ed. (New York: The American Press, 1966), #30.

From my view, the continued decline in the numbers of priests will motivate many people to accept a broader understanding of ministry. As the laity assume responsibility for ministry and mission, it is incumbent on the ordained priests, not to suppress the charism of others out of fear that laity are trying to take over the clergy's necessary place, but to integrate and coordinate them through a *ministry of leadership.* Again, from my perspective, ordination (of priests and deacons) will increasingly be the exception rather than the rule by which Catholics enter formal ministries. It's quite traditional to say that *ordination presumes ministry, but ministry does not demand ordination.*

There is an essential link between faith and justice.

Where issues of racism, sexism, social justice, peace, and human equality were concerned, most of the Christian churches have historically found it expedient to separate love and justice, piety and politics. In the past, religious education has been virtually silent on the Christian response to social issues. However, there are a number of impressive signals that seem to point the church and its educational ministry toward a clearer articulation and active demonstration of the gospel imperative to link faith and justice.

The Synod of Bishops in their 1971 pastoral statement on *Justice in the World* indicated that, "Action on behalf of justice and participation in the transformation of the world fully appear to us as a constitutive dimension of the preaching of the Gospel."[39] And liberation of the oppressed, though not identified with evangelization, is closely linked with it.

For church educators who take seriously both the Incarnation of Jesus and the "historicity of salvation" (to use the language of liberation theology), true religious education must always be prophetic. It must guide people to make an ethical response to the grave social issues of the times. For instance, when it became illegal in this country during the 1830s to teach a slave to read, religious educators were the people who taught reading and writing to the slaves.[40]

In our own times, religiously motivated "drum majors for peace

39. Text in *The Gospel of Peace and Justice*, ed. Joseph Gremillion (Maryknoll, N.Y.: Orbis, 1976), p. 597.

40. Gabriel Moran, "Religious Education As Resistance," *Religious Education* 78, no. 4 (Fall, 1983), p. 491.

and justice"—educators, clergy, businesspersons, social agitators, artists, even presidential candidates and bishops—have made an indelible impact on American social and religious life. Religious educators owe a great debt to this tradition of social and political activism.

The inclusion of the issues of social injustice—the consequences of personal and social sin—in educational curricula is *not* optional. *Sharing the Light of Faith* has unequivocally stressed a socially vital educational ministry: "Catechesis concerning justice, mercy, and peace should be part of the catechetical process. It should include efforts to motivate people to act on behalf of these values."[41]

The locus of responsibility for education for justice is in the family and extends out into social action and confrontation with the realities of injustice. As Luther put it, wherever you see God's Word preached, believed, confessed, and acted upon, there is the true church.

The narrow, pietistic individualism characteristic of church education in the past has been boldly challenged. The social encyclicals of the popes and the Council's *Pastoral Constitution on the Church in the Modern World* have played a major part in exposing the serious error of splitting faith and daily living. In the final analysis, nothing human should be foreign to a Christian's concern.[42]

Practically speaking, when teaching Joan or Johnny, a catechist never stops with the statement, "God always forgives us." Rather, he or she must add its correlative, "And this means we must always forgive one another."

The *first grade re-visioning of catechesis* returned the Bible and drew upon the insights of the social sciences, especially developmental psychology. However, a *second grade re-visioning* must engage us in learning the skills of social analysis and employing the insights of sociology to religious education. What are the catechetical implications of systemic oppression? As communities of faith, how might we provide experiences and environments where believers can interact with the tradition and one another? How might we take seriously the sociological dynamics of organizations, systems, and intentional communities in order to infuse these relationships with the Christian vision?

41. *Sharing the Light of Faith*, 170.
42. Marthaler, *Catechetics in Context*, #97, p. 195.

Changes in U.S. social and cultural patterns have increased awareness that the church is multicultural.

Parishes that have chosen to continue the unfinished business of the 1950s, with little or no planning for the future, have gradually become functionally ineffective for ministry in a changing society. A percentage of Catholic parishes and institutions, along with the ministers, have been stuck doing yesterday's work with an outdated ecclesial model, inadequate training, and a poor understanding of the "handwriting on the wall." While demographers and any serious observation point out that the complexion, social status, economy, politics, and religious needs of parishioners has profoundly changed, the instances of business-as-usual determine pastoral action (inaction) in far too many places.

With current debates around the questions of immigration and the growing number of "new" Americans, talk about cultural pluralism and cultural diversity is not misplaced. Neither should discussions about the connections between faith and culture be misunderstood among Christians. After all, our Judeo-Christian heritage has constantly emphasized the importance of history in coming to faith. If the Catholic church is to truly be universal it must be "a great tree whose branches shelter the birds of the air, a net which catches fish of every kind . . . a flock which a single shepherd pastures . . . without boundaries or frontiers except, alas, those of the heart and mind of sinful man."[43]

Today catechetical leaders are recognizing *social, cultural, and racial differences as contributing to the richness of the church rather than detracting from the fundamental unity of the faith.* The black theologian, Gayraud S. Wilmore, a Presbyterian, has observed: "Innovations, such as the display of a black Christ or images of a black Madonna and Child, remind the congregation of the universality of Christian symbols by particularizing them."[44]

The rising consciousness of the various racial-ethnic minorities has given voice to their distinctive religious expectations and educational needs. Blacks, Hispanics, native Americans, Asians, and poor whites have grown discontented with patronizing missionary approaches that have sometimes characterized their past relationships with the institutional church. Racial minorities are demanding a role in the decision making and pastoral life of the

43. Pope Paul VI, *Evangelization in the Modern World* (1975), #61.
44. Gayraud S. Wilmore, *Black and Presbyterian: The Heritage and the Hope* (Philadelphia: The Geneva Press, 1983), p. 115.

church. Those insensitive to the necessity for the inculturation of catechesis and pastoral ministry are sharply criticized by bold and eloquent spokespersons who believe they too are the church.

Some of the most outstanding examples of lay leadership training are operative in racial minority and/or multicultural parishes. However, the urgent need to retool pastoral and educational ministers (overwhelmingly white) has absorbed enormous resources, leaving the people leaderless, dispersed, and disenchanted. Racial minorities consistently pound at the door of the church demanding attention in a time of indifference to matters and issues racial. The enduring relationship between the American Catholic church and its growing numbers of minorities is frequently one of tokenism, domination, manipulation, and control.

The National Catechetical Directory states: "Ideally, the catechist will be a member of the particular social, cultural, or ethnic group. Those who are not should understand and empathize with the group, besides having adequate catechetical formation."[45] Ostensibly, this attitude can be viewed as one of the signs that seem to point toward minorities achieving a level of self-determination and authentic sharing in responsibility and decision making in all facets of church life. However, this is more of a dream than an experienced fact.

Edward Braxton, a Catholic theologian who is also black, told a recent gathering of evangelists that, "In many cities around the country the style of Catholic presence in the black community became almost exclusively one of education and social service while the traditional black Protestant church or the fast growing black Muslims met the religious needs of the community."

Braxton proposes that the church of the future require the union of conversion and education. Given the dearth in the number of indigenous priests and educational leaders of racial minority background, and the evidence that this situation will not appreciably change in the near future, Braxton underscores the importance of lay leadership development to the continuing vitality of the church.[46]

Critically speaking, while such leadership development and training programs are of value, the understanding of "lay leader-

45. *Sharing the Light of Faith,* #194.
46. Edward K. Braxton, "Black Catholic Laity and the Future of the Catholic Church in the Black Community," Keynote Address, Comfort My People Day, sponsored by Archdiocese of Chicago, April 14, 1984.

ship" is often too narrowly defined. Christian leadership can never exclusively or primarily be "churchy." After all, our baptism and eucharistic fellowship sends us forth to transform the world making a way for the preconditions of the reign of God. The laity as leaven are commissioned to evangelize individuals but also their own culture.

If bishops, pastors, and educators take seriously the emergence of grassroots leadership in racial-ethnic communities, as well as their legitimate demands for a culturally sensitive pastoral response, the church will be enriched by the contributions of millions. Where patterns of domination, paternalism/maternalism, and manipulation continue, the church will fail in its mission to be a spiritual home for everyone. How could we afford to overlook or hinder the enormous benefit that peoples of color bring to the faith? How could we fail to insure that the American Catholic community is truly inclusive and representative?[47] Indeed, attention to the concerns of racial minorities who are Catholic has been voiced by the hierarchy but most congregations persist with patterns, programs, and ministry styles that alienate and frustrate many peoples of color.

Finally, racial minorities have also drawn attention to the diverse learning styles determined by one's culture. We will undoubtedly observe a wider appreciation for the value of right-brain educational approaches—art, music, movement, drama, action, freedom of expression, spontaneity—in catechetical ministries of the future.

There is a "new" model, methodology, and approach for education in faith.

Alfred North Whitehead once cautioned, "I merely utter the warning that education is a difficult problem, to be solved by no one simple formula."[48] As Catholic educational ministries are in the process of being redefined, "new" models for doing catechesis

47. See the following resources: Nathan Jones, *Sharing the Old, Old Story: Educational Ministry in the Black Community* (Winona, Minn.: St. Mary's Press, 1982); Marina Herrera, "The Religious Education of Hispanics," *Military Chaplains' Review* (Fall, 1978); *Tell It Like It Is: A Black Catholic Perspective on Christian Education,* National Black Sisters' Conference, Oakland, Calif.; and the section entitled, "Racism, Pluralism, Bonding," *Women's Spirit Bonding,* ed. Janet Kalven and Mary Buckley (New York: The Pilgrim Press, 1984).
48. Whitehead, *Aims of Education,* p. 36.

are emerging. The educational models and approaches traditionally operative in the local congregation have a limited history and track record, whereas, the "new" models in present-day practice have a sophisticated historical precedent.

"OLD" MODEL	"NEW" MODEL
schools/classroom	community
doctrines	a way of life
children	adults
conformity	freedom

The schooling and classroom approach to the teaching of Christian doctrine has been characteristic since the Council of Trent (1545-1563) mandated catechesis for children beginning at age seven focused primarily on the memorization of doctrine as a protection against false teaching. In eras preceding Trent, the entire community, its total life, values, beliefs, and actions were the primary means of Christian education. Sunday eucharist and the preached Word were equally fundamental sources for Christian formation. The accent was upon adults with the presumption that adult believers would teach their children. The new emphasis on the role of the community-as-educator simply recognizes that there are various domains in which education in faith occurs, and one happens to be school. However, education in faith can and does go on in the absence of schools and in spite of schools.

The so-called "new" model does not diminish the value of schooling, doctrine, educational ministries to children, nor the place of obedience and the role of authority in the Christian community. It is my hope that there will always be intentional settings where the faith and its living tradition is seriously studied. However, there is a growing awareness that *everything the church does, or does not do, educates.*

In the past children were instructed in isolation from adults. Today's emphasis on adult learning does not mean there are no children around. According to John Westerhoff, catechesis "values the interaction of faithful selves in community, striving to be Christian together, in-but-not-of the world."[49]

49. John Westerhoff III, "Risking an Answer: A Conclusion," *Who Are We: The Quest for a Religious Education* (Birmingham, Ala.: Religious Education Press, 1978), p. 269.

While religious education may not be swinging in the extreme arcs of the past, there is evidence that we have come a long way. One of the significant breakthroughs in catechesis since the Council has been the realization that religious education is broader than Catholic schooling and more inclusive than CCD. *The community educates,* or as Berard Marthaler puts it, "Education of every kind must be seen in the context of total life. Schooling, however primitive and informal, is only a single factor and a rather ineffective one if not reinforced by social patterns and institutions and compatible symbols systems. . . . As one matures, a person 'internalizes,' that is, understands and consciously affirms the worldview mediated by the church's symbol system."[50]

Having grown up in a church that was an exponent of docility and unquestioning acceptance, the recent atmosphere and jargon about freedom has been certainly welcomed.

A fresh openness to the insights of the social sciences have enabled us to recognize that cultural differences shape both the articulation as well as the content of one's faith. Studies in developmental psychology have shed greater light on the development of persons and its relationship to growth in faith. Therefore, contemporary catechetical models and approaches use an experiential basis for Christian nurture. The methodology proceeds inductively rather than deductively.

The period of experimentation that followed the Council has largely waned and a more careful, reflective, and sound approach to catechetical innovations and developments seem to be standard today.

Conclusion

I have attempted to reflect on and assess the wave of renewal and re-vision sweeping Catholic-Christian education. Something new is being born out of the old. Honoring our past, we are invited to imagine a whole new way of pastoring and educating in the example of Jesus.

We are a church in search of its "American identity." We are stumbling along toward a clearer view of our mission and ministry. As we approach the start of the third millennium, it is a healthy sign to pause and look how far God has brought us and how much God has taught us.

50. Marthaler, "Handing On the Symbols of Faith," p. 30.

Chapter 8

Musings on Sunday School in the Black Community

MARY A. LOVE

The Sunday school in the black church and community has played and is playing a vital role in the lives of blacks in the United States. In the late 1700s through the 1800s, these Sunday schools were basic settings for teaching slaves to read and write. It must be noted that the early Sunday schools for blacks existed for the purpose of Christianization of those who had been transplanted in America from Africa and their indoctrination to accept slave status. This trend changed and blacks began to reinterpret the gospel and the task of the Sunday school, thus giving birth to many local congregations. The above factors point to the recognized need on the part of blacks to teach and to enable persons to increase their knowledge, not only of the Bible, but also of the everyday occurrences in life.

Early Sunday schools used the Bible as their major textbook, not unlike Robert Raikes in the Sunday school movement in England. It served as a textbook in two ways: 1) to aid in the teaching of persons to read and write, and 2) to interpret and bring meaning to dehumanizing and oppressive situations. Some blacks were able to read the Bible, while others had to be content simply to hear the accounts of the life of Job, the struggles and victories of the nation of Israel, the significance of the ministry of Jesus, and other biblical records. This was necessary to comprehend and acknowledge the hand of a caring God at work. This personal sense of God made it possible to face the physical misery with perseverance and endurance, affirming that God loves black children just as equally as children of other races are loved. The Sunday school was the place where those first positive concepts of God, Jesus Christ, and the nature and mission of the church were experienced and reinforced.

Blacks need opportunities for growth and self-expression which Sunday schools have offered and are continuing to offer. Various talents were and are discovered such as the ability to write creatively, be dramatic, compose musical selections, give instrumental and vocal renditions and orations. Within Sunday schools many blacks experienced their first audience and thereby gained the necessary skills to compete and share their God-given talents in the secular world. Consequently, America, the world, and certainly the black church and community are richer because of black Sunday schools.

Many of the teachers in black Sunday schools were capable of demonstrating the law of love in a more eminent manner than any story written in the best illustrated curriculum. This experience fostered the sensitivity to care in a station of life where the masses of blacks witness some form of oppression and need to find avenues of hope and liberation.

The ideas offered thus far reflect the past and the present. The contemporary setting may be different, but the intentional effort continues to be that of assisting persons of color to obtain the necessary tools for survival in a dehumanizing environment. William R. Johnson states the matter in this fashion:

> Survival was of paramount importance because if one is freed, and one is not able to maintain his presence in a society, freedom then is of little consequence and is without substance. So it was that the Black Church saw a part of its mandate for being, that of providing a methodology for survival, and this methodology of survival included that of the founding of predominantly Black denominations and Black churches through which Black people would be able to come together and to find solutions to their immediate problems.[1]

This motif of survival created institutions which have undergone many transformations but remain viable in the black community. Therefore, what follows is a more detailed analysis and assessment of Sunday schools in the black church and community accompanied with breakthroughs for renewal.

1. William R. Johnson, "The Black Church and the Sunday School Movement," *The Church School Herald-Journal* 66, no. 2 (December, January, February, 1980-1981), p. 11.

Points of Vitality

Every group or organization possesses strengths of which it can be proud. These strengths also often provide the ingredients for continuity, longevity, unity, and cooperation. What follows is a discussion of several factors which are perceived as vital strengths of Black Sunday schools. However, they are not given according to any sequential spiral.

Catalyst for Theological Nurturing and Inquiry

Black Sunday school classes are places where theological doctrines are taught, disputed, discussed, and clarified. Much of the theologizing takes its root in liberation because the concern is "that Blacks come to understand themselves as a part of the human race thus liberating themselves from the belief or the concept that Blacks were sub-human beings."[2] Blacks are seeking ways that will empower their ability to make sense out of the issues, beliefs, and challenges which confront them. In this process, many begin by seeking only a simplified explanation of these beliefs, but this forum also provides the means whereby formal liberation theology is concretized and the base for theological inquiry is established.

To nurture theologically means that persons are given the necessary nutrients or succor to maintain growth and development. To the Christian who is black, the Sunday school teaches the basic tenets of the Christian faith so that meaning can be gained in relation to life as it relates to the omnipotent, omnipresent, omniscient, moral, just, and loving God. A child can learn to pray and believe in the worth of prayer without the ability to read as a result of the exposure to certain experiences. Likewise, an adult's theological interpretation of the "at-one-ment" or any other theological concept may be distorted, but the opportunity to teach and correct can occur in the Sunday school classroom. It is in this setting that the seed for deeper theological inquiry may be received by the learner. Then this seed can produce new light, vigorous growth, and the possibility of sharing the gospel with others in meaningful ways.

The Recognized Need to Teach

Educational experts say that one is most ready to learn when a recognized need is present and the teachable moment exists. Most

2. Ibid.

leaders in black churches recognize the need to teach or teachable moments and put forth the effort to make the best use of each one as it occurs. The school of the church is not just a forum for the study of the Bible, but also a laboratory where the application of the scriptures to the problems and concerns of a people occurs. As a result of this recognition, much of the social activism in the black community begins in the church. This could not happen if the need to teach was not recognized as vital to the survival and perpetuation of a people. In other words, this is the performance of ministry and the meeting of needs.

The Great Commission[3] is affirmed by Sunday schools in the black church and most persons in this setting are willing to study and learn and proceed to tell and teach others. The aim becomes that of fulfilling the charge given, which instructs followers of the Way to teach newly made disciples along with older disciples (not in reference to age but to the length of time one has been involved in the Christian community), so that they are enabled and empowered to go and convince others likewise to become followers of the Way. This brings in the dimension of evangelism, because many who were unchurched have accepted the call after being led to Sunday school.

In many congregations the Sunday school is the only arena for structured teaching. But yet this arena often applies a wholistic approach to its task as a teaching unit. That is, the Sunday school and its constituent members involve themselves in areas other than mere study of the Sunday school curriculum. They often find it necessary to put into practice what they are studying on the job, at play, in the political arena, and wherever concerns present themselves. With the foregoing in mind, the need to teach is a vital strength that often provides the buttress for the educational ministry in the local congregation. Therefore, where there is a highly recognized need to teach there is usually a strong Sunday school and a strong department or strong board of Christian education. Consequently, one tends to feed the other, and likewise the local congregation grows and extends its tendrils to reach out and embrace all segments within the community.

It should be noted that the same birthing ground for black Sunday schools and black churches also gave birth to institutions geared to provide secular instruction for blacks. These institutions include the parochial, elementary, and secondary schools;

3. Matthew 28:19-20.

junior and four year colleges; universities; seminaries and institutes. This again illustrates the fact that blacks still feel it is an absolute must that proper nurture be accessible to people of dark pigmentation to insure survival, racial success, and the ability to compete in a pluralistic society.

Base for Black Talent Development

Many blacks have accomplished some goal in life as a result of a Sunday school teacher, superintendent, parent, or other concerned and caring individual who encouraged their involvement in Sunday school. The talents of many black youth and adults are being used to provide music, keep records, and to enhance the visual appearance of the environment. As the development of talents is encouraged in the home, the Sunday school becomes a place where these diverse talents can be displayed, polished, and reinforced. Often a black child may receive the inspiration to develop his/her unique skills and work diligently toward the goal of mastering the art. Within Sunday schools there are opportunities for a wide variety of arts and skills to emerge if leaders are willing to give the challenge and work with the learners. What arts are promoted in any particular congregation will largely depend upon the talents present among leaders of the church or members of the community. Examples and good role models play a vital role in the development of blacks.

Even the opportunity to learn to read and write occurs in Sunday schools. Cases have been observed where children in the Sunday school class were having difficulty reading and a concerned teacher would take them aside for tutoring. This greatly improved their reading skills and the experience of caring helped the child achieve at a higher level in the public school system. This also provided a means whereby the child could gain self-confidence and self-esteem that is so often difficult to develop within a large group where less individual instruction is possible.

Dedicated Lay Leadership

Those persons who have assumed leadership positions in the Sunday school who are dedicated to the task, provide a strength to the achievements of black Sunday schools. Leaders who are able to give good positive examples for others to follow aid in the growth of any group. Douglas E. Wingeier states in his discussion of the biblical images of teaching that we are to be "reminded by the biblical image of leaven of the potential of example for either good or evil; the Christian teacher is careful and intentional about making the influence of his or her life consistent with the message taught in the classroom."[4]

It is no secret nor mystery that any leader who endeavors to provide a good Christian example will most likely be effective. If one is using the supreme leader, Jesus, as an example, selfishness, lovelessness, harsh criticism, and pretense will not be a part of the leader's style. Thus, the doors are opened for genuine sharing of the gospel to occur among others.

When the leader's style provides a good example, comradery develops along with the willingness to cooperate and participate without fear. A vision is provided which is realistic, and systematic planning and evaluation are practiced to structure dreams into realities. Also, the responsibility for accomplishing the tasks may be delegated and shared so that the leader does not feel that he or she must do everything or that the tasks to be done must be completed exactly as the leader desires without regard to the talents and abilities of others.

Another aspect of the vitality of dedicated leadership is the role leaders play in evangelizing others. Good Christian leaders or teachers are about the business of sharing the good news of Jesus Christ. Often the process of evangelization is unplanned, but in loving and caring ways the gospel is not only verbally shared but visually demonstrated in the life lived before the learners. The enthusiasm about the message of the gospel and sharing it in Sunday school is contagious. Lessons are taught in a way that challenges are posed and the learner is encouraged to make a decision or strengthen her or his level of commitment. Many leaders and teachers recognize the value of insignificant acts as potential sparks to set persons aglow for the Savior. Thus, the sermon lived is a powerful supplement to the sermon preached and taught, and the challenge for persons to walk with God is always present.

Creativity and the Ability to Improvise
Most black Sunday schools do not have all of the media arsenals such as projectors, video recorders, screens, printed resources, or even enough space with which to augment the teaching/learning process. This is where creativity has surfaced, and many cannot

4. Douglas E. Wingeier, *Seven Biblical Images of Teaching* (Nashville: Discipleship Resources, 1978), p. 14.

understand how such meaningful learning/teaching experiences can occur with limited resources.

Many Sunday school superintendents and teachers have found themselves in need of various materials which were unavailable. They did not panic and say that nothing could be done until the resources were secured. Rather, they used their imaginative skills and created meaningful alternatives or innovative approaches to accomplish the goal and to communicate the gospel through the lessons. Any Sunday school with personnel who possess creative skills and the willingness to venture to try the untried is stronger.

Creativity builds a sense of liberation which is a priority in the black church. According to Elizabeth Allstrom, creativity is "involving my feelings, emotions and all the dimensions of myself in whatever I do. It's putting my own spark, my own mark upon it. Then no one mistakes my work for another's or another's for mine."[5]

This innate creative ability is found in unique proportions in everyone, but it must be nurtured to produce abundant fruit. When it is allowed to emerge, new insights, experiences, and possibilities also emerge. One action leads to another, and the enthusiasm and inspiration generated within persons who are creative become contagious. Then, according to Allstrom, this process of spontaneous combustion "helps to set the conditions for creativity. Sooner or later the signs of creativity are certain to break through doubts and disbelief and bring a transformation within and without the doubting individual."[6]

It is the opportunity to use the imagination that has made noteworthy contributions to the black church. Likewise, individuals have been freed to be themselves and not be puppets controlled and managed by another individual, thus yielding to conformity. As a result, they are able to make the necessary changes in the curriculum to address the needs and interests of a particular group of learners adequately, regardless of the limitations imposed.

Use of the Uniform Series

Most of the predominantly black denominations use the Uniform Lesson Series, which is developed through the National

5. Elizabeth Allstrom, *You Can Teach Creatively* (Nashville: Abingdon, 1970), p. 27.
6. Ibid., p. 35.

Council of Church's Division of Education for Christian Life and
Mission. The lessons developed from the outlines provide opportunities for all ages to study identical basic themes with respect to
the level of understanding. In many instances, the lessons for the
adults and youth will point to the biblical story while the lessons
for the children have story lines that allow a contemporary approach to the same Christian principle. Systematic study of basic
themes is needed and valuable in that it provides for reinforcement on all levels. It is difficult for reinforcement to occur in the
home when three or four different lessons are studied each Sunday. With similar themes, one does not need to do additional study
of the biblical background to be able to discuss the lesson in a
knowledgeable manner.

The black denominations that prepare their own lessons from
the outlines advocate more systematic teaching in Sunday
schools. With the freedom to develop the curriculum, the particular denominational history, heritage, and theological stance is
communicated. Also, the opportunity to address the same biblical
issues from an ethnic perspective is available. By the same token,
this promotes denominational loyalty and summons the resources
of the denomination (both human and nonhuman), while encouraging theological inquiry.

Impairments

No one wants to acknowledge deficiencies, but recognizing the
existence of a problem or impairment is the first step toward a
solution or improvement. Thus, what follows is an analysis of
several factors that need reassessment and improvement in black
Sunday schools.

Absence of Good Black Images in Curriculum

Many black Sunday schools use curriculum developed by nondenominational agencies or publishers who follow the mode of modern marketing techniques aimed to achieve profit and satisfy the
majority market. Repeatedly, these publishers will be tokenistic
and give some semblance of concern for the black market by
strategically placing and timing one or two black images. However, few, if any, blacks are involved in the development of this
curriculum. What type of image does this convey to the black
child? As a result, the image firmly planted is that of the majority,
which leads to the development of an inferiority complex. In some

instances, the absence of pictures is preferred over the use of pictures that brainwash and lead toward the development of distorted concepts.

The image of Jesus is a good example to illustrate this point. A small child who has only seen pictures of Jesus with blue eyes, straight hair and a fair complexion will have difficulty accepting any other image. The child's response to a picture with different characteristics would most likely be, "That is not Jesus, he does not have _____." If a child formulates an image without visual aids, it would probably have characteristics closer to those of her or his own. Plus, a part of the teaching process is to enable persons to discover who they are and what makes them unique. Thus, concepts of identity become key factors in the development of black people.

One's identity or concept of self is influenced by the images and role models made available for emulation and imitation. Once that individual identity has emerged, one needs to feel positive about it. This positiveness can provide motivation, guidance, or the inclination to think and act in a certain manner. Otherwise, one is ashamed of one's physical appearance and will go to great lengths to alter it to become like those who are accepted and regarded highly.

Curriculum writers and publishers must be more cognizant of the subtle and sometimes unintentional messages which are conveyed through pictures or the way the word "black" is used. Too often the word "black" is attached as a modifier to emphasize the negative or to discredit or condemn. If one only hears the negative and knows that she or he is black, it is fair to assume that one will begin to develop a negative self-image.

Where a picture is needed, a line drawing may serve the purpose and allow the child to be creative. If everything is prearranged or rigid, very little room is left for one's imagination to enter the windows of the mind. Everything must be done to destroy the inferiority, valuelessness, and disrespect associated with blackness. The signals communicated must be monitored so that wrong signals do not permeate the being and "reinforce already present feelings of inadequacy and low self-esteem based on socio-cultural determinants."[7]

---

7. Paul Nichols, "Blacks and the Religious Education Movement," in *Changing Patterns of Religious Education*, ed. Marvin J. Taylor (Nashville: Abingdon, 1984), p. 189.

Although this is an impairment, efforts have been made to improve the image projected in curriculum used by black Sunday schools. The curriculum developed by the *Black Educational Resources Development* (BERD) is one such example. According to Paul Nichols, the BERD curriculum "has as educational and pedagogical aim the correlation of biblical stories and texts with black liberation theology ideas."[8] This curriculum is still in the development stages and does not span the entire age range for use in black Sunday schools. It is hoped that this project will continue and become available for all ages.

Urban Ministries, Inc., in Chicago, Illinois, is supplying curriculum for the black church emphasizing black images and the black experience. The lessons are based on the *Uniform Lesson Series.*

Predominantly black denominations that are developing their own literature usually use black visual images and illustrations accompanied with meaningful interpretations from a liberation theme. However, some of these groups have encountered enormous roadblocks disguised in the clothes of insufficient funds, lack of personnel, and inadequate equipment. This poses limits but every effort is made to do the best with the resources available.

Teacher Training and Enrichment

According to John Milton Gregory, "The teacher must be one who knows the lesson or truth or art to be taught."[9] In other words, every teacher must be a student. This indicates that anyone who accepts the responsibility to nurture disciples in the household of faith should be first trained and constantly undergoing renewal, refreshment, and enrichment. Too often in black Sunday schools, there is a shortage of avenues for this to occur.

Teacher's meetings on a weekly, bi-weekly, or monthly basis are experiences designed to aid teachers gain confidence, explore theological concepts, and build a supporting community of teachers. Sharing with teachers of other denominations who use the same curriculum or the *Uniform Lesson Series* is one possible way to reduce the level of this impairment.

Methods used by teachers may be innovative and varied. This indicates that teachers may assume various roles in the teaching/

---

8. Ibid., p. 187.
9. John Milton Gregory, *Seven Laws of Teaching.* (Grand Rapids, Mich.: Baker Book House, 1954), p. 18.

learning process. Richard E. Rusbuldt[10] describes those roles as those of organizing, translating, communicating, planning, facilitating, motivating, and creating. Donald L. Griggs[11] adds to this list the role of counselor, friend, and learner. This implies that the responsibility taken by any teacher in the Sunday school classroom involves diversity. Too often teachers allow themselves to become fixated and render themselves unable to change roles as the need arises. Sufficient opportunities for teacher training and enrichment, plus teachers who are willing to take advantage of the opportunities, are required if black Sunday schools are to continue to be relevant to the black church and community.

Congregational, Parental, and Pastoral Support

Sunday school should be seen as the school of the church. It has already been stated that the Sunday school serves as the catalyst for theological nurturing and inquiry. For some congregations, however, there is a misinterpretation that Sunday schools are for children and youth and are a separate entity of the local congregation, rather than a corporate part. As a part of the corporate whole, the Sunday school should serve as one of the agencies for nurturing *all* members of the household of faith. Persons of the Way should constantly seek avenues that promote growth, improvement, and becoming. Furthermore, there is no point at which any individual knows all there is to know about the Christian faith, and all members of the congregation need to accept this fact.

The provision of good examples and role models has been discussed, and it is in this area that persons can build effective Sunday schools by becoming involved. Parents become lax in their commitment, and the child begins to interpret the parental example to mean that the Sunday school does not claim a high ranking on the scale of priorities. In the effort to achieve on the secular level, some parents fail to place an equal amount of emphasis on moral and spiritual development. For a person to be well-rounded in all aspects of life, there must be balance.

The example of involvement or noninvolvement on the part of the clerical staff can boost or destroy a local Sunday school. Pastors are busy people with numerous obligations, and they

10. Richard E. Rusbuldt, *Basic Teacher Skills* (Valley Forge, Pa.: Judson Press, 1981), pp. 25-35.
11. Donald L. Griggs, *Teaching Teachers to Teach* (Livermore, Calif.: Griggs Educational services, 1974), pp. 2-3.

should not be expected to do everything. However, a pastor should support the Sunday school in the local congregation by constantly highlighting its concerns during the regular worship services and teaching the teachers, if possible. Pastors may also visit classes periodically, conduct dedication services for the workers, and encourage persons to become involved along with cooperating with the trustees, superintendent, and other officers to provide a comfortable environment which is conducive to learning and teaching.

Acknowledging Christian Education as a Vocation

Many black Sunday schools and departments of Christian education have functioned successfully without the benefit of persons who were trained for educational ministry. Many limit seminary training to the realm of pastoral ministry, and educational ministry is not really accepted as a vocation for which one formally prepares. This is probably the result of two problems: First, many local black congregations are unable to hire persons for educational ministry due to the inability to provide adequate salaries and comparable benefits, thereby reducing the job market for the same. Second, some black ministers are unwilling to share responsibilities of administration with others, and congregations are not encouraged to move toward multi-staff employment with one of the positions reserved for a professional Christian educator.

If more interested individuals are encouraged to pursue seminary training in the field of Christian education, the ability to enhance the training of Sunday school teachers will increase. Also, the potential will be present for more contributions to the world of curriculum development from blacks. Congregations must move beyond the practice of pastor as the only full-time staff person serving the congregation, particularly in the larger urban and inner-city congregations. This especially holds true for congregations of the predominantly black denominations. Where there are associate ministers available, few serve in the area of Christian education and the teachers are often untrained volunteers with work responsibilities other than those with the local congregation.

Breakthroughs for Renewal and Strengthening

Change is inevitable, therefore innovations are necessary for Sunday schools in the black church and community to remain viable with a meaningful impact on their constituency. What follows is a brief explanation of several suggestions and observations which could empower black Sunday schools for the future.

From Sunday School to the School of the Church.

The traditional Sunday school meets before the 11:00 A.M. Sunday worship service, which is posing problems because the rigid time schedule causes many to cease participation or to do so sporadically. Congregations must survey their members to ascertain workable schedules and make the necessary adjustments. The future may hold a renaming of the Sunday school to that of "the school of the church" which meets anywhere and at any time convenient to the participants. This would open doors for nurturing in various settings, with various groupings and convenient times. People tend to respond more favorably when the program offered is more convenient to their needs and situations. This may gravitate toward less structured Sunday schools and more small groups studying various issues in various settings such as the home and the community recreation building. Those planning for restructuring must consider the economic conditions under which blacks operate, the work schedules, and the family structure. Increased intergenerational sessions should evolve to accomplish learning and sharing with and among persons from the various stages along the human life span.

Today, as Sunday schools are transformed into the "school of the church," the world of technology must be used to benefit the educational process in the church. It was previously noted that finances for such technological investments are often limited, but this is one avenue where the more affluent congregations can reach out in ministry and share resources. Not only sharing of material resources could occur, but sharing of human resources and experiences, which would enhance the liberation efforts on all fronts. The American society has become a wasteful society and has not sought ways to obtain the maximum use of the available goods and services. Thus, more efficient utilization of resources is needed on the part of all Christians as we strive to be good stewards of the earth's bounty.

Many have noted that the church has become the most segregated entity in American society. Can it remain in this state and continue to be functional? This is not to advocate the loss of individual identity and ethnic heritage, but to become eminently involved in mutual sharing, thereby providing a ministry with the goal of alleviating oppressive conditions. Be cognizant of the fact that one can be oppressed and really not recognize the existence of the oppressed state because it is comfortable and nonthreatening. But on the other hand, liberation from oppressed conditions means the destruction of many centuries-old traditions and it means sacrificial denial.

Development of Curriculum by Local Congregations or Clusters

Developing curriculum for a diversity of denominations does not allow writers to address the unique concerns and problems of a particular congregation adequately. Many issues are seldom addressed because they are not a part of the systematic curriculum at the time when the need is present for emphasis. Teachers, superintendents, and directors of Christian education are summoned to orchestrate an aggressive role in structuring and restructuring the curriculum to address the specific concerns of congregations. This does not mean that denominational materials should be abandoned but that supplementation is essential.

Sunday schools of close proximity should form cooperative clusters for the purpose of curriculum development and the utilization of resources. In light of the unique needs of an area, this could conceivably involve political education in view of the scriptures or documentation on the historical contributions of blacks of the locale to the life of the church and community paralleled with scriptural examples. Any curriculum writer who is removed from the locale would be unable to develop such indigenous materials.

Vacation Bible school leaders in the communities could operate joint schools and develop their own curriculum. To do so, sufficient time must be available for adequate research and compilation of the material for use in the teaching/learning process. Otherwise, it is thrown together and everyone loses.

Family Sunday Schools

Modern day society has produced a number of variations of the nuclear family. In some instances families have been destroyed as a result of the conditions placed upon them in American society. By the same token, the church must support the family and provide nurture for its enrichment and survival. The family can be viewed and used as an extension school of the church. Predominantly black churches have not applied enough energy to the area of family ministry in order that families of various configurations may be endowed with sufficient coping mechanisms in light of the Christian faith. Much of what has been produced in the area of family ministry is focused on crisis ministry. In other words, the occurrence of a crisis provokes the addressing of a problem, need, or concern. Sufficient nurturing is required before the appearance of a crisis situation so that the additional emotional strain will not enter into the teaching/learning experience whereby crises may be prevented.

Resources for family utilization such as cassettes, video tapes, and films, should be developed to address the many aspects of black family living. Since many congregations have families that do not live close to the church, the possibility of nurturing sessions in the neighborhood or family clusters becomes an innovative possibility.

A Curriculum that Orchestrates Left and Right Brain Development

A curriculum developed for use in black Sunday schools must be challenging and appealing to both hemispheres of the brain. Too often the imaginative realm (right hemisphere) is not explored or allowed to burst forth as a result of the abundance of "cut and dried" or prearranged curricula. God continues to speak to earthlings in all shapes, forms, and fashions, and it might be that well-chosen creative challenge that performs as the hook with the power to convince someone to become a newly committed disciple of Jesus. As Christians we are each commanded to be "fishers of individuals," thus the evangelistic zeal should be an underlying goal of every effort in the Sunday schools of black churches and all other churches. A curriculum that has everything outlined succinctly, with every answer clearly given, tends to destroy one's opportunity to explore lessons and materials imaginatively.

When imagination exists in a positive atmosphere of love and control, creative learning often results. Otherwise, feelings of anxiety, helplessness, and aloneness emerge.[12] Thus, imaginative teaching should be a goal for all teachers in black Sunday schools so that both hemispheres of the brain are challenged.

This is not to encourage the development of a curriculum which only challenges the imagination, or the right hemisphere. Accord-

12. Ruth Mastin Anderson, "Imagination in Teaching," *JED Share*, 10, no. 1 (Spring, 1981), p. 8.

ing to Jeannine Sweet, "The right hemisphere controls emotion, nonverbal language, memory, and concrete thinking. The speech of the right hemisphere is less colorful."[13] Gabriele Lusser Rico further describes the right hemisphere as "superior at handling the unknown, the novel, the ambiguous, the paradoxical, the uncontroversial, attempting to make sense out of all by discovering workable patterns."[14] In contrast, the left hemisphere of the brain is analytical and controls verbal language, logical thought processes, linear mathematical ability, reading, writing, and complex motor control.[15] With the increased understanding of the manner in which the brain functions, it is necessary to insure that both hemispheres are adequately developed. Thus, a curriculum that is developed for use by blacks and all others should incorporate a design which orchestrates bilateral hemispheric cooperation. In other words, the curriculum must be balanced.

How teachers function and fulfill their responsibility will be affected by this thrust. Various teaching methods encourage certain avenues of development while others do not. This further affirms the need for increased teacher training and enrichment and a larger number of blacks who are willing to pursue Christian education as a vocation or career.

Conspectus

Sunday schools have been and are continuing to be of vital importance to the life and development of the blacks in America by providing the means for nurturing persons who have encountered uprootedness and oppression. Within these Sunday schools, blacks have learned to read, write, theologize, be creative, and develop their God-given talents. Likewise, the overwhelming recognition of the necessity to teach or nurture persons of color led and continues to lead to the establishment of institutions for nurturing and preparing blacks for many of life's vocations.

The black Sunday schools have not existed without problems or impairments. Those noted previously include the inadequacy of the portrayal of good black images in the curriculum; the need for sufficient teacher training and enrichment opportunities; the

13. Jeannine Sweet, "Human Brain: Untapped Potential," *JED Share* 12, no. 2 (Summer, 1983), p. 6.

14. Gabriele Lusser Rico, *Writing the Natural Way* (Los Angeles: J. P. Tarcher, 1983), p. 70.

15. Sweet, "Human Brain," p. 6.

need for congregational, parental, and pastoral support; and the shortage of black professional Christian educators. Although these impairments exist, they should not invoke any feelings of despair, because hope is present and liberation is occurring.

Innovations that are assisting in the transformation of the Sunday school in the black church involve a rethinking of the traditions of time, space, and agenda for the Sunday school. Demands for an indigenous curriculum from the congregation are emerging along with the challenge to be more wholistic in our approach to mental development. New structures and settings must evolve to include singles, young adults, families, step-families, integenerational settings, and other configurations.

The Sunday school may change its name, setting, and structure but the underlying purpose will remain, which is to provide the help persons need to grow and nurture others in the Christian faith.

Chapter 9

Sunday Schools in the Armed Forces

ALFRED W. HANNER, JR.

The military community functions as a microcosm of society in general in many ways. There are some very marked differences in religious education in the military, just as there are some predictable similarities. The information in this section will deal specifically with the U.S. Army, which employs a number of professional religious education workers.

A survey was circulated to the civil service employees in the job called "Educational Specialist; Religion." One of these Directors of Religious Education, when asked to describe the difference between religious education in the military setting and in a civilian setting, wrote the following:

> My experience is that there is a world of difference if we are meeting the needs of our audience. It is true that we have some of the traditional models and programs that one would find in the civilian church. However, we do not have cross generation participants, stable congregations, long-term volunteer support, single denominational belief systems, or established traditions. Our main audience is of an age of questions and doubts about religious commitments and values. Our audience is of a single profession that requires twenty-four hour duty commitments and deployments at a moment's notice. While retaining some of the familiar in religious education we in the military must look to alternate and sometimes unknown plans and programs to do religious education. It is a challenging and very frustrating task that calls us to creativity and innovation that is simply not necessary in the civilian world.

Not every religious educator would state the case in such sharp terms, but the facts are true as stated. The age-level segment of the population with which the local church has the least effective contact, post-high school to twenty-five, comprises the largest segment of the military population. These young adults are involved in a profession that is periodically held up to question by society in general. The interaction from both sides can be stereotypical. I recall a week-long retreat where a military chaplain and a minister from a traditional peace church were to work all week in the same group. Neither wanted to do so and came to me as director to be moved into more "compatible" groups. I refused. At the end of the week they had developed not only a strong friendship but a much more sympathetic understanding of the other's position. It is the stereotype of the Army and society that provides some of the background against which the shape of religious education ministry must be performed. Some of the stereotypes are based on fact and some are fantasy. This exploration will seek to put more of the facts as discovered in our data gathering into the discussion.

Because of the diversity in the situations and personalities in the field of religious education in the military I undertook a survey of the professionals working with the U.S. Army. The results surfaced their views about strengths and weaknesses as well as the present and future issues they felt were confronting them. The overarching conclusion of the survey effort is that the field is very diverse and most generalizations would be false. The respondants were in all sections of the country and three foreign areas. (N=52.)

The results below are reflected in the comments of this chapter. They point up the similarities and the differences in civilian and military settings for religious education.

Table 1
THE STRONGEST ELEMENTS IN R.E. PROGRAMS

The Religious Ministries Team	35%
Administration of program	17%
Innovative program ideas	40%
Quality of training being provided	8%

THE WEAKEST ELEMENTS IN R.E. PROGRAMS

Logistical support, building funds	35%
Personnel, military and volunteer	26%

Mobility of participants 11%
Weak program. 20%
Poor or unsuitable literature 8%

THE ISSUES AND CONCERNS DEVELOPING

Mobilization, peace, and war 17%
Religious Ministries Team needs 15%
Family concerns 12%
Specific program development 28%
Theological or value issues 21%
Volunteers, use and training 7%

THE TYPE AND DIRECTION OF THE CHANGE YOU SEE

Increasing pluralism. 10%
Vitalization of religion 37%
Religious Ministry Team works 21%
Family more involved in religious education 16%
Decline in religious interest. 16%

What is Different Because of a Military Setting?

When the audience of the religious education program is all
bound into one vocational bundle there is a sharp difference in the
enterprise. The many qualities of military life which make other
areas different, change the religious education enterprise also. In
the military the needs are provided by the system in special shop-
ping privileges, health care, housing, and numerous other things
prescribed by regulation or custom. The net effect is both limitation and freedom. The limitation is that the regulations and cus-
toms can be very inflexible. The freedom is that many areas that
would concern a civilian parish are not burdens to a military
congregation. The leadership is provided in the form of the chaplain and the religious educator by the system and not by the
choice of the parishioners. Their salaries are paid by tax monies
and not by congregational offerings. The resources are in large
part provided by monies appropriated by Congress, including curriculum materials, audiovisual equipment, buildings, and support
resources.

At a recent workshop a leader wanted to present a unit on low cost resources for educational ministry. The group of military educators asked if they could change the presentation to one dealing with the best use of a resource-rich situation. The leader could not even understand the request to say nothing of complying with it. He was used to working in a civilian setting where the problem was limited resources. The religious educator in the military who will plan and work within available channels may have many more kinds of resources and equipment.

The question is a legitimate one of how to function effectively when you can borrow video production equipment for the fifth grade, or requisition 100 gallons of punch for Vacation Church School simply by knowing the forms to use.

There is a side effect of the resource-rich environment. It resembles a situation I first encountered in the South in the early 1950s in a small mill town. The company owned the church, hired the minister, and paid the bills. The consequence was that the congregation did not feel responsibility for the program. If there was a problem, they expected the company to take care of it. Some of that same kind of thinking occurs in the military religious education program. The lay person often does not own the need to be resourceful or creative because the "system" can provide what may be a more expensive and perhaps less effective solution. Frequently institutions of this size do not reward innovation.

Although the program in the military setting is just as dependent upon the lay volunteer as in the civilian sector, the volunteers can be different. Since there is seldom a long-term congregational history there is no appeal to local tradition. The rapid turnover of personnel is common. This means that both the volunteers staffing the program and the participants in the educational enterprise are in flux. There is seldom a lack of volunteers but the turnover means that persons experienced with an age level either are not trained or have been trained in a previous assignment and may be unfamiliar with the local program. It means too that the persons who are trained will have a short useful life to the religious education program at that post. Every change of assignment means that teachers must volunteer again if they are to remain in the program. Thus personal tradition is also lost along with congregational tradition. The constant redecision of persons to be involved or not means that the reservoir of volunteers is in flux.

Religious Education Programs in the Military

One of the issues of religious education, choosing the best curriculum materials, is not present for military religious educators. Selections for the Protestant program are made for them.

> The resources are selected annually by Army, Navy, and Air Force representatives from a wide range of recommendations by consulting church educators who are invited for a selection conference each year by the Chiefs of Chaplains of the three services. The process is supervised by the Religious Education Advisory Group of the Armed Forces.[1]

These selections are from church-owned publishers of Protestant curriculum materials and are changed from year to year. The system had its beginning as a money-saving step to provide a central source for all armed forces Sunday schools. The only materials that can be purchased with congressionally appropriated funds are those listed in the *Resource Guide*. The Advisory Group does an excellent job in the selections. They do have some limitations that would not exist in a local church education committee. The units that deal with a specific denomination's history of polity are, of course, eliminated. There is also the issue of providing an equitable distribution of selections among the twenty-seven publishers who participate in the Protestant Church Owned Publishers Association.

The selection process does mean that continuity is a problem and that an annual change of material format and style is a given. The teacher may have to adapt to a series with teaching packets and many classroom enrichment materials one year and a series which leaves more to the creativity of the teacher the next.

To those who have used the materials from their own publishing house for a number of years as a matter of course this may sound disruptive. In experience it is not much more so than the change of authors may be. I have heard less complaint about "the literature" in the Army system than I did in a denominational setting.

The Catholic program offers more local selection but does presently demand that a single supplier be used. The same limitations

---

1. *Protestant Armed Forces Resource Guide for Christian Growth and Nurture* (Nashville: Protestant Church Owned Publishers Association, 1984), p. 1.

as to listing in the *Resource Guide* in order to be purchased with appropriated funds applies.

Identified Weaknesses

One of the most common perceived weaknesses of the religious education program in the military setting is the lack of dedicated space. There are few installations where there is space used exclusively for classrooms for religious education. A much more common situation is shared space that is also used by a school or in some cases a child care facility.

The problems of being without permanent teaching space are both emotional and physical. The participants, teachers, and administrators have a constant problem of leaving the space in which they operate as they found it. It is perceived by the public school teacher and the Sunday school teacher as belonging to the public school. There is not the same sense of responsibility on the part of the former as the latter to leave the room usable by the counterpart. Administrators spend time dealing with minor problems of displaced items or erased chalkboards.

The physical side of the problem involves setting up the classroom for effective religious instruction when the teacher has access to the room for only a few minutes prior to the arrival of the students. The teacher must remove all items brought into the room and at times be out in a very few minutes because the same room may be used by a Protestant or Catholic class immediately following the first class.

The limitation this puts on all projects of long standing, the use of progressively developed class art, the familiar kinds of activity areas needed for pre- and early elementary children is obvious.

Another area of weakness identified by several professional religious educators is the relationship with clergy. In a local church the director of religious education is an identified part of the team and may be selected by the pastor. The religious education program is a central portion of the church's ministry, so the work is valued by the pastor. In a military setting the Sunday school or CCD may be in a separate place and treated as a separate or even competing program by the chaplain. Let me hasten to add that this is not a universal problem. It is much more possible and probable in the military setting however. In the Army especially the chaplain is identified as a "Unit Chaplain" meaning having primary responsibility to an identified group of military personnel. Since many, and usually most, of the persons in the religious education enterprise are family members and not themselves military the seeds are sown for a divided loyalty.

Some other identified weaknesses are similar to civilian churches and need not be examined in depth. These include: the working parent who is not available for teacher training through the week; the fickle loyalties of persons to religious education vis-à-vis youth sports, scouts, family recreation, etc.; and the high level of transitions of both students and teachers.

Issues

An issue that is being faced by religious educators in the Army is the court challenge to the constitutionality of the Army chaplaincy. In 1979 two Harvard law students filed a suit in federal court challenging the work of the chaplains in the Army as being a violation of the First Amendment. One of their objectives was to restrain the financial and other support for religious activities. The plaintiffs wanted a privately funded and administered chaplaincy program. The issue of "free exercise" of religion was raised along with the background issue of separation of church and state.

There is no attempt to debate the elements of the suit here. That particular legal case has been closed, yet the issue that is facing the religious educator in the military is the uncertainty of its impact.

The complaint specifically mentioned "religious education facilities, the distribution of denominational literature to military personnel . . . (and) the provision of religious education." This means that the educator is not a bystander but is in the center of the issue. The future of the enterprise, the positions of DREs, the basis of the religious education effort, and the use of the materials produced by various denominational bodies for curriculum in these programs all were being challenged.

There is a feeling among many that the chaplaincy predated the Constitution and that the framers could have prohibited it specifically if that had been their intention. There is also the argument that Congress has debated the issue in the past and decided to provide funds and structure for the chaplaincy. The legal issue is not a daily item of conversation within the ranks of religious educators, but it is one of the background uncertainties. It is amplified by the growing religious pluralism in the Army.

A second unique issue to the religious educator in the military setting concerns wartime operation. The military has as a constant fact of life that armies and navies fight wars. What is the role of the religious educator in the event of a mobilization? In most cases the professional religious educator is one of the long-term personnel. The "institutional memory" is in this civilian's mind as a radical change takes place in the military chaplains around. There is a concern about the radically changed nature of the ministry to the family members who will be left behind and will be in new stress situations. The character of religious education programs immediately will broaden and the demands become heavier at the very moment when the system will be least able to provide additional support for that need. The Army develops plans for these events, but the needs of religious education will be frequently overlooked unless the professional educator has some input.

When this is added to the fact that the religious educator is frequently the one who has dared to raise the issues of the peace concern of Christian faith, you have an ambiguous situation. In a recent conference of professional religious educators working in the Army the most important concern was peace. There is ambiguity in the role.

A third issue facing the religious education community in the military is the movement toward a conservative theology. There are increased pressures from conservative and fundamentalist theologies, both Protestant and Catholic, on religious education. The tendency of the most conservative groups is to view the role of religious education as indoctrination and/or conversion of the students. The contrast between this and the idea of education as leading to deeper understanding of God, self, other, and the world is marked. There is a stress in two ways. One is pedagogical. The other comes from the necessary pluralistic setting in which the ministry is taking place.

There are many more issues raised by the wave of conservative theology that must be dealt with in a larger context than this chapter. The inherent conflict between a specified right solution and the demands of a multi-religious parish is one that the religious education worker in the military feels acutely. One educator expressed it this way, "There are the extremely liberal, the mainline, and the fundamentalist here. How can we find the common needs and meet them with our limited time resources?"

A fourth issue facing the military religious educator is the unique needs of families. The demands of the military place some added stresses on the family in an age when the family is already at a breaking point. In combat units the military member may be called to alert or deployment and not be able to tell the spouse where or for how long. The secrecy is demanded by the nature of the situation. Add to this the fact that the family has been moved away from any base of support save the nuclear family itself. These family members are the major portion of the persons involved in the various religious education endeavors. The children and spouses are in Sunday school or CCD and they need a special kind of understanding and support during the times of the most stress.

Even in times when there is no deployment the incidence of family problems is heavy in the military. The abuse of spouse and child are too common. In the military system when they occur they are not given the quiet cover-up frequent in the civilian setting but are known widely in the system. There is a special need to offer support ministry to persons who have been physically abused by a loved one and are in jeopardy of still another kind of ridicule—abuse by those outside the family. Special religious education opportunities are here and so are special problems.

Changes

The most frequently mentioned change by the professionals surveyed was the pluralism they experienced in the military today. There are more diverse groups. These groups are given much more freedom to operate. The pressure to be in one of the major denominations has declined. Some of this change is fueled by the changes in the times. Some is probably from the free exercise issue before the courts.

The pluralism has some positive effects. There is a growing awareness of the diversity of positions. No longer is it assumed that persons are neatly divided into Protestant, Catholic, or Jewish elements. There is even a healthy interchange about the varieties of religious expression among service personnel in informal gatherings and conversations. We hear the unanswered questions later in adult study groups. Persons seek to become clearer about what they believe, and are willing to devote some time to that study.

Coupled with this awareness is a pressure for cooperation. When multiple groups must use limited facilities there is a real interchange about the best use of time and space. There is also the discovery that there are common pursuits that may have application to many of the groups. Interdenominational, or more accurately, nondenominational Bible study groups have an appeal beyond a narrow band of belief. Where these are being formed and presented as nonsecretarian there is good response.

There is also a negative aspect to pluralism, as noted in some reports by persons who despair because they fear the loss of some unique values of a faith group as the boundaries blur. The fear is that the belief systems may become so diluted that people will lose the ground to stand upon.

A seemingly paradoxical result when compared with some of the comments above is the increasing insular nature of the small groups. People who have built a great deal around their inclusion and separation tend to move away from other groups and to isolate themselves. The followers tend to be very committed to their faith and at the same time very fearful that their faith may become tainted by association with others.

A second major area noted in the survey as an important change is increased parental involvement in certain programs of religious education. The Catholic programs of sacramental training are a fine example. These now require the involvement of the family in the process. This demand has been difficult to enforce in some instances, but the response has been very positive.

The family involvement has been noticeable in other areas such as families helping with liturgies, modeling family observances for a larger congregation, and initiating extended family groups. In this we would need to include the growth of home Bible study groups and a whole wave of intergenerational learning experiences that have been on the rise over the past few years.

Innovations

The most important new thing noted by the DREs in our survey was the expansion of their role as educators. This was not universal, but was happening in enough places to indicate that there may be a trend of some kind. These persons reported that they were more valued in the ministry team and asked to provide training in new settings. For example, some were being asked to consult with the chaplain in designing training for soldiers in a unit. The new ideas of ways to communicate values and to deal with the intangibles of the religious life were asked for and used.

Another example was of a religious educator who has begun to manage the continuing education program for the chaplains at a large installation.

Another innovation or trend was identified as the increased use of need-centered short-term courses. This demands a whole planning process of needs assessment, evaluation, and planning for specific training in the area of faith development. The use of limited objective classes is new in some places that are more accustomed to the ongoing setting as the only way in which to do religious education.

The addition of the "support group" dimension to the learning group. While this is not a new kind of experience in many of the civilian churches, where they have been operational for some years, the discovery of the importance of caring groups in the military setting is somewhat new.

There are some innovations which are technological. The use of the resources mentioned earlier make some new ideas more feasible. One installation is finding the combination of video production facilities and access to the post cable network a new vehicle for education. There is a rise and fall of the use of these kinds of innovations because of the amount of energy required to coordinate them in a complex system.

The Nature of the Team

The Religious Education Team on an Army installation has several characters in its cast. The person responsible for the entire religious ministry is the installation chaplain who is in charge of all the personnel in the Chaplain Section. This senior chaplain is the supervisor and director of all the programs. Most of the tasks are delegated to various members of his staff, but their success depends largely on his support.

The director of religious education is the staff person responsible for the educational portion of the team ministry. This would include such things as the Sunday school and CCD as well as a variety of other programs. The kind of other responsibilities should vary with the gifts of the individual, the needs of the team, and the degree of delegation of nontraditional tasks to the DRE. Some have responsibility for the professional development programs of the chaplains. Others have libraries and resource centers to manage. Still others assist in personal growth and/or leadership training for unit personnel. Some are directly involved

in the development and administration of financial resource programs for the post. Many have limited "unofficial" counseling
responsibilities. Most have some enlisted personnel who work under their supervision to perform the office tasks and the interfac-
ing with the military support system. On several posts there are
two directors of religious education, and one is designated the
civilian supervisor of the other and has certain personnel responsibilities such as annual evaluations, approving leave, and coordinating team responsibilities.

The enlisted persons called "Chaplain Assistants" have already
been mentioned. These persons are assigned to the religious education program and function as "paid assistants" to the DRE.
Many of them have excellent backgrounds in religious education,
but many have no such history. The DRE must determine the best
use of these persons and put them to work where their talents
will be best utilized without jeopardizing programs by assuming
more skill or background than actually exists. Because of the
mobility of the Army system, very often the best trained of these
assistants is designated for promotion and must leave the religious education field to perform other duties. A recurring difficulty mentioned by almost all the DREs is the constant
evaluating, training, and then replacing of the assistants. The nature of the Army dictates that this area will remain one of some
difficulty.

The volunteer worker is the backbone of the religious education
ministry in the Army just as in any local church. Much has already been said about the volunteer and the nature of the system.
In all the favorable comments of the surveyed directors the warm-
est praise is reserved for these persons who avail themselves of
training opportunities, serve with distinction, and frequently receive scant notice.

These then are the main players in the enterprise; the post
chaplain, the DRE, the assistants, and the volunteers. The experience of "team" by workers in the field is very diverse. I would
expect the same to be true in the local church setting. Many say
that the team spirit is controlled from the top and changes with
changes in top leadership. Others speak of team as being only the
team in the Religious Education Section. There are frequent la-
ments like, "They say we have it (Team Ministry), but it is hard to
tell." These cries of discomfort are frequent enough to assume
that many lonely DREs feel they are left out of the inner circle.

The unique environment of the military community contributes to the nature of religious education, making it different in many ways. Yet there are many similarities that give the religious education endeavor characteristic tasks and functions that it shares with the civilian church setting. In the midst of the problems and challenges there may be as much variation between two congregations from different traditions in the same town as exists between the military and civilian setting for religious education.

Chapter 10

Sunday School Renewal

D. CAMPBELL WYCKOFF

Some years ago, the pundits gave up on the local congregation. It was dead, they said, and needed to be replaced with things like "task forces." Today, the local congregation is very much alive, and many of the pundits are serving it in one capacity or another. Even earlier, they had given up on the Sunday school, but the Sunday school, though in decline in some quarters, is very much with us.

But it is not in the best of health. Where it is in decline, that decline cannot be attributed entirely to the birth rate. Where it is growing, there is anxiety about its quality and results. Is it doing well a job that the church really needs to have done? Does it need to be replaced, reformed, renewed? We opt for renewal.

The purpose of this chapter is to bring together what is being said on the matter, to reflect on it critically, and to suggest avenues for renewal. First, the "futurizers" are heard; then the contributors to this volume who deal with the Sunday school; then other voices. This sets the stage for exploration of the conditions for renewal.

In sum, it is proposed that genuine renewal comes to the Sunday school as its character and responsibility are defined in the process of rediscovery, as it knows and draws on the sources of its power, as it focuses on meeting imperative needs, and as it is realistic about the resources that it needs to accomplish its tasks.

Responsible "Futurizing"

Renewal immediately suggests consideration of the future. Applied to the project of proposing possibilities for renewal of the Sunday school, some sort of "futurizing" is called for.

In the broadest context, the need for responsible consideration of the future by Christian educators leads Douglas W. Johnson[1] to stress both continuity and change. He distinguishes between life patterns, which are more likely to be enduring, and lifestyles, which are more likely to change. Life patterns are based upon values that are not as easily swayed as are lifestyles, which are dependent upon the inevitable ups and downs of economics. Thus the future is likely to carry on the life patterns that reflect basic values, but is at the same time likely to embody change that is occasioned by limitations of choice that are already present, identifiable, and enduring.

A number of factors making for limitations of choice are cited by Johnson, among them changed patterns of housing (more apartments, townhouses, and condominiums), the women's movement with the changes it has effected in attitudes about women's roles and capabilities, the dependence of certain career plans upon accelerated college costs, the impact of the personal computer (which he predicts will do for the present generation what the automobile did for previous generations), the population bulge of older people at the end of the century (which will for the first time in history place the responsibility for more older people upon fewer young people), and the impact of international politics (including terrorism, war and the threat of war, military stockpiling, and the place of the military in the national and world economy).

Using the method of looking at the future that this suggests, Johnson analyzes the probable continuities and changes, the dynamics and pressures, in the Christian growth of a hypothetical person, Jill, by five year periods from 1990 to 2010.

In a more specifically institutional frame of reference, that of Christian education in the parish, Marion E. Brown and Marjorie G. Prentice,[2] in order to look at "Christian education in the year 2000," studied what are considered to be today's most successful Sunday schools before they consulted the work of professional "futurizers." As a result, they are in a position to propose six guidelines for Christian educators as they prepare for the coming decades:

1. Douglas W. Johnson, *Growing Up Christian in the Twenty-First Century* (Valley Forge, Pa.: Judson Press, 1984), pp. 9-14.
2. Marion E. Brown and Marjorie G. Prentice, *Christian Education in the Year 2000* (Nashville: Abingdon Press, 1984), pp. 11-12.

Intentionality—Knowing our goals as we listen to God's call, and knowing how we may reach them as stewards of God's resources.

Mutuality—Shared ministry, extended to the educational ministry.

Empowerment—Of both laity and clergy, not just the clergy.

Spiritual enrichment—Bible study, prayer, and intentional spiritual growth, at the center of things.

Voluntary simplicity—A style of life requiring a reassessment of personal values.

Interiority—Struggle with values, beliefs, and behavior, guided by the gospel, and leading to the deepening of care and concern for the poor of the world.

One of the most ambitious enterprises in "futurizing about Christian education in recent years—Joint Educational Development's Consultation on the Future of Christian Education—concentrated on the same area of institutional responsibility. According to Donald L. Brown,[3] who chairs the Joint Educational Development Executive Committee, the question became, "Will the real and projected global changes of the next two decades require a more radical change in the church's educational ministry during that period than was evident in the past two decades?"

Brown reports that the result of the Consultation was "not a clear call to specific forms of educational ministry, but the identification of eight 'threads' that were perceived to be integral to that ministry." He cites in particular three of the "threads":

Mutuality and leadership. Education will respect the gifts and needs of each person and draw upon gifts for mutual benefits. Teaching/learning will be a shared experience toward the goal of "building up the body of Christ."

Community of faith (congregation) and company of strangers. Education will hold in dynamic tension its responsibility for nurture of those in the community of faith and equipping the community for a faithful discharge of its ministry in the world. There can be no separation of spiritual and social, private and public, sacred and secular. There can be no separation of the book of faith from the events of our lives.

Global and particular. Education will respect individual and

3. Donald L. Brown, "The Consultation on the Future of Christian Education," *The Association of Presbyterian Church Educators Advocate* (November, 1984), pp. 3-4, 8.

local church needs and aspirations while affirming God's sovereign compassion for the whole inhabited world. The person and the particular congregation are to be valued and nurtured in the context of global imperatives for peace and justice.

Encouragingly, Brown sees that "the foundation for a new educational future is to be found in current theory and practice."

But in the more specific setting of the Sunday school, Jack Seymour[4] calls attention to "a sharp wall . . . between the theory of Christian education and its implementation in the school of the church." In his view, the key issues of separation and simplicity have caused the confusion. He puts his finger on the Sunday school's real problem when, in discussing the problem of inertia, he says, "Without a clear awareness of what needs to be changed, or whether it does; how the change would affect 'the system' of church education; and how church education, church, and culture relate in an institutional ecology, efforts at change or reform are difficult."

Thus the three matters that church educators must fundamentally address, according to Seymour, are:

—The question of the nature of the church and its ministry.
—The relation of church to culture and consequently the present ecology of and for Christian religious education.
—The actual desired effect of church education on the church, individual character, and the culture.

These, he insists, are theological issues about the character of the Christian life.

More specifically still, Seymour follows Cremin in analyzing the "ecology" of Christian education, transcending the formal institution of the school to include family life, the whole religious life, and organized work. Mass media, voluntary organizations, public libraries, museums, child-care facilities are all included. The necessary conceptual shift is from school to education.

Key Ideas Reviewed

Renewal is the theme to which the authors of the chapters in this book have addressed themselves. Among those who have looked at the Sunday school, what key ideas have emerged?

4. Jack Seymour, *From Sunday School to Church School, Continuities in Protestant Church Education in the United States, 1860-1929* (Washington, D.C.: University Press of America, 1982), pp. 160-169.

Jack Seymour tells us what we need to know about past strategies, the waves of zeal for reform that have determined the
changing character of the Sunday school. Each wave was pro-
pelled by aims more grandiose than were possible of realization,
yet the Sunday school remained the church's movement for popular education, whether its focus was chiefly the moral education
of the disadvantaged, progressive reform, or theological awaken-
ing.[5] Present wisdom, then, calls for "study in more depth [of] the
power and effect of strategies of popularization." More specifically, the Sunday school is to provide "an entry point into the faith,
personal support in the quest for understanding, and a broad
knowledge base."

Seymour also establishes a realistic context for the Sunday
school when he recognizes the validity and necessity for "a more
comprehensive program of Christian formation around it which
takes life and decision making in the community of faith seriously
as well as other opportunities for more rigorous study."

Warren J. Hartman, examining the findings of research, rein-
forces the importance of the Sunday school's popular character
with his metaphor of the two doors—the front door, in which the
Sunday school is a major factor in bringing children and youth
into the church, and the back door, in which adults' loss of interest in the Sunday school and its concerns correlates with dimin-
ished interest and activity in the church.

Hartman sees an enrichment of the Sunday school and a clearer
specification of its context in the identification of the five audiences for Christian education that exist in the contemporary
United Methodist Church—those who continue to ask for the
traditional Sunday school, those whose motivation is to find fellowship, those eager for serious study, those who would use it as a
base for study of social concerns and a launching place for action,
and those whose interests encompass two or more of these per-

5. Boardman W. Kathan has written an unusually perceptive critical
historical account of the growth and change in the Sunday school, "The
Sunday School Revisited," *Religious Education* (January-February,
1980). The finest study of the Sunday school yet published is Thomas
Walter Laqueur's *Religion and Respectability, Sunday Schools and Working Class Culture, 1780-1850* (New Haven: Yale University Press, 1976).
Laqueur sees the Sunday school as an indigenous institution growing out
of and serving the working-class community, and combining aspects of
secular education, the new attitude toward children, and the renewal of
evangelical Christianity. He makes a convincing case for the independent
and lay character of the movement. See also Gerald E. Knoff's *The World
Sunday School Movement* (New York: Seabury Press, 1979).

spectives. Whether or not the Sunday school can be a suitable
vehicle for all of these may be open to question. If it is not, then
the activities through which the church fosters these interests
may maintain a linked relationship with the Sunday school, within a more broadly defined program of Christian education. In
other words, the Sunday school may give rise to such related
activities, and they in turn may feed back into it. The Sunday
school thus serves as a hub for activities that meet more specific
needs and that offer more challenging educational opportunities.

Additional possibilities within and beyond the Sunday school
are suggested by Hartman's drawing implications for teaching
and learning styles and groupings from the research data. Multiple audiences and divergent expectations as to theological orientation and teaching style call for several different options in the
congregation. Criteria such as teaching style, subject matter, and
group life expectations, as well as age and experience, are taken
into consideration in organizing the program. Recruitment and
training of teachers and leaders honors a wide variety of teaching
styles.

Recognizing that lay people are generally more positive about
the Sunday school than are professionals, Locke Bowman is constructive and specific about the ingredients of strong educational
effort and better schools: a firm sense of purpose, appropriate
organizational structures for maintaining order and communication both at the local level and at the national and regional levels,
vision and continuity in adequate teacher training, good teaching
materials, and adequate facilities.

Bowman notes significant advances that are taking place: more
and better professional leadership, well-equipped resource centers available to churches, increased curriculum choice coupled
with wiser and more effective local planning, and a new volunteer
situation that calls for richer and more specific teacher training.
Promising innovations, in his judgment, are not lacking: clarity
and variety of lesson planning format, variety in media, more
comprehensive and relevant sets of electives for adults, increase
in the use of learning centers, and a tendency toward orienting
cycles of teaching and learning to the common lectionary.

Thus, Bowman "favors renewal of the Sunday school, believing
that such a strategy has the best chance of helping the churches
of our time to offer a strong and much-needed ministry of teaching for the people of God." But renewal, in his opinion, hinges on
six factors that add up to taking the Sunday school more seriously:

—The positive leadership that clergy and professional Christian educators take, locally and nationally, to secure the structures of Christian education and to empower the laity.

—Sharing with the laity what is now known about teaching and learning, and in particular about growth and development, and putting this knowledge to work in curriculum and in teaching and learning methods.

—Forthright and thorough use of biblical and theological scholarship at every level, from national planning to the local classroom.

—Accepting the "school" in a positive sense, and making it work well through smooth and effective administration.

—Rebuilding widespread regional and national support structures, with adequate and resourceful personnel, so that local decision-making responsibilities may be fulfilled wisely and in a coordinated way.

—Throughout the system, from local learners to national leaders, a prayerful sense of openness to the leading of the Spirit.

The Sunday school as a successful popular movement is most evident at present in evangelical circles, where it is growing rather than dwindling. Robert J. Dean sees a balanced emphasis on outreach, Bible study, and fellowship as a key to its continuing vitality. Not blinking at its weaknesses, nor at its inner tensions, he sees it as a prime vehicle for the transmission and development of values. Like Seymour, he affirms the Sunday school as a popular movement with essential but limited aims, asking lay teachers to become better trained, but not asking them to provide educational opportunities beyond their capacities. He values the Sunday school as "a time for mutual sharing of faith and love within the context of Bible study," complemented by other Christian education experiences. The Sunday school emerges again in a larger context, the necessary hub of a varied and rich Christian education program.[6]

In the black churches, as Mary Love makes vividly clear, the Sunday school has special significance and functions. Uprooted and oppressed, and lacking essential resources and services, black Christians used, and continue to use, the Sunday school as a major educational institution. In a "do it yourself" situation

6. Dean's analysis of the evangelical Sunday School is further documented by G. Temp Sparkman, "The Southern Baptist Sunday School," *Religious Education* (January-February, 1980), and by Clifford V. Anderson, "The Practice of Evangelical Christian Education Since World War II," in *Changing Patterns of Religious Education*, ed. Marvin J. Taylor (Nashville: Abingdon Press, 1984).

(which has been generally both a strength and a weakness of the Sunday school), black talent has been developed, leadership has been enlisted and trained, and people with teaching ability have emerged. Not the least of its uses has been its encouragement and training of persons who have entered the public arena prophetically.

In the process, the black Sunday school has developed a special character—with a vigor, spirit, and variety—that gives a different flavor to the standard emphases on Bible study, outreach, and fellowship.[7] Thus Love is able to point to its creativity and to its ability to improvise. Quite in character, and quite promising, is her call for attention to "a curriculum that orchestrates left and right brain development."

The black Sunday school's dependence on existing patterns, however, leaves it with a limited tradition in curriculum, a tradition in which good black images are absent. It also results in a marked need for concentrated teacher training and enrichment; a lack of congregational, parental, and pastoral support; and a failure to develop Christian education significantly as a professional field.

The call for indigenous black curriculum, only hinted at in the lack of black images in traditionally "white" curriculum patterns and resources, is shared by other minorities in the United States and abroad. Attempts have been made to provide resources, mostly developed from within the groups themselves, that reflect and embody the values and ways of American Indians, Appalachians, Hispanics, Asian-Americans, and the Caribbean. There is no question but that Sunday school renewal today requires a special attention to the culture, character, and needs of every particular people that it serves.[8]

7. James D. Tyms' *The Rise of Religious Education Among Negro Baptists* (Washington, D.C.: University Press of America, 1979) is useful as a reference work in the history of black religious education. Unfortunately, it only reflects the interests and concerns of the 1940s (when the study originated), brought up-to-date to the early 1960s. Yet the emphasis is on the development of an indigenous church and its adaptation of the Sunday school to meet its educational needs.

8. My own interest in culture-specific curriculum began in the late 1930s with a project in which an indigenous curriculum for weekday religious education among the Navajo Indians was constructed. Later, I participated at various points in helping to develop and introduce the curriculum of the Caribbean Conference of Churches, "Fashion Me a People." More recently, I have co-edited with Henrietta T. Wilkinson

Correspondingly, Love analyzes the need to adjust the Sunday school's notion of and program for the family to the realities of the situation. Mentioning singles, young adults, and step-families, she draws attention to the fact that the present-day family that the Sunday school seeks to serve, and that it seeks to enlist integrally in the process of Christian education, is no longer stereotypical, but comes in many configurations, some of which are quite new and critically challenging. Alfred W. Hanner, in his discussion of the Sunday school in the armed forces, picks up this same issue by citing responsibility for families under special stress—in this case, the family where one member is suddenly on alert or deployment, and the family that is required to be unusually mobile and to live under abnormal and rather isolated conditions. Among other things, this heightens awareness of the need for the Sunday school, as an aspect of its renewal, so to define its ministry that it incorporates significant pastoral functions.

Basically, Hanner's picture of the Sunday school in the armed forces shows how usefully it may be adapted to a very special situation. With all its problems—red tape, staff relations, a constantly shifting clientele, institutional dependence, and a potential for serious moral conflict—it is employed to serve a large, pluralistic constituency of families and single persons with a diversified and unusual professional staff, a markedly multidenominational curriculum, significant parental involvement, a special sensitivity to learners' needs, a conscious pastoral dimension, and a willingness to deal with hard ethical issues occasioned by the juxtaposition of the church and the military.

Other Voices

A great deal of careful attention has been given over the last ten years to analysis of the Sunday school and prescription for its future health. In part this has been occasioned by the fact that its two hundredth anniversary took place during this period, but much of it would have come in the normal course of events as concerned persons worked on its renewal.

Beautiful Upon the Mountains, A Handbook for Church Education in Appalachia (Memphis: Board of Christian Education of the Cumberland Presbyterian Church, 1984). The handbook proposed three models, indigenous to Applachian culture and values, supplementary to the Sunday school. Not incidentally, it would never have come into existence without the work of John Spangler and Harold Davis.

Wesley R. Willis,[9] whose fundamental plea is for a biblically based Sunday school, attributes decline to a too exclusively experience-centered curriculum and to a heavy-handed centralization of authority and denominational control. His stress is on the local church that is biblically alive, since life is given to the church that adheres to biblical guidelines, and since the Sunday school finds its meaning as a basic aspect of the church's life and work. The heart of a biblical theology, as he sees it, is to "make disciples: to help persons accept Christ and then mature in their Christian walk." It is within such a biblical theology that the Sunday school is to operate.

Willis maintains that Sunday school ministries, then, are to be designed to build biblical qualities and accomplish biblical tasks for the church. Three guidelines follow:

—Emphasize the Bible, study biblical doctrine, and communicate effectively.
—Demand teachers who are committed to sharing themselves personally with their students in the context of the life of the church.
—Insist that lay persons have an essential role.

John H. Westerhoff III has been one of the most persistent and fruitful of the critics of Christian education. The schooling model has been one of his main targets. Thus, the Sunday school has been singled out for special criticism. So negative has he been, that in a 1975 article,[10] he confesses that when asked to deal with the topic of the Sunday school's future, his first thought was, "That will be easy, there isn't any." Reflecting deliberately and in context, however, it became his judgment that "the Sunday school can provide *one* context for church education, an environment where people can strive to be Christian together as they become conscious of their identity as a tradition-bearing community of faith." He develops specific examples of what he calls "the new-old school," insisting that its programs "need to aid us in thinking, feeling, and acting socially."

9. Wesley R. Willis, *200 Years—And Still Counting: Past, Present, and Future of the Sunday School* (Wheaton, Ill.: Victor Books, 1979), pp. 75-132.

10. John H. Westerhoff III, "A Future for the Sunday School," *The Duke Divinity School Review* (Fall, 1975). Two other articles in the same issue provide careful assessments of the Sunday school and its possibilities. They are Sara Little's "A Badly Organized Miracle," and Richard Murray's "Myths of the Modern Sunday School."

In his 1983 book, *Building God's People in a Materialistic Society*,[11] Westerhoff develops his views more systematically, and in a more thoroughly theological way, than previously. His focus is practical theology, and within that, "catechesis," which aims

> to establish ways to transmit, sustain, and deepen a Christian perception of life and our lives; to aid us to live individually and corporately in a consciously responsive relationship to God; and to enable us to acknowledge and actualize our human potential for perfected personal and communal life.

Mere instruction cannot achieve such aims. Neither can an education that "tends to perceive the learner as one who associates with others and forms institutions." Westerhoff prefers a term like "socialization," which he claims "tends to perceive the learner as a communal being whose identity and growth can only be understood in terms of life in a community that shares a common memory, vision, authority, rituals, and familylike life together." That community, to serve at all adequately, is "a converted, disciplined body" that serves as an "agent of God's work in the world." Catechesis, then, is a process that cannot be satisfied with less than the transformation of knowledge into a shared living faith.

Furthermore, catechesis touches every dimension of the church's life, work, and witness. It is in profound interplay with the community at worship (the liturgical dimension), the acting community (the moral dimension), the praying community (the spiritual dimension), and the caring community (the pastoral dimension), as it focuses on life in a learning community.

One of Westerhoff's most appealing concepts in the recent past has been his "four stages of faith," which he has now transformed into "three pathways or trails to God," of which he says, "None is superior to the others. While the first path is a natural place to begin . . . each may be traveled at any time, in any order." The first is a slow, easy path [in which] "the community focuses its concern on the passing on of its story and thereby framing its identity and that of its people." On the second path, as persons journey along together, they are "encouraged to establish a sense of their independence and are urged to explore their own way, sharing their discoveries (on the meaning of community, of trust, and of intimacy) with the community." The third way "encourages persons to move back and forth between the two previous

11. John H. Westerhoff III, *Building God's People in a Materialistic Society* (New York: Seabury Press, 1983), pp. 8-9, 16, 44-45, 50-52.

ways and thereby create a new way. [They are] aided to discern what they should live for and give their life to, and they are provided opportunity to assume responsibility for community life."

A total program of Christian education in a congregation provides for all three ways, recognizing the presence, validity, and power of both formal and informal elements. A unified and integrated program seeks for the most fruitful interaction among the three ways. In my judgment (although I am sure that Westerhoff would not go quite this far), the Sunday school is most appropriately concerned with the first, but may also provide various opportunities for the others, even though they are primarily implemented elsewhere. Focus (on the first) and interaction (of all three) is the necessary business of the Sunday school.

Howard Grimes, looking to the future, suggests four emphases:[12]

—A more careful planning of the life of the congregation, including its teaching ministry, so that structures and approaches are chosen with greater deliberation, and the old is not discarded for the sake of what might turn out to be nothing more than a gimmick.
—A recovery of the three-part function of instruction, caring, and evangelism, and a recovery of mass appeal.
—A recognition of three kinds of teaching: the mass movement of the Sunday school, the socialization that occurs through the entire life of the congregation, and special in-depth teaching of content for a minority.
—A major thrust toward the family, with clear recognition of the changes that have taken place in the modern family.

John C. Purdy, from the viewpoint of the seasoned curriculum expert, sees signs of four significant trends:[13]

—Change will be forced upon us by improved technology (more than by theory).
—The church will press education for greater integration into the life of the congregation.
—Tradition will prove to have surprising vitality.

12. Howard Grimes, "Changing Patterns of Religious Education Practice in Protestant Churches Since World War II," in *Changing Patterns of Religious Education*, ed. Marvin J. Taylor (Nashville: Abingdon Press, 1984).
13. John C. Purdy, "Signs of Things to Come," *The Association of Presbyterian Church Educators Advocate* (November, 1984), pp. 1-2.

—Curriculum development will continue along lines laid down by previous efforts.

The pastoral possibilities of the Sunday school have been most thoroughly explored by Billie Davis.[14] She makes excellent use of both the behavioral sciences and the resources of faith to enable the ministries of the church (particularly the teaching ministry through the Sunday school) to deal sensitively and effectively with a variety of life crises—single parenting and blending families (resulting from remarriage); adolescence; midlife; illness, dying, death, and grief; work, unemployment, and money; and identity. The pastoral dimension is also emphasized by Merton Strommen.[15] He advocates a family model, one that reflects and deals with both family values and family problems and tensions, and he shares the programs for ministry to people in stress that have developed from his research. While he uses "Sunday school" in a broader sense than is customary, his suggestions are applicable to the Sunday school as it is ordinarily more strictly defined.

Jack Seymour, Robert T. O'Gorman, and Charles R. Foster challenge church education to have a public function.[16] Actually, they challenge today's church to recapture its historic function of helping to shape the public mind, but in contemporary terms. The church today tends to focus its energies upon itself, thus diminishing its contribution to the forming of public life. However:

> Faith communities, including Christian churches, are the primary agencies for the mediation of a religious perspective on all matters affecting our personal and corporate welfare. That contribution is dependent upon the presence in the public of a people whose visions, meanings, and skills have been given content and refined by participation in faith communities that seek to be responsive both to their heritage and to the agenda of the world.

The central dynamic is imagination. Religious education that takes on the task of infusing the public imagination with the religious, gives promise of providing the public with "that certain

14. Billie Davis, *Teaching to Meet Crisis Needs* (Springfield, Mo.: Gospel Publishing House, 1984).

15. Merton Strommen, "The Future of the Sunday School: A Researcher's Reflections," *Religious Education* (Summer, 1983).

16. Jack Seymour, Robert T. O'Gorman, and Charles R. Foster, *The Church in the Education of the Public* (Nashville: Abingdon Press, 1984), pp. 135-136, 151, 153.

power of imagination that is capable of self and society recreation. It is only when our self images and social images are reformed that we then change our beliefs, values, and judgments
about the meaning of our life together, our public being, and thus
change our actions."

A corollary is that church education "needs to make connections with other public-minded agencies of the community, which,
in spite of their potential differences, share a common commitment to shape the emerging *paideia* or vision of the common life."

Conditions of Renewal

Clearly, among the "futurizers" who have been consulted on the
matter of renewal, among the contributors to this book, and
among the other voices we have heard, there has been no will to
do away with the Sunday school. Rather, they see it as a useful
instrument, performing certain key functions for Christian education.

There are, however, critics who see the Sunday school as an
encumbrance with no good in it—tired and bored bureaucrats, an
occasional theorist, and educators whose expectations and standards leave no place for what they consider to be a trivial and
nonprofessional enterprise. There are some who look on the Sunday school as a totally detestable enterprise, of which the church
should rid itself. There is some justification for this in light of its
"tendency to survive by avoiding controversy: hesitancy on race
relations, and on the Bible and biblical criticism"; [17] blatant "mor-
alism" in some of its curriculum materials; its resort to the razzle-
dazzle of contests, stunts, and extrinsic reward systems to boost
membership and attendance; and its all too often offering of
"cheap grace" through a distorted and oversimplified gospel.

Others have sought to root out such abuses and are in general
agreement that the Sunday school is here to stay for the foresee-
able future, that it has values that are worth conserving, and that
it is worth the effort to try to make it live up to its potential.

But how is renewal to be understood? Even as the secret of
church union is to find and realize the unity that Christ has
already given, so the secret of renewal of the church or any of the

17. Robert W. Lynn and Elliott Wright, *The Big Little School, 200 Years
of the Sunday School,* 2nd. ed. rev. (Birmingham and Nashville: Religious
Education Press and Abingdon Press, 1980), pp. 158-159.

aspects of the church's work is to rediscover what God in Christ intends for it, to be prepared for new things as that rediscovery comes clear, to reconstruct the enterprise faithfully, and to pursue its revitalizing purposes with commitment, joy, and wisdom.

The basis for the renewal of the Sunday school (within the larger context of Christian education) is Christ's gift of teaching, which with his other gifts constitute ministry, "building up the body of Christ, until we all attain to the unity of the faith and of the knowledge of the Son of God, to maturity, to the measure of the stature of the fullness of Christ." (Ephesians 4:12-13.) The writer of the epistle is speaking to the church of underlying conditions for renewal when he says, "Be renewed in the spirit of your minds, and put on the new nature, created after the nature of God in true righteousness and holiness." (Ephesians 4:23.)

Renewal begins when we look to Christ and to his body, the church, and acknowledge that we are missing the mark. When the Sunday school is characterized by abuses like those cited above, such sin calls for repentance and new direction.

More often, missing the mark is a more subtle matter of failure to set appropriate aims; failure to plan adequately and faithfully; failure to make the necessary provisions for time, curriculum, supplementary resources, leadership, and equipment; and failure to make the enterprise a serious, gripping, and absorbing one for those who participate in it. There is a missing of the mark, as well, in domesticating the Sunday school to the easy constituency of the church's own members and their children, not reaching out to the larger community. Repentance for the sins of being lackadaisical, unplanned, unprepared, and comfortably at ease in the midst of need—of not being seriously biblical, theological, educational, or evangelistic—is called for.

There is a spurious renewal to be avoided, a "renewal" that is effected when we are worried about or lured by the wrong things. C. Ellis Nelson, in a challenge to representatives of two educational departments about to merge in the National Council of Churches, warned them "not to look for what is *new,* but for what is *true.*"[18]

Genuine renewal comes to the Sunday school as its character and responsibility are defined in the process of rediscovery, as it knows and draws on the sources of its power, as it focuses on

18. Referred to by J. Blaine Fister in his introduction to Lynn and Wright, p. 11.

meeting imperative needs, and as it is realistic about the resources that it needs to accomplish its tasks.

What is the character and responsibility of the Sunday school?
Working from the specific to the general, the Sunday school is an
aspect of Christian education, which in turn partakes of religious
education. Working back from the general to the specific, what is
the special character and the specific responsibility of the Sunday school?

Richard F. Tombaugh, of The Education Center, St. Louis, is not
optimistic about our defining our terms in any agreed way:

> I am beginning to wonder whether the term "religious educa-
> tion" has *any* commonly agreed upon meaning. To some it
> means learning about people, places, and ideas in the Bible. To
> others it means learning to act in certain approved ways. To
> others it means exploring one's feelings about God, or becoming
> more pious, or growing in awareness about the presence of God.
>
> [We use the term] to describe a process of discovery of self-in-
> relations. The process is "religious" in the sense that it address-
> es fundamental questions that have an ultimate meaning. The
> process is educational because it seeks to lead a person out from
> the self. This journey to find meaning and self-understanding is
> basically a search for personal wholeness.[19]

The process thus lends itself to diverse interpretations. There
are those who see religious education not as self-realization in the
search for meaning and value, but as vocational training for discipleship and mission, or as instruction (biblical, theological, and
ethical), or as socialization or enculturation in the family and the
community of faith, or as the gaining of certain methodological
skills (primarily hermeneutical and theological).

But precision of definition is not entirely a lost cause. Tombaugh's use of "religious education" is quite proper, for religion is
the search for, and devotion to, meaning and value. It is "the
ability to see all life as making sense," and as such is "alive and
well."

> Scientific rationalism has brought us war, famine, pollution,
> hopelessness, and normlessness. We cannot accept this as the
> real world. We must hold fast to visions and utopias that au-

19. Richard F. Tombaugh, "Process and Spiritual Development," *In Process* (St. Louis: The Educational Center, March, 1985).

thentic religion offers us, not out of cold, hard logic, but because "the religious soul has to leap over the abyss, toward the evidence of feelings, of the voice of love, of the suggestions of hope."[20]

Religious education, in this sense, is a necessary aspect of general education, for education itself does not reach the point of fulfillment without discrimination of meaning and value in experience and studies, and without such commitment to that meaning and value that life direction is indicated and appropriate behavior and action undertaken.[21] Religious education is also integral to Christian education, in that Christian meaning and value lend themselves in special ways to the dynamics of religion and education. While religious education consists in teaching and learning as modes and means of commitment to value, Christian education consists in teaching and learning as modes and means of response to revelation.

There are intriguing current explorations of what Christian education in this sense is and does. Mary Elizabeth Moore's "traditioning" is a possibility that "maximizes persons' connectedness with the past so that transformations taking place in their life will be rooted and will be all the richer," at the same time that it "maximizes persons' changing so that their connectedness with the past will help them live in the changing world and with God's call forward."[22]

Lois E. LeBar emphasizes a wholistic approach to the learner (with particular attention to affective needs), fundamental nurture in faith, the centrality of Christology, the integrity of worship and education, and the problems of influencing Christian practice.[23]

Thomas H. Groome's proposal is for "shared Christian praxis,"

20. Nathan R. Kollar, reviewing Rubem Alves, *What Is Religion?* (Maryknoll, N.Y.: Orbis Books, 1984) in *Books and Religion* (January-February, 1985).

21. See, for instance, Mortimer J. Adler, *The Paideia Proposal, An Educational Manifesto* (New York: Macmillan, 1982) and David Arthur Bickimer, *Christ the Placenta* (Birmingham, Ala.: Religious Education Press, 1983).

22. Mary Elizabeth Moore, *Education for Continuity and Change, A New Model for Christian Religious Education* (Nashville: Abingdon Press, 1983).

23. Lois E. LeBar, *Education That Is Christian* (Old Tappan, N.J.: Fleming H. Revell Company, 1981).

a process that puts our personal and collective story and vision into critical interplay with the Christian Story and Vision.[24]

Lawrence O. Richards maintains that the institutions for Christian nurture (the home, the church, and the school) must be rooted in a theology of integral participation in the life and worship of the Christian community and in Piagetian developmental understandings.[25]

Craig Dykstra values "vision" over standard predictions in relation to character, interprets revelation as an experience of the imagination, and sees Christian education as part of the experience of the repenting, praying, and serving community (a context of interpersonal and imagistic mutuality, established and sustained by Christ whom it follows and in whom it lives).[26]

Shirley Heckman, maintaining a good balance between educating into the community and educating for freedom, creativity, and responsibility, develops what it means to be an educating community, and comes as close as anyone today to "a whole Christian nurture."[27]

Such ferment of thought does not lend itself easily to reduction to *a* point of view. Nor should it. Renewal requires the creativity and spontaneity evidenced in these explorations. It also requires critical and fruitful give-and-take on them, live experiments with them, and widespread sharing of the results.

Within the context of Christian education, the renewing Sunday school serves indispensable functions. More significantly, it provides an entry point for new persons (be they children, youth, or adults) where they are oriented to the Bible and to the Christian life; a hub from which other more intensive and probing experiences of study, action, and exploration of the Christian faith and life stem, keeping them related to one another through the provision of a church-wide forum; and a continuous source of new interests, concerns, and insights.

The renewing Sunday school focuses the learning function of

24. Thomas H. Groome, *Christian Religious Education* (San Francisco: Harper & Row, 1980).

25. Lawrence O. Richards, *A Theology of Christian Education* (Grand Rapids, Mich.: Zondervan, 1975) and *A Theology of Children's Ministry* (Grand Rapids, Mich.: Zondervan, 1983).

26. Craig Dykstra, *Vision and Character* (New York: Paulist Press, 1981).

27. Shirley J. Heckman, *On the Wings of a Butterfly, A Guide to Total Christian Education* (Elgin, Ill.: Brethren Press, 1981).

the church, helps to clarify and direct the learner's purposes, and assists the leader to develop and maintain self-identity as a teacher. It is a symbol of the interdependence of ministries, and thus of the ecology of the church and Christian education as a unifying, dynamic system. It may spark anything that has to do with learning in the church, from individualized study plans to training in the skills of Christian social action.

There are, of course, areas of responsibility that need further development. To cite a few:

—The specific relations of Christian learning in the Sunday school to the other educational functions of the church, to the role and functions of the Christian school, and to learning in other contexts (e.g., public schools, colleges and universities, seminaries, and community institutions and agencies, as well as the home and neighborhood).[28]

—The almost totally neglected role of the arts and aesthetic experience in the dynamics of Christian nurture, and how they may serve to enrich the exploratory and integrative functions of the Sunday school.[29]

—The functions of the Sunday school in pastoral care.

—The interplay of the Sunday school and social ministry (which may be seen as a major factor in congregational revitalization).[30]

—The rootage of the Sunday school in and enriched and deepened spiritual life.[31]

28. See, for instance, David M. Evans, *The Pastor in a Teaching Church* (Valley Forge, Pa.: Judson Press, 1983), Richard C. McMillan, *Religion in the Public Schools* (Macon, Ga.: Mercer University Press, 1984), and Ronald P. Chadwick, *Teaching and Learning, An Integrated Approach to Christian Education* (Old Tappan, N.J.: Fleming H. Revell Company, 1982).

29. See Nicholas Wolterstorff, *Art in Action* (Grand Rapids, Mich.: Eerdmanns, 1980). Wolterstorff says, "Works of art are objects and instruments of action. They are all inextricably embedded in the fabric of human intention. They are objects and instruments of action whereby we carry out our intentions with respect to our world, our fellows, ourselves, and our gods." Some rather specific clues for Christian education are found in the final section.

30. See Dieter T. Hessel, *Social Ministry* (Philadelphia: Westminster Press, 1982).

31. See Iris V. Cully, *Education for Spiritual Growth* (San Francisco: Harper & Row, 1984).

The renewal process is one in which such concerns are worked through with the character of the Sunday school clearly in mind, and in which diversity of thought about it and vision for it are shared toward common purpose and action.

The renewing Sunday school knows and draws upon its sources. Chief among these sources is the Bible, through which its knows and responds to the Word of God and comes to know and follow the living Word, Jesus Christ.[32] Renewal comes as the Sunday school knows itself as belonging to God in Christ, as it listens to and speaks the Word, and as, guided by the Holy Spirit, it responds in prayer, worship, and faithful action.

It is imperative that the church's educational ministry think and plan theologically in order that its biblical roots may feed everything that it does. As it seeks to understand and engage in learning, it needs a theology of learning.[33] As it probes the dynamics of human growth in faith, it needs a theology of faith development.[34] As it prepares for service and social responsibility, it needs a theology of Christian social action.[35] As it enlists and trains teachers and leaders, it needs a theology of volunteer service as Christian calling.

The renewing Sunday school focuses on imperative needs. The traditional three are still central—the need for biblical faith, the need for the fellowship of the community of faith, and the need for evangelistic thrust. For decades, the Sunday school has also

32. The current resources on the Bible and Bible study provide rich and varied possibilities. Some of the most thorough and stimulating are David L. Barr and Nicholas Piediscalzi, eds., *The Bible in American Education* (Philadelphia: Fortress Press, 1982), Lucien E. Coleman, Jr., *How to Teach the Bible* (Nashville: Broadman Press, 1979), HansRuedi Weber, *Experiments with Bible Study* (Geneva: World Council of Churches, 1981), Walter Wink, *Transforming Bible Study, A Leader's Guide* (Nashville: Abingdon Press, 1980), and Robin Maas, *Church Bible Study Handbook* (Nashville: Abingdon Press, 1982).

33. See Donald B. Rogers, *In Praise of Learning* (Nashville: Abingdon Press, 1980).

34. See, in particular, James W. Fowler, *Stages of Faith, The Psychology of Human Development and the Quest for Meaning* (San Francisco: Harper & Row, 1981). See also, Edward Robinson, *The Original Vision, A Study of the Religious Experience of Childhood* (New York: Seabury Press, 1983), and other theologically oriented treatments of faith development like Neill Q.Hamilton's *Maturing in the Christian Life* (Philadelphia: Geneva Press, 1984) and Bruce P. Powers' *Growing Faith* (Nashville: Broadman Press, 1982).

35. See Hessel, *Social Ministry.*

served as a seedbed for discipleship, that long-term growth in faithfulness through which the Christian life deepens, concerns broaden, and Christian action becomes more effective. There is a new urgency in the need for spiritual growth (in light of rampant self-centeredness and materialism) and of personal and social morality (in light of decay in moral standards). Today the Sunday school is also charged with dealing specifically with changing needs at home and abroad—stewardship of the created world, the scourge of world hunger, liberation of the oppressed, minority and human rights, the rise of religious and political tyranny in the form of ideologies, and the need for peace and deliverance from terrorist and the nuclear threat. The Sunday school shares in the church's present calling, strikingly put in a recent statement by the Presbyterian Church (U.S.A.):

We are called to say "no" to the powers that threaten to destroy God's people.

We are called to identify with the less powerful in the world.

We are called to learn from Christians of other cultures.

We are called to repent of our individual selfishness and greed, and of our conscious or unconscious complicity in corporate sinfulness.

We are called to become aware of the crushing effects of militarism, economic imperialism, and systemic racism.[36]

While the Sunday school is not the context for dealing with or solving such problems in depth, it *is* the context in which the greatest number of people may be exposed to them and begin the deal with them in a responsible way. The Sunday school that ignores or avoids such imperatives is irrelevant and is not likely to experience significant renewal. The Sunday school that takes them seriously opens itself to the possibility of a new vitality because it is clearly confronting serious matters.

The renewing Sunday school is realistic about the resources it needs to accomplish its task. It knows that it needs people, both leaders and participants, and that it needs to be alert to the many more persons and groups that it may serve and from whom it needs to gain acceptance.[37] It has not been spectacularly success-

36. *Presbyterian Outlook*, April 1, 1985, p. 9.

37. See Charles Arn, Donald McGavran, and Win Arn, *Growth, A New Vision for the Sunday School* (Pasadena: Church Growth Press, 1980) and John T. Sisemore, *Church Growth Through the Sunday School* (Nashville: Broadman Press, 1983).

ful in its approach to families, but new insight is available.[38] And there are challenging areas of service opening up to such groups as the handicapped.[39]

Leaders and teachers, seeing their work as a calling, deserve more thorough and effective approaches to recruitment and training. The renewing Sunday school is not staffed by people who are serving reluctantly, but by people who have been carefully chosen and equipped, and who have had a hand and voice in determining the roles in which they may best serve and the kinds of help— both pre-service and in-service—that they most need. They have immediate access to supervisory help, which requires that professional Christian educators be available to them in the persons of ministers, directors of Christian education, and specialized consultants.

> The new structures of the church and Sunday school will demand more of the professional Christian educator, not less. Who should be better equipped or more competent to aid the congregation in study, diagnosis, goal-setting, planning, designing, testing, evaluating, resourcing, leader development? . . . The need is for persons with biblical and theological knowledge, first, and then a knowledge of planning, leading, resourcing for the total life of the congregation.[40]

Persons of this kind are in a position to provide a variety of kinds of guidance: a clinical approach, a standard leadership curriculum, and personal supervision.

In renewal, curricula are not only more adequate in scope and in approach, and richer and more varied in method, but also more localized and specific. Materials are less stereotyped and more adaptable to local needs and to cultural and ethnic particularities. We may not be far from the time when the computer makes it possible for teachers and learners to build into their

38. For instance, Charles M. Sell's *Family Ministry* (Grand Rapids, Mich.: Zondervan, 1981) and Ross T. Bender's *Christians in Families* (Scottdale, Pa.: Herald Press, 1982).

39. See, for instance, the definitive reference work by Gerald Oosterveen and Bruce L. Cook, *Serving Mentally Impaired People, A Resource Guide for Pastors and Church Workers* (Elgin, Ill.: David C. Cook Foundation, 1983).

40. R. Harold Hipps, "Confrontation: Sunday School," *The Duke Divinity School Review* (Fall, 1975), p. 149.

educational experience both completely current information and their own concerns and questions.

The computer may also facilitate good communication throughout the system, making it possible for national and regional leaders and curriculum planners to hear what local people are saying and asking for, and at the same time making it possible for local people to get immediate guidance, thus helping to heal the rift between the distant leader and the local worker.

The Sunday school, so far as space, time, equipment, and money are concerned, has been a pretty marginal enterprise. Few churches are really adequately equipped at these points, while many still operate on a "hear the pennies dropping" basis. Renewal today does not call for affluence, but it does call for adequacy of undergirding.

The idea of the "church school" has been around for a long time, and still has potential for Sunday school renewal if it is a multifaceted ministry, a service activity, and if it is not a substitute for other church activities—an imperialism.

One might predict that in the near future, if conditions of renewal are met, the church school will become increasingly diversified, with the Sunday school as its hub. The Sunday school's purpose as a popular, mass activity will be clarified. It will be seen to be basic, caring, and evangelistic. It will recognize and serve a variety of audiences. Around it will be grouped a wider variety of other more intensive activities for different groups and functions.

Its lay character will be intensified. Lay people will continue to provide the leadership, and will tend to regain control. Their sense of vocation will be more specific and they will be better trained and more permanent. They will have more of a sense of membership and ownership in an enterprise that extends beyond the parish and beyond the present.

There will be greatly increased access to adequate supervision, with augmented professional guidance at local, regional, and national levels. The minister will take on strategic roles as initiator, enabler, evaluator, and teacher. Planning, provision of resources and guidance, and evaluation will center in well-equipped committees of Christian education in the parish.

All of which will result in greater local initiative and control and call for augmented and improved resources from national boards and from publishers.

Chapter 11

CCD Renewal

JAMES MICHAEL LEE

Introduction

The Confraternity of Christian Doctrine (CCD), the American Catholic counterpart of the Protestant Sunday school, enjoys an unenviable position in the contemporary church in that it is often neither loved nor respected by a large number of Catholics. Advocates of Catholic schools have always tended to disdain the CCD as an inept and faint shadow of what they maintain is "the real thing," namely day-long Catholic schooling. More recently, proponents of the "local-faith-community-as-a-whole-is-the-best-religious-educator" point of view frequently regard the CCD as a tottering relic of what they consider to be a severely outmoded and grossly ineffective form of religious education, namely schooling.

Despite all the sneers and denunciations directed at it, and despite all the nihilistic wails that it be abolished, one existential fact of overriding importance remains: the CCD is here and in all likelihood will be around when all those persons who seek to ignore it or liquidate it are rotting in their graves. Consequently, a central imperative facing contemporary Catholic religious educators is not one of foolishly trying to bury the unburyable but rather one of creatively striving to bring the fullness of life into what most honest persons freely admit is a relatively ailing and enfeebled form of religious education.

Creative solutions to the currently ailing state of the CCD must be grounded in reality rather than in fantasy or in naiveté. It is pure fantasy to expect that in the near future Catholic parents en masse will suddenly begin to send all their offspring to Catholic schools. This fantasy is all the more unreal when we consider that

211

about half of all Catholic parents currently do not send their children either to Catholic schools or to the CCD.[1] It is gross naiveté to expect that the CCD will soon be dissolved so that the local faith community as a whole can move right in and provide optimal religious education for Catholic children when one realizes that the local faith community as a whole is itself in a somewhat religiously unhealthy state and hence not in a favored position to optimally educate anyone in religion. For example: less than half of the nation's Catholics attend Mass weekly; the staggeringly high divorce rate in the nation is roughly the same for Catholics as for other Americans; most of the local faith community has little time or inclination to religiously educate the young. Indeed, it would appear that by and large the local faith community is itself religiously undereducated.

Let me candidly and forthrightly state the central theme of this chapter: The CCD has not failed because it has never really been tried. The persistent undercurrent of this chapter, then, is an optimistic one, namely that the CCD can become imbued with that kind of quality and excellence to make it *a* truly effective force in religious education. In order for the CCD to attain its full potential, fundamental and far-reaching realignments must be made in its structure and operation. Such extensive and wide-ranging realignments necessitate a thoroughly honest assessment of the current situation in the CCD together with concrete, empirically verified suggestions on basically improving the present structure and operation. There can be genuine optimism only when the mechanisms and the realities upon which this optimism is founded are allowed to flow and encouraged to flourish.

Throughout this chapter I will blend a critique of the relatively unhappy present state of affairs in the CCD with concrete and growth-directed proposals on how the CCD can attain its full and rightful potential.

Nomenclature

A major obstacle facing the CCD is its name, the Confraternity of Christian Doctrine.

The name Confraternity of Christian Doctrine is unwieldy. It is a gagging mouthful to utter, a fact which explains why the name

---

1. This is the statistic given by Andrew D. Thompson in his chapter found earlier in this present volume.

is usually shortened to its initials CCD. As initials, CCD reveals nothing about the organization.

Another sizable difficulty with the name Confraternity of Christian Doctrine lies in the word doctrine. Rightly or wrongly, the word doctrine implies exclusive or near-exclusive emphasis on cognitive content. Yet the scope of the substantive content of religious instruction is, or at least ought to be, much wider than cognition. The proper content of religious instruction is holistic, namely subject matter which is not only cognitive but even more importantly affective and lifestyle.

Still another significant problem brought on by the nomenclature Confraternity of Christian Doctrine is that the very mention of the name conveys to most American Catholics an organization devoted entirely to the teaching of religion to children and youth attending public schools. Programs for older parishioners are usually given such names as adult religious education or the like. Thus the name CCD tends to be divisive in terms of what should be a unified and integral parish religious education effort.

I strongly recommend that the name Confraternity of Christian Doctrine be changed to a term which is more intelligible, more holistic, and more inclusive. The obvious choice for a new name is religious education program. *First*, this name is intelligible in that virtually all Catholics know, or can at least imagine, what the term religious education means. The name CCD is an obvious bafflement. The term religious education unambiguously describes what the program does, while the name CCD does not of itself indicate the functions of the program. *Second*, the term religious education is holistic since it intrinsically suggests that the substantive content of what is taught and learned necessarily includes cognitive, affective, and lifestyle content. *Third*, the term religious education is inclusive because it encompasses both school and nonschool programs. Religious education is essentially religious education regardless of whether it is conducted in a school or in a nonschool setting. An inclusive title, when accompanied by an inclusive structure which would place school and nonschool programs in a unified organic framework, could contribute significantly to the healing of the unfortunate rift and lack of integration between religious education programs conducted in Catholic schools and those conducted in CCD. An inclusive title, when accompanied by an inclusive structure, could also contribute to the closer coordination between what is now the parish's CCD program which is for children of school age and the parish's other nonschool religious education programs which are typically for adults.

Because of my commitment to the necessity of changing the name from CCD to religious education, I will not use the term CCD henceforward in this article. Instead, I will employ the term nonschool religious education to signify the CCD.

The Imperative of Empirical Research

A major problem plaguing nonschool religious education programs is the lamentable fact that there is a severe lack of adequate empirical research on the nature, composition, funding, and effectiveness of these programs throughout the country. About the only empirical research which does exist is an occasional demographic study dealing with the characteristics of parish directors of religious education programs,[2] one or another demographic study of the attendance rates of children and youth in parish nonschool religious education programs,[3] and a cluster of some small, interesting, but statistically nonrepresentative empirical investigations of one or another element in parish nonschool religious education programs. As Andrew Thompson pointedly observes in the opening pages of his chapter in the present volume, it is really impossible to make any definitive or even minimally confident statements about the quality and effectiveness of parish nonschool religious education programs because nationwide and statistically representative empirical studies of these programs have been practically nonexistent.

A solid base in empirical research is typically requisite for a truly successful religious education program.[4] Therefore, if these programs are to be what they can be, then careful, systematic, comprehensive, and ongoing empirical research of all the relevant

2. See, for example, Eugene F. Hemrick, *A National Inventory of Parish Catechetical Programs* (Washington, D.C.: United States Catholic Conference, 1978); Thomas P. Walters, *A National Profile of Professional Religious Education Coordinators/Directors* (Washington, D.C.: National Conference of Diocesan Directors of Religious Education, 1983).

3. See, for example, Eugene F. Hemrick and Andrew D. Thompson, *The Last Fifteen Years* (Washington, D.C.: United States Catholic Conference, 1982).

4. For an elaboration of this crucially important point, see James Michael Lee, "Toward a New Era: A Blueprint for Positive Action," in *The Religious Education We Need*, ed. James Michael Lee (Birmingham, Ala.: Religious Education Press, 1977), pp. 119-120.

variables in these programs must be undertaken on both the national and local levels.

The kind of empirical research I am advocating is two-tiered. The *first tier* consists in survey or nose-counting empirical research. This research is important because it provides data on critical surface phenomena such as the percentage and characteristics of persons of school age attending nonschool religious education programs, the achievement scores of students enrolled in school and nonschool religious education programs, the level of funding in school- and nonschool programs, the religious beliefs and attitudes of adults in nonschool religious education programs, and the like. The *second tier* consists in more sophisticated empirical research into the deeper and more influential variables operating in nonschool religious education programs such as the differential effects of various kinds of religion curricula, the relative success of assorted pedagogical procedures in the teaching of religion, the consequences of liturgical participation on the religious lifestyle of learners, and so forth.

To put Catholic nonschool religious education programs on a solid empirical base, a four-stage process will have to be initiated. This four-stage process is not aimed at improving empirical research itself, but rather at stimulating the willingness of religious education officials to sponsor the two-tiered empirical research I discussed in the previous paragraph.[5]

The first stage consists in breaking down that kind of residual or even active resistance to empirical research which many nonschool Catholic religious education officials seem to harbor. Much of this resistance seems to be consciously or unconsciously rooted in fear, namely the fear of discovering and making public the fact that there are numerous and serious defects in the current programs.

The second stage consists in developing the cognitive understanding that empirical research is helpful and indeed necessary for the significant improvement of nonschool religious education. Nonschool religious education officials can be shown specific examples of how empirical research has concretely helped the

5. The basis of this four-stage process is not arbitrary but is deliberately grounded in the holistic nature of persons and in the empirical research about the way persons actually do change. The first stage is aimed at eliminating negative blocks to learning (change). The second, third, and fourth stages center around cognitive activities, affective activities, and lifestyle activities respectively.

church resolve various problems besetting it, such as financing
Catholic schools, ascertaining the religious outcomes of children
in Catholic schools, assessing attitudes of parishoners, and so
forth. These officials can also be shown the historical account of
how John Paul II energized empirical research on American seminary education in the mid-1980s.

The third stage consists in fostering a positive affective "feel"
and appreciation for empirical research and its necessary role in
nonschool religious education. Nonschool religious educators
might be afforded the opportunity to talk at length on various
occasions with empirical researchers, perferably in a warm, inviting, and nonthreatening atmosphere such as over a dinner in a
cozy restaurant. Such friendly conversations should center on the
affective human dimensions of empirical research activity such
as the hopes for the church which the researchers feel can be
brought to reality through empirical studies. As part of the third
stage, the religious education officials might be invited to share
their own dreams for and frustrations with their own programs.
Such sharing will tend to produce an affective bonding between
them and the researchers and also provide a good connector with
the fourth stage.

The fourth stage consists in incorporating empirical research
activity directly and concretely into the professional lifework of
nonschool religious educators. These educators might be given the
chance to become personally involved in some ongoing research
study conducted by the National Catholic Educational Association, by the Center for Applied Research in the Apostolate
(CARA), by church-related universities, and the like. During the
course of this personal and concrete involvement in empirical
research, the religious education officials might be offered the
possibility of working directly with an empirical research to
study first-hand one of the dreams they have for their religious
education programs or one of the difficulties they have experienced with those programs.

Adequate Funding

As far as I am aware, there are no reliable national data on the
amount of money spent annually on parish nonschool religious
education programs. The lack of such basic data provides a key
insight into the fundamental problem, namely the pathetic lack of
genuine interest on the part of parochial and diocesan officials

for adequately funding their nonschool religious education programs. Genuine interest breeds basic knowledge of the facts. Genuine interest demands basic knowledge of the facts.

My own observations, combined with the observations of Catholic religious educators around the country with whom I have spoken, indicate that parish nonschool religious education programs are grossly underfunded.

Many years ago I read in some report or other that a certain midwestern diocese annually spent an average of $468 for each pupil enrolled in its Catholic schools and an average of 56¢ for each pupil enrolled in its nonschool religious education programs. If a parish spent only 56¢ a year per student, that is about all that it received from its investment.

There was a popular song some years ago which, referring to certain people playing the jukebox of life, contained these lyrics: "They put a nickel in and they want a dollar song." It is difficult to escape the impression that this is the same mentality which characterizes many parochial and diocesan officials with respect to funding parish nonschool religious education programs.

I am not implying that money will solve all the problems large and small which beset nonschool religious education programs. What I am suggesting is that it is exceedingly difficult and perhaps impossible to operate a quality religious education program over the long haul without adequate funding. Money does not comprise the total solution to the problems facing nonschool religious education programs, but it is a major and indispensable ingredient of the total solution. In short, adequate financial funding of nonschool religious education programs is necessary but not sufficient.

There are many empirical research investigations which conclude that the one factor most closely correlated with high quality education in formal settings is the annual amount of money which is spent on each pupil in average daily attendance.[6] In what has probably been the most carefully controlled empirical study ever conducted on this whole issue, the investigators discovered that the only tested school/structural characteristic that seems to significantly influence the disparities among states and regions in terms of the quality of public school education is the

6. These data come from empirical studies conducted since the 1940s on students in public schools. There is no reason to suppose that the correlations found in these studies fail to apply validly to education conducted in nonpublic settings.

amount of money actually spent on students in the schools.[7] This study concluded that independent of all other predictors of quality education in formal settings, the greater the student funding, the higher the quality of education. Unlike most other empirical studies on this general topic, this sophisticated investigation carefully controlled for such factors as the time students spent in academic courses, the degree of curricular tracking, presence of private schools in the area, percentage of students eligible to take special achievement tests, gender variables, racial variables, and family income. Of particular interest to religious educators are the study's data which suggest that median family income does not remain a significant predictor of quality education. Once public expenditures come into play by being factored in, the significance of median family income for quality education disappears.

Of the many crucial reasons for adequately funding nonschool religious education programs, three stand out as worthy of special mention. *First,* adequate funding is absolutely necessary for quality education. As has been previously demonstrated, the quality of an educational program tends to vary directly with the amount of funds spent on each learner in the program. *Second,* adequate funding is inextricably related to the local church's actual concrete commitment to religious education. Financial support does not just enflesh commitment; it is commitment. Jesus hit the nail right on the head when he stated that a person's heart lies where that individual's money is (Lk. 12:34). If the local church wishes to find out what its priorities in ministry really are, it only has to look at its budget allocations. *Third,* adequate funding is itself a form of education. The level of funding which the local church (parish and diocese) gives to nonschool religious education activities directly teaches parishoners the actual value which parish and diocesan officials place on nonschool religious education. Teaching is both verbal and nonverbal. If the local church teaches its members through sermons and bulletins and letters that nonschool religious education is important, and then nonverbally teaches these selfsame members through its budget allocations that nonschool religious education is not important, the members will believe the nonverbal teaching. The empirical

7. Brian Powell and Lala Carr Steelman, "Variations in State SAT Performance: Meaningful or Misleading?" in *Harvard Educational Review* LIV (November, 1984), p. 409. The researchers operationalized educational quality as concrete performance on the SAT.

research indicates quite clearly that when verbal and nonverbal messages contradict one another, people typically believe the nonverbal messages.[8]

Sufficient Time

Most parish nonschool religious education programs for children and youth last for an hour to an hour-and-a-half for a period of about thirty-five weeks. This typical time frame is sometimes supplemented with teaching-learning activities necessitating a greater amount of time per week, as, for example, open and closed retreats, sacramental preparation programs, apostolic service work in the community, and the like.

The time which children and youth typically spend per week and per year in parish nonschool religious education programs is considerably less than the amount of time spent by children and youth in religion classes conducted in Catholic elementary and secondary schools. In those Catholic schools in which religion does indeed permeate other areas of the curriculum, the amount of time spent in the study of religion by students in nonschool religious education compares even more unfavorably with the amount of time which Catholic school students devote to the study of religion.

It is impossible to exaggerate the detrimental influence of insufficient time on both the quality and the lifestyle impact of nonschool religious education programs. Indeed, the lack of sufficient time is one of the root causes of what most candid religious educators privately concede is the relative lack of success of nonschool religious education programs.

There is simply no way in which nonschool programs for children and youth can be made educationally adequate without sharply increasing the amount of time spent per week and per year in these programs. In my view, an effective parish nonschool religious program is one which actively involves children and youth in religious education activity from three to eight hours a week and continues in one form or another throughout the entire year.

I must underscore the fact that my proposal does not state that

8. For a summary of the pertinent empirical research on this point, see James Michael Lee, *The Content of Religious Instruction* (Birmingham, Ala.: Religious Education Press, 1985), pp. 381-383.

children and youth in nonschool religious education programs should spend three to eight hours per week in the classroom. Rather, my proposal states that these children and youth should spend from three to eight hours per week in religious education activity. Parish nonschool religious education ought not to confine itself solely to classroom settings.

At least two important arguments can be brought against my proposal.

The first argument is that children and youth will resist spending from three to eight hours per week in a nonschool religious education program. Consequently, many students will withdraw from the program, and the result will be a situation which is worse than that which currently prevails. My response to this argument is that the present grossly insufficient time afforded students in elementary and secondary nonschool religious education programs all but precludes the probability that these persons will learn much religion. I suspect that there is little or no significant difference between what students learn presently in the typical parish nonschool religious education program on the one hand and what public school students not enrolled in a program live/feel/know about religion on the other hand. In other words, the loss of students from the program will not be all that adverse when viewed from the perspective of the amount and quality of religious learnings they are missing by not being enrolled. Furthermore, those students who remain in the new and longer program will be given an adequate amount of time to acquire religious outcomes in that depth and breadth which is necessary for making a significant impact on their personal lives. It is educationally more sound and ecclesially more fecund to provide a quality high-impact program to a small number of persons than to offer a fundamentally ineffectual program to large numbers of students. Finally, we should underestimate neither the thirst for quality nor the generosity of young people. Once they find out that the new nonschool religious education program will be of such a quality and duration as to be truly worthwhile, they might not leave the time-extended program in such droves as some of their less idealistic elders predict. Indeed, an extended time frame might even attract some new students who had been searching for a high-quality religious education program but who had refrained from enrolling in the time-constricted program because the latter is perceived of low quality.

The second major objection which can be brought against extending the time which learners must spend in nonschool religious education programs is that few volunteer teachers can spare the drastically increased time and effort. The overwhelming number of teachers in Catholic nonschool religious education programs are volunteers. My response is that this objection is invalid because it is aimed at the inadequacy of the faculty rather than at the requirements of a satisfactory educational program. Indeed, this objection highlights, from yet another vantage point, the fact that no religious education program, school or nonschool, should be staffed by volunteers except when these persons serve in a decidedly ancillary capacity. A first-rate religious education program (and for that matter, even a minimally adequate program) requires that the faculty have plenty of time and plenty of professional preparation. As a general rule, volunteer teachers lack both. I shall deal at greater length with the issue of volunteer religious educators later in this chapter.

The Curriculum

In many instances the parish nonschool religious education curriculum is seriously deficient in at least seven respects: (1) its primary emphasis is often not on religion but is restricted to something less than religion, as for example, theology; (2) its breadth is usually not holistic but is limited to something less than holism, as for example, cognition; (3) its locus of enactment is not customarily the whole community but is usually confined almost exclusively to a classroom milieu; (4) its latitude is commonly not the whole parish but is constricted to something less than the whole parish; (5) its base is generally grounded in subjective impressions rather than in solid objective empirical data; (6) its textbooks frequently are not especially designed for the nonschool program but are written for quite different kinds of educational programs; (7) its sphere of involvement regularly fails to include adequate parent involvement.

In this short section I will deal very briefly with each of these major curricular shortcomings with special emphasis on remedying these deficiencies.

Breadth of the Curriculum

If the curriculum of the parish nonschool religious education program is to be effective, then it must do what its name indicates it does. By virtue of its name, the religious education curriculum is one in which religion is the over-arching and all-inclusive substantive content. Religion is a composite of many molar contents which are meshed into a basic lifestyle or pattern of living. Consequently, religion is not theology, not psychology, not human relations. Theology is simply one way of cognitively exploring religion. Theology is just one way of thinking about religion. Religion is holistically experiential, while theology is only cognitive. Indeed, theology is fundamentally areligious in nature because as a cognitive science it does not intrinsically necessitate lifestyle religious practice on the part of the person engaging in scientific inquiry of a theological nature. Theology is intrinsically targeted toward the improvement of cognitive thinking about God and religious phenomena. Religion, on the other hand, is intrinsically targeted toward the improvement of holistic religious living.

The primary emphasis of many parish nonschool religious education programs is currently not on religion but on theology. This state of affairs is most regrettable. Theological content can never of itself yield Christian living because the cognitive domain is of an essentially different order of reality than the lifestyle domain. If thinking about religion could of itself directly yield holistic Christian living, then all church members past and present would be very holy—something which appears not to be the case. If the parish nonschool program aims at educating persons in religion, and if this program strives to empower learners to live deep religious lives, then its curriculum must be wholly and fully religious rather than largely theological. Substituting theology or psychology for religion as the overall substantive content of the curriculum is to substitute rationalism for real pulsating life. Religion is life, and learners want life and improvements in their lives. Religion in its full dimension turns persons on, while theology in itself often turns younger learners off, especially adolescent learners. For most persons in the parish nonschool program, theology is important only to the extent to which it illumines religion.

Holism of the Curriculum

A truly successful parish nonschool religious education curriculum is one which is holistic, namely one which integrates into a unified whole all the fundamental domains of human functioning. A religious education curriculum which is holistic is one which interjoins the psychomotor domain, the cognitive domain, and the affective domain into one overarching domain, namely the lifestyle domain. A holistic curriculum is also one in which the pedagogical activities are congruent with the desired learning outcomes. Since the desired outcomes of a holistic curriculum are in the lifestyle domain, it follows that a holistic curriculum must feature teaching procedures which are as fully and as integratively lifestyle-grounded as possible. An especially effective pedagogical way of making both the teaching procedures and the goals of a religion curriculum as lifestyle soaked as possible is to transform the entire program into what I have described elsewhere as a laboratory for Christian living.[9]

As a general rule, religion curricula in parish nonschool programs are not holistic. These curricula frequently are centered on cognitive teaching procedures which in turn are targeted to cognitive learning outcomes. The result is that such religion curricula are not integrative and indeed are disintegrative. They fail to do what holistic curricula are supposed to do, namely to intrinsically integrate for the learners the basic domains of personal and religious existence. Interestingly enough, a carefully conducted empirical study discovered that both religious educators responsible for planning parish religion curricula and parents with offspring studying these curricula definitely preferred affective and lifestyle outcomes to cognitive goals as the desired end result of the religion curriculum.[10] There is no legitimate basis either in holistic curriculum theory or in the actual dynamics of human learning to assert that the task of the religion curriculum is primarily cognitive, leaving affective and lifestyle outcomes to the home and to the church's liturgy. Such a division of labor is not only unwarranted in religious education, but also seriously cripples the effectiveness of the religion curriculum to successfully empower learners to live deeper and better Christian lives.[11]

Locus of the Curriculum

A superior parish nonschool religious education curriculum is one which is not confined solely to classroom settings but also includes selected learning experiences in fruitful community mi-

9. For a further discussion of the laboratory for Christian living, see ibid., pp. 618-626, 656-657, 707-708.

10. Dean R. Hoge et al., "Desired Outcomes of Religious Education and Youth Ministry in Six Denominations," in *Living Light* XVIII (Spring, 1981), pp. 18-35. This conclusion is also valid for the other Christian denominations studied in this research investigation.

11. On this point, see Burton Cohen and Joseph Lukinsky, "Religious Institutions as Educators," in National Society for the Study of Education, *Education in School and Nonschool Settings*, Eighth-Fourth Yearbook, Part I (Chicago: The Society, 1985), pp. 149-150.

lieux. When it is utilized to its full holistic and experiential potential, the classroom is an extraordinarily powerful and synthesized setting for facilitating focused learning outcomes. But even when a classroom is organized around holistic experiential laboratory processes rather than life-isolated cognitive didactic procedures, the learners need to participate in those kinds of important religious and religiously related community activities which are intrinsically lush with learning opportunities. These community learning opportunities should not be regarded as low-level experiences or as activities lying outside the regular curriculum. Rather, community activities of a religious or a religiously related nature should be planned for, enacted, and evaluated on a level commensurate with classroom work. In a well-balanced religion curriculum, community experiences should be regarded as pedagogically coordinate to classroom experiences and not subordinate to them. In order to be educationally effective, classroom and community experiences must be carefully integrated in terms both of organizational structure and of complementary learning activities. In the latter connection, the classroom and community experiences in which the learner participates must revolve around a single curricular axis. The learner should be aware of this axis. In terms of the time allocation to religious education which I mentioned in a previous section, an ideal program would comprise five hours per week in selected community activities and three hours per week in classroom work. Examples of fruitful community experiences for learners in nonschool religious education programs include planning and celebrating liturgies in one or another parish church and apostolic service such as working with the poor and needy of the diocese, helping the elderly, or participating in evangelization programs.

Generally, parish nonschool religion programs around the country do not feature a great deal of curricularly integrated community activities in which the learner participates for the entire duration of the program. Yet such activities are essential for a truly life-centered religion curriculum.

Latitude of the Curriculum

A strong parish nonschool religious education curriculum is one which inclusively involves the entire parish as an entire parish. Such inclusive parish involvement is one which is preeminently organic in character, namely a unified structure in which the various aspects of parish life are functionally interconnected with one another. Such an organic structure has at least two major advantages. First, it enables the nonschool religion curriculum to become a focused watershed for parish life, thus insuring that the curriculum is relevant to that to which it should be relevant, namely, corporate and sacramental religious living. Second, it enables the rest of the parish to be enriched and fecundated by its nonschool religious education program. In the latter connection it should be noted that the purpose of every dynamic religion curriculum is twofold, namely conservative and progressive. In other words, a religion curriculum should serve as a situation in which (1) the objectively best and subjectively most useful Christian traditions can be mediated to learners, and (2) these Christian traditions, combined with contemporary post-tradition develop ments, can become a powerful engine for reconstructing the parish and larger church in a manner broadly continuous with but not identical to the original tradition. Thus the parish's nonschool religion curriculum flows in some significant degree (but not totally) from the parish to enrich the curriculum and flows back again to the whole parish to enrich the whole parish. It cannot be sufficiently emphasized that an organic structure involving the productive interaction between the whole parish and its religious education program does not simply happen. Rather, an organic structure must be carefully planned and systematically implemented.

While some better-known Catholic religious educationists have been urging the integration of nonschool religion curricula with the entire parish,[12] it would appear that such integration, at least on an organic and total basis, is not widespread throughout the United States. Part of the failure to achieve this organic and total integration is due to the fact that its proponents typically engage in high-sounding rhetoric such as "the entire parish community educates" but fail abysmally to provide the requisite concrete blueprints of those structures and functions necessary to achieve organic and total integration. Part of the failure can also be placed at the doorstep of those diocesan and parish religious educational officials who have not developed their own programs which organically and totally integrate the nonschool religious education curriculum with the whole parish.

12. See, for example, David O'Neil, "Building a Parish Community: Some New Concepts in Catechesis," in *The PACE Reader*, ed. Sheila Moriarty O'Fahey and Mary Perkins Ryan (Winona, Minn.: St. Mary's College Press, 1976), pp. 197-200.

Base of the Curriculum

A worthwhile parish nonschool religious education curriculum is one which is based on empirically proven effectiveness. The religion curriculum is an integrated group of planned experiences which are intended to produce certain desired learning outcomes. In the final analysis, a religion curriculum is no better than the learning outcomes it actually yields. The only—repeat, the only— way in which a teacher or administrator can know the degree to which any packaged commercial religion curriculum is doing what it claims to do is to find out the degree to which its results are validated by empirical research. When considering which packaged commercial religion curriculum to adopt for use in the parish's nonschool program, the religious educator should first ascertain the degree to which the effectiveness of the curriculum under consideration has been empirically proven.

Almost invariably, the effectiveness of packaged commercial Catholic religion curricula have not been empirically demonstrated in a satisfactory way. Only in rare instances have these curricula been constructed primarily on the basis of what is empirically known about teaching and learning. Only in rare cases, also, have these packaged commercial curricula been subjected to rigorous and thorough empirical field testing before they are released for sale. Yet such field testing is absolutely essential to ascertain the degree to which these curricula facilitate the learnings which their publishers claim they facilitate. Smaller publishers of packaged Catholic religion curricula employ a few facile and imaginative writers who grind out the curricula from their own homes. Larger publishers employ two or three named authors together with a fleet of unnamed subordinate methods persons, editorial technicians, and subject-matter consultants. This team holes up in a motel complex or in the company office for a set period of time in order to churn out the religion curriculum. The decidedly nonempirical manner of composing Catholic religion curricula stands in marked contrast to the careful empirical way in which religion curricula are composed in many advanced Protestant denominations. The United Methodists, for example, developed a religion curriculum in stages, with each stage undergirded by rigorous empirical testing. A preliminary curriculum is drafted incorporating the findings of relevant empirical research on teaching and learning. A tentative pilot religion curriculum is then empirically tested with a large representative sample of religion teachers in a wide variety of settings. As a result of this scientific field testing, the curriculum undergoes further refinement, after which it is published in its final form. During its lifetime, the religion curriculum undergoes continual empirical testing so that even greater fine-tuning can result. As C. Ellis Nelson aptly remarks, "No major Protestant denomination will ever again formulate an instructional program costing three to four million dollars to design without a thorough testing of the materials. Moreover, this testing and evaluation will continue as the materials are used, in order both to eliminate the units that are not effective and to discover why good units of instruction are useful."[13]

I once asked a nationally revered Catholic religious education official why he and his colleagues had strongly recommended that the nonschool religion teachers of his diocese adopt one particular packaged commercial Catholic religion curriculum. The septuagenarian religious educator smiled and responded: "Because that curriculum resounded well in my heart and in the hearts of my administrative colleagues." This response, lovely though it was, represents one of the pedagogically poorest ways of selecting a curriculum for use in nonschool and school religious education programs. The fact that one or another religion curriculum resounds well in the hearts of religious education officials is only marginally relevant. What is totally relevant is the degree to which a particular religion curriculum actually yields the learning outcomes which it claims to yield and which religious educators in a particular program wish it to yield. The answer to these central issues can only be determined by actual empirical research—research carried out in the extensive pilot studies which the publisher should have conducted prior to releasing the curriculum for general distribution, and research conducted by the diocese on the demonstrable learning outcomes which the curriculum yields for students in their own locality.

Textbooks in the Curriculum

An effective parish nonschool religious education curriculum is one in which the basal textbooks are specifically designed for this special kind of curriculum. Though sharing many of the same substantive contents as a school curriculum, the nonschool cur-

13. C. Ellis Nelson, "Religious Instruction in the Protestant Churches," in *Toward a Future for Religious Education,* ed. James Michael Lee and Patrick C. Rooney (Dayton, Ohio: Pflaum, 1970), p. 178.

riculum perforce must be distinctively different for a wide variety of reasons. Three examples should suffice to illustrate this point. First, learners who come to the nonschool program probably differ in some significant respects from those enrolled in a school program, notably in RI and RQ.[14] Second, there is, at least for the present, a great discrepancy in the amount of time spent in nonschool religion curricula as contrasted to school religion curricula. Third, there is no reinforcement or expansion of the nonschool religion curricula from other areas of the curriculum as there is in a religious school program. It should be emphasized that the religion curriculum which is designed for the nonschool program should be genuinely distinctive and deliberately targeted to that program, rather than simply an "adaptation" or a watering-down of the school's religion curriculum. This statement holds true for the nonschool religious education of adults as well as that of children and youth.

The basal textbooks used in a large number of nonschool religious education curricula in parishes around the country do not seem to have been specifically designed for nonschool programs. This unfortunate situation is regrettable and should be promptly corrected.

Involvement Sphere of the Curriculum

A first-rate parish nonschool religious education curriculum for children and youth necessitates as close an involvement with parents as possible. Parent involvement is in some respects even more crucial in nonschool religion curricula than in Catholic school religion curricula because the former currently are of much shorter weekly duration than the latter. A potent nonschool religion curriculum is one which structurally involves the parents as fully as possible in every major phase of the nonschool religion curriculum, ranging from planning it, enacting it, extending it into the home situation, and evaluating it. Such heavy parent involvement requires considerable time and expertise on the part of the teachers and the administrators in the nonschool program. These two necessary qualities tend to sharply militate against staffing the program with volunteers. Planning the curriculum should be an ongoing process which takes place on a regular basis. Curriculum planning includes such devices as: unmet needs

14. RI is educational shorthand for religious interest. RQ is for religious quotient.

conferences so that parents can indicate what they believe the curriculum ought to be doing but is not accomplishing; parental input into the scope, range, and design of the curriculum; parental suggestions on the required and especially the supplemental materials to be used in the curriculum. Parents should also be involved, as appropriate, in enacting the curriculum both in formal settings such as the classroom and in informal setting such as field trips, in liturgical milieux, and the like. Most certainly the curriculum should be architected in such a way that it formally extends into home life, a fact which will necessitate parent involvement. Materials for that religious education which is taught by parents in the home should be prepared in such a way as to be a complement, not a supplement to the classroom curriculum. Finally, parents should be a vital part of the formative and summative evaluation process. Such evaluation should include both assessment of learning outcomes which the student gained from the religion curriculum and also the relative worthwhileness of the current religion curriculum itself.

It is fairly common knowledge that most parish nonschool religion curricula provide for very little parental involvement of an influential or decisive nature. Parish and diocesan religious officials would do well to alleviate this educationally indefensible condition.

Attention to the Teaching Act

It should be obvious that the essence of religion teaching is the effective facilitation of desired learning outcomes. Teaching is basically an activity which is reciprocal to learning. Therefore the degree to which an activity can properly be termed teaching is directly proportional to the degree to which learning takes place as a consequence of that activity.

The teaching act, then, is the most important thing which can be said about religious instruction. The knowledge which the religious educator possesses about the subject matter, the level of the educator's spiritual life, the amount of love which the educator has for learners—these count for naught in the work of religious education if the teacher cannot teach. Put more accurately, the religious education value of the teacher's knowledge of subject matter of the teacher's spiritual life or the teacher's love for learners lies in direct proportion to the educator's actual skill in facilitating desired learning outcomes.

In the short run and in the long run, the success of parish nonschool religious education programs will be determined more by the pedagogical skill of the teachers than by any other single factor. Consequently, the most effective thing which diocesan and parish religious education officials can do to directly optimize the success of their programs is to give top priority to the development and improvement of the pedagogical skills of the persons who teach in the program.

Despite the fact that successful teaching is the most fundamental and most important characteristic of religious instruction, the sad truth is that the one area most neglected in parish nonschool religious education programs is the teaching process. The most prevalent criticism directed against parish nonschool religious education programs, especially those for children and youth, is that the teachers do not know how to teach. (As the various chapters in the present volume attest, the poor quality of teaching also constitutes the major complaint voiced by Protestants against their Sunday schools.) Catholic religious education officials typically spin out lofty statements of program goals but almost never pay requisite attention to cultivating the complex of teaching procedures necessary to achieve these goals. Indeed, these educational officials seldom even translate these high-sounding goals into performance objectives or into any other kind of doable instructional targets, thus all but precluding the possibility that these goals will ever be rendered teachable.[15]

In chapter 5 of the present volume Locke Bowman writes that professional directors of religious education in Protestant churches tend to concentrate on current ethical concerns and world problems, on the latest developments in theology, on new trends in educational psychology—on everything except the day-to-day tasks of helping religion teachers improve their pedagogical skills. This sad situation is unfortunately ecumenical. It is equally characteristic of Catholic religious educationists and educational officials.

The pathetic inattention to the dynamics of teaching on the part of religious education officials is due in no small measure to the lack of adequate professional preparation in religious instruction which these officials received in the seminary and/or in

15. For a brief description of how educational goals can be rendered teachable, see James Michael Lee, *The Flow of Religious Instruction* (Birmingham, Ala.: Religous Education Press, 1973), pp. 230-233.

university-based graduate religious education programs. Catholic seminaries generally offer few if any courses in religious instruction and virtually none in the dynamics of teaching—despite the fact that most of the parish priest's time is spent in religious instruction activity whether or not he is affiliated with the parish's formal religious education program. Graduate programs in religious education housed in Catholic universities are scandalously deficient in course work in the scientific study and practice of teaching religion. Therefore it should come as no surprise that most diocesan and parish religious education officials, trained as they were in seminaries and/or university religious education programs, are woefully ignorant of the nature and importance of the teaching process. Ignorance breeds neglect, and neglect breeds failure (or at least a grave minimization of effectiveness).

In the ongoing preservice and inservice training of teachers for the nonschool religious education program, parish as well as diocesan officials should accord unremitting and central attention to helping teachers improve their pedagogical skills. The preservice and inservice teacher training program should have its hub in the teacher performance center. Such a center ought to be a permanent fixture in every parish or at least in every diocesan deanery. A teacher performance center is a pedagogical laboratory in which any aspect of the religious educator's instructional behavior can be scientifically analyzed and improved. For example, a religion teacher in the nonschool program wishes to sharpen his instructional skills in higher-order questioning. A staff member from the teacher performance center makes a videotape of an on-site lesson in which that teacher employs higher-order questioning. Returning to the center, the staff member and the teacher analyze the videotape with a number of scientific devices such as the Flanders Interaction Analysis System to assess the verbal shape and teacher-centeredness of the lesson, the Galloway Interaction Analysis System to examine the nonverbal contours which took place in the lesson, the Withall Interaction Analysis System to appraise the affective dynamics in the lesson, and so on. After the religion teacher and the staff have thoroughly analyzed what actually occurred in the higher-order questioning sequence, the teacher, with the assistance of the center's staff member, engages in actual practice sessions designed to enhance the effectiveness of the higher-order questioning technique.

Coordinate with the work which religion teachers do in the teacher performance center, the parish, deanery, or diocese should offer a diverse menu of top-quality preservice and inservice courses on the nature, structure, and dynamics of the teaching process. These courses must be intellectually respectable. A course is intellectually respectable when it is solidly grounded in appropriate theory, when it is shot through and through with relevant research, and when it involves the learners in acquiring the basic (as contrasted to superficial) skills in those areas covered by the course. There is no intrinsic reason why a practical course in teaching methodology should be less intellectually respectable or personally demanding than a course in Elizabethan literature, experimental psychology, or biblical exegesis. If teaching process courses have been weak in the past, the fault lies not with the subject area itself but with the person offering the course. A practical course it not one which dispenses "tips to teachers" or "Mr. Fix-It" remedies. Such courses are at bottom not practical at all. Indeed, they are impractical because they fail to do what all real practicality requires, namely insertion into appropriate theory, grounding in relevant research, and engagement in actual practice under scientifically controlled conditions.

The preservice and inservice courses which are offered in the area of the teaching process should minimally include all of the following: (1) an understanding of the theory of teaching, namely the fundamental explanation of why and how teaching functions as it does; (2) the development of carefully framed goals for the experiences which the teacher is providing to learners; (3) skill in translating these goals into performance objectives, a process which enables the goals to become teachable; (4) an understanding of and actual practice in the most basic underlying dynamic of all teaching activity, namely antecedent-consequent behavioral chaining;[16] (5) competence in the use of protocol materials;[17] (6) proficiency in the concrete deployment of a wide variety of teaching procedures including role playing, the project technique, action-reflection and reflection-action processes, group discussion, problem-solving methods, the discovery strategy, the inquiry procedure, panels and symposia, case and contrary case techniques, the cell, committee work, affective strategies, and so

16. For a brief description of teaching as antecedent-consequent behavioral chaining, see James Michael Lee, *The Flow of Religious Instruction*, pp. 196-197, 207, 212.

17. See David C. Berliner et al., *Protocols on Group Process* (San Francisco: Far West Laboratory for Educational Research and Development, 1973).

forth. Proficiency in these pedagogical procedures requires both an adequate understanding of the principles which they enflesh plus skill in their effective enactment.

A rigorous and high-level certification examination should constitute the culminating activity of preservice programs for prospective religious educators in nonschool settings. Analogous to the practice prevalent in the other professions such as medicine, law, and psychology, the certification examination should be administered by a licensing committee established by the profession rather than by the university or seminary in which the courses leading to certification were taken. In the ideal situation, all religious teachers in school and nonschool settings would possess a master's degree in religious education. In such a situation, preservice courses offered by the parish, deanery, and diocese would supplement rather than replace university or seminary course work. Until this ideal is realized, however, dioceses will be forced to operate their own preservice programs. In such cases, persons who successfully complete the entire preservice preparation program conducted by the diocese, the deanery, or the parish, should be awarded an emergency certificate rather than a regular license.

Whether administered by a licensing committee established by the profession or as a last resort by the diocese, the certification examination should not be watered down but should represent a high level of demonstrated religious instruction competence. Three discrete but interconnecting elements should comprise the certification examination. *First,* the prospective religious educator should demonstrate a stated degree of knowledge of the substantive content of religious instruction, namely religion. The certification examination should require cognitive competence in the major areas of religious studies, including theology, psychology of religion, sociology of religion, religious literature, and so on. Since the religious educator teaches religion and not theology per se, this portion of the examination should cover the gamut of religious studies rather than be restricted simply to theology. *Second,* the prospective religious educator should demonstrate a stated degree of knowledge of the structural content of religious instruction, namely the teaching process. The certification examination should require cognitive competence in the major areas of pedagogical endeavor such as the historical theories of education, educational psychology, teaching theory, and instructional methodology. *Third,* the prospective religious educator should demonstrate a stated degree of performance in concrete here-and-now teaching. In other words, the certification examination should require competence in actually teaching a religion lesson. The degree of pedagogical proficiency should be evaluated as far as possible by objective instruments which assess the levels of teaching performance rather than by the subjective impressions of an observer. In addition to these three tests of competence, the certification process should include a psychological examination to screen out any prospective religious educator who might be afflicted with a psychological difficulty of such a nature as to impair that individual's effectiveness as a religious educator.

The results of a carefully conducted empirical research investigation by Catholic sociologist William McCready bear considerable relevance for the preservice and inservice training of nonschool religious educators. McCready's study found that those Catholic religious educators who identified their work as ministry tended to have unclear goals and unformulated objectives about their religious instruction work. These individuals also tended to minimize or even disparage the importance of working assiduously to sharpen their pedagogical skills, of assessing as precisely as possible the cause-effect relationship between their teaching and the learner's learning, and of scientific evaluation of the outcomes of the lesson. In contrast, those Catholic religious educators who identified their work as education tended to have clear goals and well-formulated objectives about their religious instruction work. These persons also tended to emphasize the importance of working hard to improve their teaching skills, of ascertaining as exactly as possible the antecedent-consequent relationship between their teaching and the learner's learning, and of the necessity of scientific evaluation of the outcomes of the lesson.[18] The overwhelming preponderance of empirical research on teaching suggests that clarity of goals, precision of objectives, unremitting attention to the improvement of pedagogical skills, careful assessment of antecedent-consequent instructional events, and scientific evaluation of learning outcomes are all highly correlated with teaching success. Consequently, a preservice or inservice training program for parish nonschool religion teachers should empower the persons in that program to function as educators rather than simply ministers.

18. Personal conversation with William McCready in his Chicago office, April 4, 1985.

Preservice and inservice programs should be structured in such a way that religion teachers will come to the realization that their own personal spirituality is intimately tied in with their religious instruction activity.[19] The religious educator's growth does not occur in a vacuum, but is inextricably intertwined with that person's life. Teaching religion is an important aspect of the religious educator's life. It follows, then, that the quality of the religious educator's teaching performance constitutes an essential source and context of that person's spiritual life. For religious educators, pedagogical competence and personal spirituality are two sides of the same coin.[20]

Volunteers

One of the most serious problems facing the parish nonschool religious education program is the fact that its teachers are mostly volunteers. The disastrous effects of this situation cannot be sufficiently stressed.

Of the many reasons accounting for the generally meager educational outcomes facilitated by volunteer religion teachers, two stand out. Volunteer religion teachers are typically untrained. Volunteer religion teachers are typically unpaid.

Teaching is a profession. Adequate performance in any profession demands a great deal of preparation in the theory, the principles, and the specific practices which characterize the activities of that profession. The purpose of all preservice and inservice professional training is to maximize the probability of success in all the activities falling under the rubric of that profession. Without adequate training, success in professional activities is exceedingly difficult to attain. Whatever success is achieved by untrained persons in effectively discharging professional tasks

19. Joseph Collins recognizes the validity of this crucial point when he writes: "One would like to see developed during these days a formal and practical system of spiritual formation for the faculty members of the CCD in our country. It should be of such a nature that the CCD itself is a potent means of [spiritual] perfection." Joseph B. Collins, "Spiritual Formation and Its Development in the CCD," in *Spiritual Formation and Guidance-Counseling in the CCD Program* (Washington, D.C.: The Catholic University of America Press, 1962), p. 16.

20. The points made throughout this paragraph are treated at some length in James Michael Lee, "Lifework Spirituality and the Religious Educator," in *The Spirituality of the Religious Educator*, ed. James Michael Lee (Birmingham, Ala.: Religious Education Press, 1985), pp. 7-42.

can usually be attributed to luck or to accident or to a combination of both. Intelligence, love for learners, personal piety, and good will are no substitutes for adequate preservice and inservice training. The thesis of this paragraph is nicely illustrated by the story of Jack Degnan. This fine man has worked as an administrative marketing specialist with IBM for thirty years, is a devout Catholic, and is quite apostolic. Reflecting on the service which he and his wife gave to his parish as religious educators of youth, Degnan said: "We didn't have the slightest idea what we were doing."[21] What is true of Degnan's experience as a volunteer religious educator is probably true of most untrained religious educators, namely that at bottom, they do not know what they are doing. How can they know—they have never been trained. It is hard indeed to adequately discharge the responsibilities of a profession if the practitioners do not know what they are doing.

It is extremely difficult to establish and especially to maintain those professional conditions necessary for effective religion teaching if the teachers are not financially compensated for their work. Unpaid volunteer religious educators generally believe that they are doing the parish a favor by offering their time and energies free of charge. Indeed, when recruiting volunteers for the nonschool program, parish officials usually stress that those persons who volunteer are doing the parish a favor by devoting their time and effort. Because volunteer religious educators are unpaid and hence doing the parish a favor, there is no compelling motivation for these teachers to give top priority to their teaching activities. As result volunteer religious teachers miss classes from time to time when seemingly more important duties suddenly arise. Or again, volunteer religious educators will not give much effort to significantly enhancing their subject-matter knowledge or pedagogical skills because their regular salaried jobs, their family lives, and their legitimate recreational pursuits leave very little time remaining for the development of religious education knowledges and skills. For good reasons, then, the nonschool program cannot count on volunteer religious educators rain or shine to always do even the minimum required of an adequate teacher. Inasmuch as the unpaid volunteer is doing the parish a favor, it is the volunteer rather than the parish that is in control. When a

21. Robert J. McClory, "Their Deductions Are Disappointing," in *National Catholic Reporter* XXI (January 25, 1985), p. 20.

practitioner is paid, then the group or agency which is paying that person is in control. It is only human nature for a person to accord top priority to those who pay him on a regular basis. There is a certain healthy and fruitful compulsion to human behavior which paid employment brings. Even Jesus did not expect his followers to be unpaid. In fact, when sending out the seventy-two disciples to teach religion to the Jews, Jesus specifically told them that a worker deserves to get paid for his work (Lk. 10:7).

Because volunteer religion teachers are unpaid, there is the natural tendency on the part of the parish officials, parents, students, and indeed the whole ecclesia, to expect rather little of them. After all, it is unreasonable to expect the same level of preparation and competence from an unpaid teacher as from a paid professional religious educator. The low expectancy which parish officials and professional religious educators have of volunteer teacher is in itself an extremely potent factor in influencing volunteer teachers against preparing themselves adequately and against devoting large amounts of time and effort in discharging their pedagogical responsibilities competently. There is an abundance of empirical research evidence which clearly indicates that persons tend to perform or not to perform in direct proportion to what other individuals expect of them.[22]

More often than not, diocesan and parish officials manufacture faint and even sometime bizarre excuses to justify the heavy presence of untrained and unpaid volunteers in parish nonschool religious education programs. This lame concoction of excuses is by no means a uniquely Catholic phenomenon; it is a pervasively ecumenical disgrace. Writing of the fanciful excuses which Protestant officials fabricate to absolve their religious education programs from the stain of heavy volunteerism, Ellis Nelson trenchantly states that these officials "justify inexperienced and untrained teachers in our church schools with the notion that their religious life is so fine that the children will 'catch' the more important aspects of religion, such as devotion and faith, even if

22. For a book which examines various theories explaining the effect of expectancy on performance, see Norman T. Feather, ed., *Expectations and Actions* (Hillsdale, N.J.: Erlbaum, 1982). For a classic treatment of one major effect of teacher expectation on learner performance, see Robert Rosenthal and Lenore Jacobson, *Pygmalion in the Classroom: Teacher Behavior and Pupils' Intellectual Development* (New York: Holt, Rinehart & Winston, 1968).

the intellectual work is substandard or the classroom is poorly managed."[23] Ethel Johnson has written movingly of the devastating effect which the almost exclusive use of volunteer teachers has had on efforts in the black churches to make religious education a quality experience for learners and congregation alike.[24]

When all is said and done, the presence of untrained and unpaid volunteer religion teachers essentially constitutes an abject disvaluation of the worth of the nonschool religious education program. No sphere of activity can be deemed to be of more than inconsequential worth if it is staffed by practitioners who are untrained, unpaid, and who spend very little time or effort in the discharge of their total responsibilities. The more valuable a sphere of work, the more does society demand that the practitioners within that sphere of work have a longer period of preparation, greater theoretical background, greater overall grasp of basic principles, and greater demonstrated practical skills.

One can only wonder if officials of a nonschool religious education program which is staffed by volunteers would send their mothers to be operated on by a physician who was a volunteer having no professional preparation, who was unpaid, and who performed cardiac operations as a very minor sideline. Religious education officials should ask themselves whether the body is of such much more worth than the soul in that these officials demand that the care of the body be undertaken by full-time professionally prepared practitioners while at the same time permit and even encourage the care of the soul to be undertaken by practitioners who are part-time and untrained.

There is no legitimate place in the parish nonschool religious education program for volunteer teachers. However, there is an educationally legitimate and positive role which volunteers can play in the parish nonschool program.

The general principle undergirding the positive role of volunteers is this: volunteers should work only in positions within the program which are contributive and ancillary to the regular, professionally prepared, salaried staff members. Put negatively, "vol-

23. Nelson, "Religious Instruction in the Protestant Churches," pp. 173-174.

24. Ethel R. Johnson, "Black Women as Professional Religious Educators," in *Women's Issues in Religious Education*, ed. Fern M. Giltner (Birmingham, Ala.: Religious Education Press, 1985), pp. 115, 117, 124.

unteers should not supplant or decrease the need for suitably qualified, regularly employed staff."[25]

Volunteers can help enrich the parish religious education program because they represent the grass roots of the ecclesia and thus bring with them some fresh ideas and insights which can enrich the nonschool religious education program. Some volunteers also bring special skills which can contribute significantly to the quality of the program. All of the above notwithstanding, it should be reiterated that volunteers are helpful to the program when and only when they are utilized in a decidedly supplemental capacity and to the level to which they are trained.

The well-staffed parish nonschool religious education program should employ two discrete kinds of instructional personnel, namely professional teachers and paraprofessional auxiliaries. The rightful role of a volunteer is to lend occasional assistance to the regular instructional staff or to any other phase of the program including help with the physical plant and the financial operations.

Properly speaking, a volunteer is basically a walk-on, a person who does not belong to the essential structure of the program but who occasionally helps out during times when the program needs temporary outside assistance. A volunteer is typically unpaid and generally requires relatively little preparation. A paraprofessional, on the other hand, belongs to the essential structure of the program. A paraprofession is a regular and salaried job, though it frequently does not consume as much time on-site and off-site as does a professional position. As an auxiliary staff person, the paraprofessional has input, as appropriate, in relevant decision-making processes. A paraprofessional is paid, and is prepared at the theoretical and practical level required for the effective discharge of the duties demanded by the particular paraprofession.

One of the major reasons accounting for the relative ineffectiveness of nonschool religious education programs is that volunteers have been used in ways wholly inconsistent with their proper and legitimate roles. Specifically, volunteers have been asked to assume the roles and functions of paraprofessionals and more often

25. Ahlgren Haeuser and Florence S. Schwartz, "Developing Social Work Skills for Work with Volunteers," in *Voluntarism and Social Work Practice*, ed. Florence S. Schwartz (Lanham, Md.: University Press of America, 1984), p. 28.

of professionals without being provided the requisites for effectively fulfilling these roles, notably inclusion in the program's essential structure, adequate preservice and inservice training, and a paid position on the regular decision-making staff.

Paraprofessionals are regular salaried persons who are employed to assist professional religion teachers in the educational efforts of the program. They are paraprofessional in the sense that it is not their primary responsibility to innovate or to initiate instruction. They are assistants who take direction from the professional religion teachers in an effort to further enhance the effectiveness of the learning process. Paraprofessionals are not substitute teachers, nor can they be expected to take over the major instructional responsibilities of the professional religion teacher, except in a highly unusual case or in an emergency.[26]

Paraprofessional religious educators[27] perform a wide variety of pedagogically related tasks including but by no means restricted to the following; (1) relieving the professional religious educator of certain clerical and nonprofessional duties; (2) preparing certain kinds of educational materials; (3) performing housekeeping and monitorial duties; (4) providing supplemental one-to-one or small group assistance; (5) facilitating independent study activities; (6) assisting in advising and counseling students in an ancillary capacity; (7) helping some learners in improving their English language proficiency; (8) serving as liaisons between the nonschool religious education program and the parish.[28]

There are at least four levels of paraprofessional religious educators. In ascending order, these levels are aide, assistant, associate, and intern.[29] Each higher level is characterized by more advanced training in the theory, in the principles, and in the performance skills of teaching religion together with an increas-

26. Benjamin DaSilva and Richard D. Lucas, *Practical School Volunteer and Teacher-Aide Programs* (West Nyack, N.Y.: Parker, 1974), pp. 28-29.

27. A helpful book in this regard is Alan Gartner, Vivian Carter Jackson, and Frank Riessman, *Paraprofessionals in Education Today* (New York: Human Sciences Press, 1977).

28. Jewell C. Chambers, *ABC's: A Handbook for Educational Volunteers* (Washington, D.C.: Washington Technical Institute, 1972), p. 2.

29. Each of these terms properly has the word teacher in front of it, e.g. teacher aide, teacher assistant, and so on. See Jorie Lester Mark, *Paraprofessionals in Education* (New York: Bank Street College of Education, 1975).

ingly greater knowledge of the subject-matter content. One key function of the diocesan preservice and inservice program is to train interested paraprofessionals to move up the ladder and possibly even progress to the ranks of professional religious educator. In this effort, the diocesan religious education office must necessarily work in close cooperation with the local university, whether Catholic, Protestant, or church-unaffiliated.[30]

Parish and diocesan religious education officials will find that the inclusion of paraprofessionals in their nonschool and school programs serves as a potent preparation and recruitment vehicle for future religion teachers. Progress through the four ranks of paraprofessional instructional staff operates on an ideal scaled-internship program for future religious educators. Beginning with their sophomore year in college, persons wishing to explore a permanent career in Catholic education as a religion teacher can work successively in each of the four paraprofessional levels of the nonschool program.

Hiring paraprofessionals will not save the parish money. Indeed, paraprofessionals will cost the parish money. The whole concept of paraprofessional religious educators is based on the valid assumption that the parish nonschool religious education program is already staffed by one professional religion teacher per class. Paraprofessionals are hired not to supplant the regular professional religion teacher but rather to give the teacher additional and needed help of an auxiliary nature. Consequently, the parish has to pay for the cost of both the full complement of professional religion teachers plus the paraprofessional staff members. Those pastors and religious education officials who openly or secretely believe that the intrinsic worth of the parish nonschool religious education program is virtually nil will oppose the hiring of paid paraprofessional religious educators with the same mindless obduracy with which they oppose the hiring of a complete cadre of paid professional religion teachers.

Almost every book written on paraprofessionals and volunteers in educational settings states that the effective use of both of these kinds of individuals necessitates: (1) solid preservice and

30. Diocesan and parish religious education officials will generally find the education department and the religious studies department in Protestant and church-unaffiliated institutions of higher learning as cooperative, in some cases even more cooperative, than their counterparts in Catholic colleges.

ongoing inservice training; (2) periodic on-the-job supervision.[31]

Both paraprofessionals and volunteers must have adequate pre-service and inservice training. This training is not nearly as in-tense, as deep, or as long as that required of a professional religion teacher. Paraprofessionals need considerably more prep-aration than do volunteers, but it is a mistake to think that volun-teers need no training. All volunteers, including those with special talents and skills, require some sort of preservice and inservice training if they are to effectively discharge their educa-tional tasks. Some of this training will consist of familiarizing the volunteer with the exigencies, circumstances, and conditions of that phase of the religious education program in which they wish to serve. Other aspects of the training will deal with the acquisi-tion of those special skills required for successful participation in one or another component of the program.[32] An indispensable part of the preservice and inservice training of both paraprofes-sionals and volunteers is familiarity with the literature on reli-gious education as appropriate to the level of service. Unless the paraprofessional and volunteer read some solid books in the field each and every year, it will be all but impossible for that person to perform knowledgeably. Seriousness of purpose implies keep-ing abreast of the field through reading serious books in religious education. Those paraprofessionals and volunteers who are in-capable of reading serious books in the field in which they serve will most probably be also incapable of successfully fulfilling their tasks in the religious education program.

If they are to perform well, paraprofessionals and volunteers must be periodically supervised. It is a grave mistake to leave paraprofessionals and volunteers unsupervised.[33] After all, para-professionals and volunteers by definition lack the requisite the-ory, principles, skills, and knowledge of subject-matter content to

---

31. A fine book illustrating this point is T. Margaret Jones, *School Volunteers* (New York: Public Education Association, 1961).

32. Evelyn S. Byron, "Recruiting and Training of Volunteers," in *Volunteerism*, ed. John G. Cull and Richard E. Hardy (Springfield, Ill.: Thomas, 1974), pp. 33-67.

33. Much of what Linda Bennett writes about coordinating and super-vising volunteers in a school media center can be legitimately generalized to volunteers in the parish's nonschool religious education program. See Linda Leveque Bennett, *Volunteers in the School Media Center* (Littleton, Colo.: Libraries Unlimited, 1984).

exercise their organically programatic tasks in an autonomous fashion.

The parish religious education director should work carefully to coordinate the work of the professional religion teachers, the paraprofessionals, and the volunteers. Job descriptions ought to specify as finely as possible the roles, functions, tasks, and responsibilities of the teachers, the paraprofessionals, and the volunteers in such a way that all these persons are simultaneously aware of what is expected of them and how their own particular activities organically fit in with those activities carried out by the other individuals working in the overall parish religious education program. Recognizing and developing mutual awareness of the essential interrelatedness of professional, paraprofessional, and volunteer activities is a major function in educational leadership.[34]

It might be helpful for a parish or even a diocese to have a liturgically situated commissioning rite for professional religion teachers, paraprofessionals, and volunteers.[35] If done properly, such a rite could further strengthen the motivation of all the parish's nonschool religious education personnel and give these individuals some desperately needed prestige not only among the parishoners but among the clergy. However, such a commissioning rite is a sham and a disgrace if the paraprofessionals and volunteers who are commissioned lack the requisite training, or even worse, if these paraprofessionals and volunteers are commissioned to serve as teachers, a task for which they are grossly incompetent to discharge effectively.

Conclusion

To be a Christian is to be called by God to excellence. To be a Christian religious educational organization is likewise to be called by God to excellence. A parish nonschool religious education program which is not excellent, or what is worse does not even conscientiously strive for excellence, is a program which fails to heed God's call. If a religious education program does not

34. Harriet H. Naylor, *Volunteers Today: Finding, Training, and Working with Them* (New York: Association, 1967).
35. See Anne-Marie Kirmse, "The Vocation of the Volunteer Catechist," in *Living Light* XVI (Winter, 1979), pp. 498-505.

heed God's call for excellence, how can that program expect its students to heed God's call for excellence in their own lives? A primary purpose of renewing the parish nonschool religious education program is to energize and empower the program to achieve excellence.

Genuine renewal has its price. The more thoroughgoing and lasting the renewal, the higher the price. No person and no organization receives something for nothing.

There is no cheap grace in the church. Nor is there any cheap renewal. Authentic renewal is costly. This fact should not be buried under the rug or glossed over. The greater and more far-reaching the renewal, the higher the cost.

Unless church officials are willing to pay the necessary price, a first-class nonschool religious education program will never come about. Renewal requires a price. But renewal also generates rewards. If we focus on the rewards, perhaps the price will not seem so high after all. Even better, if we concentrate on Jesus who gave everything so that we may live, then surely we will not even think of the price.

About the Contributors

Jack L. Seymour is Associate Professor of Christian Education at Scarritt College in Nashville, Tennessee, and has also taught at Vanderbilt University Divinity School and Chicago Theological Seminary. He is a pastor of the United Methodist Church and is author of *From Sunday School to Church School, Contemporary Approaches to Christian Education,* with Donald F. Miller, and *The Church in the Education of the Public: Refocusing the Task of Religious Education,* with Robert T. O'Gorman and Charles R. Foster.

Mary Charles Bryce, OSB, Ph.D., was Professor of Religious Education at the Catholic University of America, Washington, D.C., 1971-1983, and served as dean of the Pastoral Ministry Program of the Archdiocese of Oklahoma City, 1983-84. During 1984-85 she was the Flannery Scholar of Theology at Gonzaga University, Spokane, Washington.

Warren J. Hartman is the Executive Director of Research for The General Board of Discipleship of The United Methodist Church. Prior to assuming that position, he held several positions in Christian Education, the last being that of the Executive Administrator of Christian Education for The United Methodist Church. His home is in Nashville, Tennessee.

Andrew D. Thompson, Ph.D., is a private consultant in religious education and family ministry. As Associate Professor of Religion and Religious Education at The Catholic University of America in Washington, D.C., he taught graduate and undergraduate courses from 1973 to 1982. He has also been Research Associate of the University's Boystown Center for the Study of Youth Development, and of the University's National Center for Family Studies. He was founding Editor of *American Catholic Family Newsletter* and Executive Assistant of the Holy Childhood Association. His most recent books include *That They May Know You*, published by the National Catholic Educational Association, and *Preparing For Marriage*, published by Abbey Press (1983).

Locke E. Bowman, Jr., is Professor of Christian Education and Pastoral Theology at the Protestant Episcopal Theological Seminary of Virginia, Alexandria. He is also editor and publisher of *Church Teachers* magazine, a publication of National Teacher Education Program, Scottsdale, Arizona. As founder of the latter organization, Mr. Bowman conducted research and served as teacher and lecturer in ecumenical events throughout the country, 1965-1983. He is a former curriculum editor for the Presbyterian Church in the U.S.A. and is a priest in the Episcopal Church.

Robert J. Dean is Editorial and Curriculum Specialist, Church Programs and Services Office Staff, The Sunday School Board of the Southern Baptist Convention, Nashville, Tennessee.

Nathan W. Jones, Ph.D., is a Religious Education Consultant for black and multicultural churches and educational institutions, Catholic and Protestant. He is also Editor-in-Chief for Ethnic Communications Outlet, Chicago, Illinois, and author of a range of educational resources.

Mary A. Love is currently editor of church school literature for the African Methodist Episcopal Zion Church, with offices in Charlotte, North Carolina. She is also former Assistant Professor of Christian Education at Hood Theological Seminary, Salisbury,

North Carolina. She holds a B.S. degree in Home Economics from Mississippi State University, Starkville, Mississippi and a M.R.E. from Wesley Theological Seminary in Washington, D.C.

Alfred W. Hanner, Jr., is Director of Religious Education and Religious Education Supervisor, Office of the Staff Chaplain, Fort Bragg, North Carolina.

D. Campbell Wyckoff is Thomas W. Synnott Professor of Christian Education, Emeritus, Princeton Theological Seminary.

James Michael Lee is Professor of Education at the University of Alabama at Birmingham. Among his many books are *The Shape of Religious Instruction* (Religious Education Press, 330 pp.), *The Flow of Religious Instruction* (Religious Education Press, 379 pp.), and *The Content of Religious Instruction* (Religious Education Press, 814 pp.) He is listed in *Who's Who in the World*, *Who's Who in America*, and *Who's Who in Religion*.

Index of Names

Index of Subjects

253